T0069045

St. Louis Politics

Also by Lana Stein

Holding Bureaucrats Accountable: Politicians and Professionals in St. Louis

City Schools and City Politics: Institutions and Leadership in Pittsburgh, Boston, and St. Louis (with John Portz and Robin R. Jones)

St. Louis Politics
The Triumph of Tradition

Lana Stein

Missouri Historical Society Press • Saint Louis

Distributed by University of Missouri Press

© 2002 by the Missouri Historical Society Press
All rights reserved
Published in the United States of America by Missouri Historical Society Press,
P.O. Box 11940, St. Louis, Missouri 63112-0040

5 4 3 2 1   06 05 04 03 02

Library of Congress Cataloging-in-Publication Data

Stein, Lana, 1946 –
     St. Louis politics : the triumph of tradition / Lana Stein.
          p.   cm.
     title: Saint Louis politics.
     Includes bibliographical references and index.
     ISBN 1-883982-43-X (cloth : alk. paper)
     ISBN 1-883982-44-8 (paper : alk. paper)
     1. Saint Louis (Mo.)--Politics and government.
     I. Title: Saint Louis politics. II. Title.

JS1385 .S74 2002
320.9778'660904--dc21
                                        2002019864

Distributed by University of Missouri Press

Designed by Robyn Morgan
Photo edited by Lana Stein and Duane Sneddeker
Index by Thelda Bertram
Cover design by Kathleen Strand and Robyn Morgan
Printed and bound in the United States by Maple-Vail, covers by Pinnacle Press

Cover: Photograph of Democratic members of the
St. Louis board of aldermen, April 1934.

∞ This paper meets the requirements of the American National Standard for Permanence
of Paper for Printed Library Materials, Z39.48-1992 (R 1997).

For friends and instigators,

Catherine Forslund and Dan McGuire

Foreword

The role of the Missouri Historical Society is to provide factual historical context for our community, in which to discuss the planning of our future. The Society also must facilitate the conversation that will develop the story of St. Louis into a story that we, to the exclusion of no individual and no group, will share and pass on. And so it is with optimistic enthusiasm that the Missouri Historical Society Press publishes Professor Lana Stein's *St. Louis Politics: The Triumph of Tradition*.

The political past of St. Louis is a complicated and fascinating story. To tell it requires a scholar of perception and endurance, a researcher of energetic determination, a writer with a penchant for clarity and a dedication to accuracy. If that storyteller has personal knowledge of and an abiding affection for this place but also the confidence to criticize, then our story will be better and more usefully told. Professor Stein and *St. Louis Politics* meet all these criteria.

The fragmentation of St. Louis, as a city and a region, is shamefully apparent, often obscuring the accomplishments and prospects of this place. The factors are many. We have allowed issues of race and racial tensions to divide us and to shatter both a shared past and a shared vision for a successful future. The complex networks of politics and political power have created a labyrinthine diversion that discourages many a well-intentioned office seeker—and ordinary concerned citizens as well. Partisan political machinery and intertwined coalitions, disruptive competition among various bureaucracies, abundant patronage opportunities, and the equally abundant potential for many levels of corruption are part of the political history of this place. Stein examines all these aspects of what she describes as our political tradition with a discerning and knowledgeable eye.

At the Missouri Historical Society we honor tradition but know we are not bound to it. We understand that change is fundamental to the human condition but also that its course is not fixed—that we who live here now can use the story of our past to shape the story for our future. Hence, the "triumph of tradition" can be utilized to create a shared narrative, a mutual exploration of what that tradition means and how we can use it to enhance this place we call St. Louis for ourselves and for those who come here after us.

Stein, like me, is not a born-and-reared St. Louisan. But she, again like me, has experienced the remarkable diversity of this place, looked on its failures but participated in its successes and attempts at betterment. Her book, as I see it, is not merely a history or a political-science treatise but also a tool that she offers with perception, affection, and criticism to her fellow citizens of the St. Louis region.

ROBERT R. ARCHIBALD, PH.D.
PRESIDENT, MISSOURI HISTORICAL SOCIETY

Preface

This work began as the unraveling of a minor puzzle. How did political figures in St. Louis decide whom to endorse or with whom to forge alliances? To even broach that question, it became necessary to explain how St. Louis's political system had evolved and how it functioned on a regular basis. The roots of today's system began in 1876 with the city's divorce from its county and in its 1914 charter. Unlike a number of other cities, St. Louis failed to centralize either its government or its political function. It has practiced factional, ward-based machine politics for better than a century, and its political culture reflects the individual ward system and a distrust of any concentration of power. Although there have been bursts of leadership, the city has continued with a complacency and lack of confidence. Changes to the system have not altered the fundamental modus operandi. This political history illustrates the importance of institutions and political culture, which combine with economics and demographics to shape a city.

In this clearly qualitative study, the most important source may well have been interviews with present and former elected officials and business and community leaders. St. Louisans were very gracious with their time and often provided introductions to other possible informants. Because St. Louis is a small town/big city, I promised anonymity to everyone I interviewed. Informants are identified in this work only by generic headings such as "veteran politician" or "alderman." Including interviews conducted for previous research projects, I relied on information from close to two hundred sources. Some were even willing to speak to me on multiple occasions. A few informants were continuously helpful by advising me when new developments occurred or by preventing me from assuming something with insufficient evidence.

As far as was possible, I tried to triangulate by using multiple sources of information for the conclusions I reached. Naturally, any errors that exist are my responsibility.

Acknowledgments

This study had its beginnings in a casual conversation that took place in a campaign office in the summer of 1992. A conversation with a fellow volunteer piqued my interest in how campaigns were waged traditionally in St. Louis and how elected officials decided whom to endorse. I jokingly said, "There's a book in this." My good friend Catherine Forslund never let me forget what I said and reiterated frequently that I had to do this project. Another friend, then Alderman Dan McGuire of the twenty-eighth ward, a history buff, agreed to help me get started and establish a bibliography. There is not a great deal of published material about St. Louis politics, and some of it is quite old. Thanks to Dan, I located many sources at the St. Louis Public Library, a fine repository. The best historical treatment of St. Louis is James Neil Primm's work *Lion of the Valley*. Primm's volume is all encompassing, however, and politics is just one of many topics. But he has an excellent bibliography that helped my research greatly.

McGuire wanted me to be as historical as possible, and his gentle prods sent me back as far as St. Louis's "Great Divorce." He also helped introduce me to some St. Louis political legends who spoke about their careers. In addition, he and Nancy Rice put me into contact with Miss Olive Dwyer, who graciously allowed me to use her father's papers (John J. Dwyer) before they were sent to the archives at Saint Louis University.

Certain individuals and institutions have made research on St. Louis politics infinitely easier. Carole Prietto helped me use the Washington University archives, which contain the papers of three former St. Louis mayors—Raymond Tucker, A. J. Cervantes, and John Poelker—that are rich fodder for a researcher. The University of Missouri–St. Louis has a collection of oral histories of African Americans who played important roles in St. Louis history. Doris Wesley helped me utilize that collection, which provides information not available elsewhere. The main branch of the St. Louis Public Library has a section devoted to city history that is both user friendly and useful, thanks to Noel Holobeck.

Kevin Coan of the St. Louis Election Board helped me access returns from many years back. In addition, back issues of the

St. Louis newspapers from the early 1900s onward provided important data.

Geraldine Osborn, Jim Shrewsbury, and Fred Steffen answered many questions about what happened and when, saving me many additional hours at the microfilm reader. Francis G. Slay, Olive Dwyer, and Georgia Buckowitz graciously furnished photographs.

I am also grateful to a number of political science colleagues for their support of this work and will mention Terry Jones, Dennis Judd, Carol Kohfeld, and Dave Robertson in particular. John Pelissero kindly read a draft of this work, as did former U. S. senator Thomas Eagleton. Sharon Carpenter also offered comments. Their questions and comments certainly helped improve the manuscript. Lana Vierdag and Jan Frantzen helped in too many ways to enumerate. Their friendship and assistance kept me going. I would also like to express my thanks to three stalwart neighborhood friends who buoyed my spirits with laughter over many a lunch and telephone call: Lois Schoemehl, JoAnn Vatcha, and Marj Weir. They and the instigators for this project, Catherine Forslund and Dan McGuire, have shared their love for our neighborhood and our city. Finally, the Missouri Historical Society Press provided a very amenable place to see this work published. I want to particularly thank editors Josh Stevens and Lauren Mitchell and director Lee Ann Sandweiss.

I came to St. Louis in 1987 to teach at the University of Missouri–St. Louis and knew quickly that I had found a home. St. Louis is a very easy place to live. In that first year, someone told me St. Louis was the country's best-kept secret. I am grateful to have found a home here and to have encountered so many St. Louisans able to help me explain why St. Louis has the politics it does.

An Introduction
to St. Louis's Political Context

Many newcomers to St. Louis look askance at the city's political life, which may seem somewhat archaic to them. St. Louis politics clearly hearken back to an earlier era in American history. The city's elections are partisan, a large number of offices need filling, and twenty-eight ward organizations serve as the focal point of campaigning, the source of endorsements, and the base of the city's patronage employment. Jobs still are provided in exchange for political support. Power is fragmented, and ward-based factionalism remains a hallmark of the system.

When the twentieth century began, most major U.S. cities shared St. Louis's form of government and its type of politics. Now, into the twenty-first century, St. Louis stands almost alone with its traditional political arrangements. Other eastern and midwestern cities—New York, Philadelphia, Cleveland, Pittsburgh, and Chicago—also display certain characteristics of unreformed government. However, these cities have altered their governance to lessen fragmentation. They have centralized administrative authority in the person of the mayor. This strong-mayor form permits leadership with less expenditure of political capital, as fewer officials have to sign off on programs or payments. St. Louis had some active mayors in the twentieth century, men able to dominate the political stage for a time. But the city's factional nature and its fragmented power made the exercise of strong leadership a relatively short-term affair.

This introduction places St. Louis political history within an analytical framework developed by various urban scholars. The terminology is widely shared and permits comparisons across cities. This work is a case study of St. Louis designed to highlight the factors that shaped political life there and could be relevant in examining other jurisdictions as well.

The nature of a city's system of governance affects its political behavior in a number of ways. The interaction between elected officials and business and civic leaders can be intimate and extensive or intermittent and project related. Urban scholar Clarence N. Stone called this interplay a relationship between business and government

Unlike in some of these other cities, St. Louis's politics have changed very little over the years. Its traditional political rituals persist despite immense changes in demography, economics, technology, and policy. Interestingly, other machine cities have moved toward greater centralization, allowing them to respond better to postwar urban decline.

Four decades ago, Edward C. Banfield and James Q. Wilson predicted the extinction of machine politics in their classic work *City Politics*.[5] Certainly the Progressive reform movement had eliminated machine practices in many places. Banfield and Wilson expected that machine practices would wither away in any city where exchange relationships continued to exist. When the machine's supporters secured middle-class status, these political scientists felt that allegiance to the ward boss would disappear. According to them, "the main reason for the decline and near disappearance of the citywide machine was—and is—the growing unwillingness of voters to accept the inducements that it offered. The petty favors and 'friendship' of the precinct captains declined in value as immigrants were assimilated, public welfare programs were extended, and per capita incomes rose steadily and sharply in war and postwar prosperity."[6]

Banfield and Wilson felt that citizens were either private-regarding or public-regarding. A private-regarding ethos typified machine politics because it was based on individual exchange relationships. Those with a private-regarding ethos were members of the working class, immigrants, and their heirs. The scholars associated the public-regarding ethos, on the other hand, with cities on the reform end of the continuum. For Banfield and Wilson, the public-regarding ethos represents "the Anglo-Saxon Protestant elite, the central idea of which is that politics should be based on public rather than private motives and accordingly, should stress the virtues of honesty, impartiality, and efficiency."[7] Banfield and Wilson make civic spirit income-related and appear quite optimistic about human virtue.

Sociologist Robert K. Merton took a different tack. He felt machine politics arose in the U.S. because of "the scattered fragments of power" characteristic of the American political system.[8] Merton found that machine politicians recognized that "the voter is a person living in a specific neighborhood, with specific personal problems that are extremely concrete and immediate."[9] Thus, machine politics, with its individual contacts, was not impersonal and did not ground its service delivery in rules and forms. "The precinct captain...asks no questions, exacts no compliance with legal rules of eligibility and does not 'snoop' into private affairs."[10] Reform meant bureaucracy; machine politics gave individually tailored exchanges. St. Louis's politicians have been any city's equal in providing such direct services to constituents, be it a job, a word with the municipal judge, or the proverbial Thanksgiving turkey.

Many writers, such as Banfield and Wilson, felt that Roosevelt's New Deal programs would help dig the grave of machine politics. Raymond Wolfinger had a different point of view. Instead of the New Deal decreasing the need for the friendly machine politician, Roosevelt's social programs increased it. The programs produced a bureaucratic labyrinth that constituents needed help negotiating. The assistance might be different from before, but it could still engender that old sense of obligation in the recipient.[11] New immigrants also continued to take the place of the old, whose children had become more affluent and suburbia-bound. After World War II, poor whites and blacks from rural areas flocked to the nation's cities. They too would need help negotiating in a strange climate. And inside central cities, poverty never vanished; in fact, it became more entrenched. For these reasons, Wolfinger felt that the ward politician still had a place in a modern city.

Banfield and Wilson, Merton, and Wolfinger all saw machine politics in functional terms. Machine politics answered needs with exchanges at the individual level. Although needs and means changed, Wolfinger found that machine politics played a continuing role. Indeed, they have persisted in St. Louis and other major cities despite the passing of time. Although the functional argument is a strong one, other factors also may help perpetuate the machine mode. In St. Louis, traditional practices remain close to their original form. Institutional structure and cultural norms may well be related to this city's enduring machine style, along with functionalism.

Institutions and Culture

A strong link exists between machine politics and certain forms of institutional arrangements: mayor-council form, partisan elections, large councils with members chosen from districts, and patronage. In turn, machine cities have a political culture that accepts the bestowing of favors in return for electoral support. However, machine-politics cities have not all evolved in the same direction. Some form of institutional change may have resulted in differences in leadership, policymaking, or behavior evident today.

In recent years, political scientists have begun to reassert the importance of institutional examination in a discipline dominated by behavioralists since just after World War II. An example of this new mode of inquiry is a study of how rules affect certain outcomes, such as election returns. Prominent organizational scholars James G. March and Johan P. Olsen have brought to the fore critical arguments for including institutions as factors in political inquiry. For example, they believe that "political institutions define the framework within which politics takes place."[12] They illustrate this point by noting that "the values and preferences of political actors are not exogenous to political institutions but develop within the institutions."[13] The institutional environment helps define appropriate means and actions, and a political actor's choice of policy and strategy is shaped by his or her location.

Looking at nations, James Q. Wilson as well as R. Kent Weaver and Bert A. Rockman have demonstrated that different sets of institutions can affect the ability to devise, change, or implement policy.[14] Certain types of institutions, e.g., parliamentary, support a more consensual style of governance than does the separation of powers and federalism present in the United States. Weaver and Rockman stipulate that form of government will not guarantee a particular outcome, but, in association with other factors, it can affect overall policymaking.[15]

Political culture, which governs style and appropriateness, has a strong association with institutional arrangements at all levels of government. It encompasses "the attitudes and beliefs of citizens about how political institutions and processes ought to work, about fellow citizens and their place in the political process, and about the proper rules of the game."[16] Political culture enables the installation of a particular institutional mix, and the institutions then sustain that political culture. Political scientist Barbara Ferman has described the importance of institutional and cultural congruence: "Changing the structure of function of an institution while leaving the underlying political (and institutional) culture untouched may amount to nothing more than moving boxes on an organization flow chart."[17]

St. Louis's political institutions and culture influence its ability to react to a changing environment. Rather than prescribing certain courses of action, they may delimit which strategies will be considered. As Daniel J. Elazar, a student of federalism, noted, "Political culture...directly determines behavior within relatively few situations or in response to relatively few particular issues. Instead its influence lies in its power to set relatively fixed limits on political behavior and to provide subliminal direction for political actors."[18] Both Ferman and Elazar acknowledge the fusion between institutions and culture in the way they structure their political arena. St. Louis may well be an exemplar of this phenomenon.

St. Louis as a Case Study

St. Louis stands out among machine-politics cities because of its perpetuation of a weak-mayor form, fragmented power, and ward factionalism. To understand the longevity of this governance pattern, the city's institutions and culture must be key foci of analysis. Economic and demographic factors interact with structure. Class and race as well as tradition have made St. Louis a prisoner of past decisions. Other cities began with similar institutional arrangements and modified them in due course. But no city had quite the same structure or number of officeholders as St. Louis, yesterday or today.

In more recent times, St. Louis's institutions and culture have affected the city's ability to work with business leaders on developmental issues. Since the late 1960s, these relationships have not been cohesive. Machine-politics traditions also shaped the pattern of African American political incorporation in St. Louis. Most black elected officials centered their ambitions on the provision of patronage, not out of step with their white brethren.

Institutions either aid or abet the exercise of leadership. In the twentieth century, St. Louis had several mayors with the drive and determination to reshape their city. Henry Kiel, a Republican, launched a major civic building program during his three terms in office. Democrat Bernard Dickmann helped change the political allegiance of many St. Louisans in the 1930s and operated New Deal programs to benefit constituents. Raymond Tucker, a civil engineer, led the city's efforts at urban renewal and served three terms. Democrat Vincent Schoemehl was a three-term mayor as well. Schoemehl stressed programs aimed at beautifying the city and making residents feel safer. He also reinvigorated housing in the city's midsection and oversaw downtown rebuilding. As will be shown, each of these men conceivably could have exercised greater programmatic leadership had the institutional structure been more centralized and power more concentrated. In St. Louis, the qualities of an individual can make the mayor's office more potent and effective, but those qualities can go only so far. Barriers in the political system destroy valuable political capital and leave St. Louis worse off than it would like to be.

This political history will describe how St. Louis's institutions developed and will explain the role of the political culture in maintaining the status quo by preventing major changes to offices, roles, and rules. Despite a considerable decline in economic significance in the last century, despite sizable losses of people, jobs, and businesses, the city totters along in its traditional governmental clothing. Old habits and old arrangements die hard. St. Louis is a comfortable place to "go along to get along." At several points in recent history, there were attempts to change the city charter. These efforts failed in part because of racial and income divisions among the citizenry. New attempts to disturb St. Louis's form of government are brewing today; whether these efforts will be more successful is still open to question.

Studying St. Louis permits a multifaceted examination of institutional and cultural questions over time. The first chapter will begin the telling of St. Louis's political development at the time it became an early home-rule city. (For a discussion of the methodology employed, see the Preface.)

St. Louis Politics

Chapter 1

Building St. Louis's
Institutional Parameters
1876–1914

This study concentrates on the Democratic ward politics that have dominated St. Louis for most of the years since 1933. However, it is impossible to attempt an institutional analysis of these politics in a more recent era without looking at the origins of St. Louis's governmental and political structure. The institutional underpinnings of this city and its factional ward politics began to develop in the middle of the nineteenth century. St. Louis's culture and form of government were rooted in the city's immigration patterns, geography and sectional associations, and path-breaking attempt to establish greater control over its environs. Past decisions do not determine future ones, but they lay a foundation that makes certain outcomes more likely than others. Many cities' political life resembled St. Louis's before 1900. By the end of the twentieth century, St. Louis remained virtually alone in perpetuating a fragmented ward system. Decisions made in the late nineteenth and early twentieth centuries continue to cast long shadows over St. Louis's political present and to circumscribe opportunities for change.

Founding and Early Years

Just below the confluence of the Missouri and Mississippi Rivers, French fur traders established a trading post in 1764 that eventually became the city of St. Louis. The city's early growth took place along the Mississippi's western banks. Its current moniker, "Gateway to the West," highlights the city's role as the starting point for the Lewis and Clark expedition and for many wagon trains of frontier pioneers.

The French fur traders who came up from New Orleans to settle St. Louis brought slaves with them. Located in the center of the United States, Missouri borders both the South and the Midwest heartland. An area in the central part of the state carries the appellation "Little Dixie" even today. It was in this region that plantation agriculture took hold. Missouri entered the union as a slave state under the terms of the Compromise of 1820. However, at that time, only 15 percent of the state's population were slaves, and only 10 percent of the state's households owned slaves.[1]

Shortly after statehood, a new wave of immigration reshaped St. Louis. Native Germans came to this river city in large numbers in the 1830s and 1840s. Predominantly Catholic, the German immigrants also possessed abolitionist views in substantial numbers, especially those who came after the thwarted Revolution of 1848. Irish Catholics also began arriving in this period, and their numbers increased markedly during the ravages of the great potato famine that struck their homeland. The arrival of large numbers of foreigners, and Catholics to boot, set the state's largest city apart from its rural brethren: Protestant, native born, and often from neighboring southern states.

Mistrust of urban entities by state legislators and rural residents has been commonplace in U.S. politics. As Dennis R. Judd and Todd Swanstrom point out, "No matter how fast and big cities grew, their representatives to the state house never would be able to exert a majority voice in state legislatures."[2] U.S. cities are creatures of the states that contain them. States make the laws that allow or forbid forms of taxation as well as bonding and local incorporation. In the nineteenth century, states often assumed control of city functions, including policing, for a period of time and then returned them to municipal rule.

The Civil War brought home the clear differences between St. Louis and the state of Missouri. Missouri's rural-dominated legislature had strong Confederate leanings. St. Louis, on the other hand, hosted an increasing number of German immigrants who sympathized with abolitionists and the Union. St. Louis also housed the largest arsenal in any slave state. Fearful that city fathers would protect the arsenal's contents for the federal government, the Missouri legislature put state government in charge of St. Louis's police force in March 1861.[3] Although other states assumed control of city police forces at various times in the nineteenth century, they always eventually returned the police function to local stewardship. Missouri did not. In St. Louis, a board appointed by the governor has run the police without interruption since 1861, even though Southern sympathizers failed to gain meaningful control of the state at the beginning of the Civil War. A continuing chasm has separated city and state, and the relations between the two entities, as well as lack of local control of the police, are critical in understanding St. Louis politics.

The 1876 Divorce

An end to easy annexation by northern municipalities in the early years of the twentieth century helped seal their fate. Legislatures in various states made it far more difficult for their major cities to add areas on their periphery that increased in population. Decades later, cities stagnated while a widening suburban ring grew in population and jobs. St. Louis became the first victim of finite boundaries, and, ironically, it sealed its own fate. The events of 1875–76 also had a profound impact on the city's political development and its continuing machine-style practices.

Not unlike other states, Missouri continuously tinkered with St. Louis's governmental arrangements after the Civil War, including "regulations of specific detail."[4] Frustrating as this was to city officials, they were troubled also by their relationship with St. Louis County (which contained St. Louis City), with the nature of county governance, and with the county residents outside city boundaries. The county court provided a particular source of problems to city officials because of how it disproportionately allocated the funds derived largely from city taxpayers.[5]

Adoption of a new Missouri constitution in 1875 enabled the selection of a board of freeholders (property owners) to draft a municipal charter. St. Louisans seized this opportunity and elected a thirteen-man board from the city and from the county. Their work had two principal components: the separation of city from county and the drafting of a charter for St. Louis City. This would be the nation's first municipal home-rule charter.

In what is referred to locally as the 1876 divorce, St. Louis City ceased to be part of any county. In the process, it expanded its borders well into undeveloped territory. Certainly the city's elders did not foresee the tremendous migration outward that streetcar technology would make possible only a couple decades later. The 1876 divorce hastened what would have occurred with a likely end to annexation early in the next century. The divorce left the city with only sixty-one square miles of territory. This premature boundary closure certainly had demographic and economic implications, but, most important for this study, it laid an institutional framework that shaped the city's style of politicking and governance.

When St. Louis City ceased to be part of a county, the state of Missouri mandated that it fulfill certain county functions. The city had to elect magistrates and constables in district elections and also fill a large number—eleven at that time—of the so-called "county offices." The heads of each of these offices would be elected at large on a partisan ballot at the time of the state primary in August and in the general election in November. The state constitution and state laws contained the duties and perquisites of each office. Subsequent court decisions have ruled that these offices are indeed state offices, responsible to Missouri's legislature.[6] The legislature has continued to set the salary of these officeholders and, with the exception of the city treasurer, the governor can fill any vacancy that occurs between regularly scheduled elections. These county offices represent an additional linkage between state and city politics. And the locally elected officeholders are not beholden to the mayor or the city's aldermen, contributing to fragmentation. Instead, they lobby and ally with candidates for state office.

The Missouri constitution also provides for partisan organization in all of the state's counties and, hence, in St. Louis City as well. It specifies electoral districts concomitant with city wards, which then select Democratic and Republican committeemen and, after 1920, committeewomen. City elected officials such as aldermen are prohibited from holding these committee posts. However, county officeholders such as sheriff or recorder of deeds can fill these positions, as can state representatives and state senators.

The 1876 St. Louis City Charter

At the time St. Louis's home-rule charter was written, many American cities had ward-based politics centered on patron-client relationships. This political genre is peculiar to the United States among western countries. Various explanations have been offered for the phenomenon. Amy Bridges has pointed to the confluence of immigration, industrialization, and a suffrage available to all white males, including those who owned no property.[7] In Europe, workingmen prohibited from voting joined political parties directly linked to the trade-union movement. Class divisions manifested themselves in the nature of political participation. The U.S. system of government is far more decentralized than its European counterparts, and, importantly, workers here were not fighting for the vote along with rights on the job.[8] In addition, in the latter part of the nineteenth century, ethnic divisions were also neighborhood divisions.

The various eastern and southern European immigrants clustered with those of the same nationality. Solidarity at the plant between Irishmen and Serbs did not reproduce itself in the precincts.[9] For these reasons, city governance moved from a system of elite-dominated committees to ward-based political entities led by members of a particular immigrant group, in St. Louis most often the Irish and the Germans, which catered to the needs of the multiplying numbers of other new arrivals.

There is general agreement that, in the 1870s, municipal politics were decentralized in American cities, with, as Martin Shefter described, "independent political operators, whose influence was a function of the size and strength of their personal followings."[10] Although Shefter documented a relatively early end to this form of machine politics in New York City, historian Jon Teaford maintained that such factionalism generally characterized urban political life through the end of the nineteenth century. Teaford felt that "urban politics was, then, a divisive arena of competition and rivalry presided over by party brokers who sought to create coalitions in the place of conflict."[11] The locus of party organization lay in the various city wards, and they could be divided by various rivalries.[12]

The exchanges of votes for services and jobs and the networks of personal obligation frequently spawned corruption as well. "Vote early and vote often" was not just a humorous phrase then, and contracts and jobs often carried hefty price tags. "Boodle," as it was called in St. Louis, enriched party treasuries and the purses of various party functionaries as well as those of some members of the economic elite.

St. Louis certainly was no exception to this general portrait of late-nineteenth-century municipal politics. In fact, Thomas S. Barclay noted that some of the freeholders drafting St. Louis's home-rule charter "frequently expressed the belief that ward representation alone had resulted in undesirable ward politics and in the control of the city council by men who have little interest in general municipal dignity and honor."[13] This pattern of urban governance was not confined to St. Louis. The adventures of Hinky Dink Kenna and Bathhouse John Couglin, who represented Chicago's first ward, provide the flavor of the times.[14] Legal shenanigans occurred frequently, and roughhousing and fisticuffs sometimes marked political gatherings. A frontier atmosphere still pervaded municipal governance, and political life was centered, more often than not, in saloons.

St. Louis's freeholders wanted especially to end the extravagance and waste they felt was typical of their rural brethren in the county.[15] In one sense, the state constitution furthered their aim. It set a "fixed maximum rate of taxation" for the city.[16] The state did not provide complete home rule, of course. For example, the state mandated that the city have an executive and "two houses of the legislature, one of which shall be elected by general ticket,"[17] or at large. Despite sentiment to eliminate contentious and sometimes corrupt ward-based politics, the freeholders finally opted for a bicameral legislature. The House of Delegates had members elected from each of twenty-eight wards to a two-year term. There was also a thirteen-member council elected at large to four-year terms.[18]

The freeholders debated whether their charge included the abolition of the police board appointed by the governor and the adoption of local control of public safety. After considerable discussion, the freeholders chose not to question the state's power in this area. State courts had "emphatically declared that control of the police was a matter of state and not municipal concern."[19]

In the end, this home-rule charter continued a very decentralized governmental structure. Aside from the two legislative bodies and the mayor, there would be fourteen more elected administrators. This new structure would do little to temper St. Louis's ward-based machine politics. Barclay, who has written extensively on the 1876 charter, noted that the political form it created would "render exceedingly difficult any cooperation save through the instrument of an indispensable political machine or political boss."[20] In truth, the framers saw no alternative to "municipal administration…permeated by the spoils system." They offered no protection against "partisan preferment."[21]

Home rule in St. Louis meant a one-time gain of territory and the embrace of state and local structures that proved to help perpetuate ward factionalism. Perhaps, in 1876, the ramifications of these decisions were not apparent to St. Louis citizens. Nor were there readily recognizable alternatives. However, a reform movement opposed to the venality and gross inefficiencies of machine operations that offered clear structural alternatives soon would appear nationwide. Interestingly, as we shall see, the movement failed in St. Louis to a greater degree than in many other locations. The familiar continued to be comfortable, in part because class cleavages worked against the possibility of significant change.

City Government in the New Century

The early years of the twentieth century saw a tremendous change in urban governance in many cities. A new wave of reformers, the Progressives, with both populist and civil-service roots, fought to root out corruption and inefficiency by depoliticizing local government. At all levels, the political party was their enemy, and efficiency was their watchword. Led most frequently by middle- to upper-class, native-born professionals or businessmen with no stake in the machine system, they changed the rules to set up purchasing and hiring standards. They wanted men of means elected to office to replace the immigrants who occupied many municipal elective posts.[22] Progressives favored at-large, nonpartisan elections for small city councils, a strong mayor (later a city manager), civil service, line-item budgets, and procedures for competitive bidding in the letting of contracts.

Many U.S. municipalities enacted the changes desired by the Progressives. Some saw only partial change, among them Cleveland, Philadelphia, Pittsburgh, Boston, and New York. According to Shefter, New York's machine politics became more centralized, especially in terms of control of the "spoils."[23] Key leaders who had elite cooperation gave New York City a party system that has maintained itself, at least to some degree, to the present. Although reformers there instituted purchasing requirements, a budget, and civil service, reform administrations alternated with those dominated by party regulars in the ensuing years. Political party influence remained strong in the other four cities as well, although centralization of patronage and other rewards of the game occurred in Pittsburgh and Boston as well. Teaford noted that in some cities, such as Cleveland and Chicago, partisan control remained despite the adoption of nonpartisan elections.[24]

Change in St. Louis during the Progressive era was more symbolic than substantive. The fragmentation inherent in the governance structure created by the 1876 charter certainly inspired calls for reform. Adherents of the Progressive cause were not out of view but, despite their strenuous efforts, they had relatively little influence. St. Louis adopted a new charter in 1914, but this document also made very little difference in the city's ward-centered political life. The factors that enabled a decentralized machine politics continued their unabated influence.

Change, but Little Change

The corruption that accompanied the inchoate machine politics of the late nineteenth century was no stranger to St. Louis. In the 1870s, the Great Whiskey Ring operated with impunity. "The

St. Louis had not been a good provider of basic services to much of its citizenry. The wealthy could build their lavish residences on private places, where they themselves assumed responsibility for basic infrastructure and service needs.[38] In addition, homes on these private places protected the wealthy from industrial encroachment and unsavory land uses.[39] Middle-class proprietors and professionals, on the other hand, lacked such protection and, often, basic sanitary services, as did the working families who toiled in factories or mines. For example, "geographic and social divisions...kept South St. Louis from having well-paved streets or easy-to-obtain mortgages."[40] According to local historian Eric Sandweiss, St. Louis continually adhered to the dictum that "public improvement was...the financial responsibility of those particular people who were directly affected by it.... (I)t continued to be earmarked primarily for those areas where people might be expected to afford it."[41] Inequalities, along with unhappiness, continued to mount.

For some reason, the wealthy West Enders, somewhat encased in myth, came to be known as the "Big Cinch." In fact, there was a high degree of connection among the prominent St. Louis families involved in big business and finance.[42] Programs tied to their imprimatur provoked bitter opposition and often meant defeat at the hands of the voters. Rammelkamp found that "the general public fervently believed there was a 'Big Cinch' and that it did control the city."[43] Many people assumed that because of the Big Cinch's control over capital, financing for new ventures not acceptable to this group would be rejected.[44] The battle for a free bridge across the Mississippi absorbed the passions of those outside the circle of power, and they promised to oppose other planning efforts. Businessman Rolla Wells, a Democrat, presided over the city as it prepared for, and then put on, its 1904 World's Fair. The excesses of his Republican predecessor helped Wells get reelected, and he managed to spruce up the city for its big moment while circuit attorney Folk prosecuted certain boodlers.

Despite cooperation for the Fair, the division between the wealthy and the rest of the populace later affected the enactment of a new city charter. The 1876 document had proved unwieldy and certainly had permitted many forms of chicanery. The Civic League sponsored a new charter and put it on the ballot in 1911. This charter would have strengthened the powers of the mayor and would have provided for a unicameral legislature elected at large, in proper Progressive fashion. The Civic League had clear ties to the Big Cinch. Curtis Hunter Porter found that the "largest percentage" of significant contributors to the League "were officers in downtown business firms, banks, or the manufacturing enterprises."[45] So, not surprisingly, voters overwhelmingly defeated this proposed charter. Men of the working class and ethnics active in ward politics worked against it, as did socialists and labor union members.[46] Opponents of the charter saw "the new proposal as a device by the 'Big Cinch' to take over the governance of the city."[47]

City voters finally managed to enact a new charter by a narrow margin in 1914. That document still governed the city as of 2001. Charter drafters included the initiative, referendum, and recall in the document to assuage the suspicions of the rank and file. However, the 1914 charter continued a weak-mayor system. It provided for a board of estimate and apportionment that would have budgetary and contractual authority for the city instead of resting it in the office of the mayor. The mayor and a comptroller and the president of the board of aldermen would make up the board; those positions would be elected citywide. A new unicameral board of aldermen would comprise twenty-eight representatives, each from one of the city's wards, although the aldermen would be elected by a citywide vote. (This peculiar electoral form lasted until 1941 and satisfied the state requirement of having a legislative chamber elected at large.) Municipal elections retained their partisan character. The charter did not provide for a civil service; all municipal jobs, as well as those in the county offices, remained patronage positions. The charter did provide for written exams as part of the hiring process, but the exams would be as practical as possible.

In numerous other cities from Chicago to Pittsburgh, patronage eventually became centralized in the hands of the party chair. However, in St. Louis, job referrals and requests for favors still were handled at the ward level. Ward committeemen of both parties supplied ready workers, and offices would change overnight when the electoral returns put a leader of the opposition in charge of city government.

The tepid path to reform taken with the 1914 charter resulted from deep class and ethnic divisions in St. Louis. To pass the charter, reformers had to appease those who identified with their ward organizations and who wanted more services for their more plebian neighborhoods. This division between the more ethnic and less affluent and the native-born men of wealth would persist in St. Louis politics and continue to hinder structural reform. Cries for efficiency would fall by the wayside if they became mixed up in a "we versus they" struggle encouraged by ward politicians. In other locations, the ethnic and class divisions over structural reform were not as sharp. For example, New York City voters elected a reformer, Seth Low, as mayor in 1903. His supporters were "disproportionately native born." However, he also received the votes of some "first generation foreign stock" residents because of his "policies on disease control and tenement regulation."[48]

Class divisions prevented reform in St. Louis during the Progressive Era that could have changed the city's ward-based factional politics. Unlike Boston, St. Louis maintained its partisan elections. It made no provision in 1914 for any kind of merit system. The city did not adopt strong executive leadership because of many citizens' fear and resentment of the Big Cinch. Coupled with state law mandating both a ward-centered party structure in the city and the maintenance of numerous county offices elected citywide, it is not surprising that the more things changed in St. Louis, the more they stayed the same.

St. Louis spruced itself up for the World's Fair of 1904, and some of the elite's City Beautiful plans came to fruition. But machine politics remained, and new immigrants—eastern Europeans, Italians, and Lebanese—arrived and looked to their committeemen for favors and jobs, as had the Germans and Irish before them. Deep social divisions had prevented any genuine Progressive-type reform. Local and state law continued to make the ward the locus of political activity and the party its vehicle. The parties did not become hierarchical.

Chapter 2

Republicans, Race, and Realignment
1914–1932

St. Louis's 1914 charter did not alter the nature of the city's politics: it kept the city's twenty-eight wards that had been established in 1876 as political units. It did little to alleviate St. Louis's fragmentation. The city's political structure remained conducive to ward-based factionalism aided by the fourteen officeholders selected citywide. Neither the Republicans nor the Democrats showed much centralization at this time. However, since elections for all city offices—including aldermen—were at large, one party could dominate St. Louis's electoral politics. In fact, from 1914 until 1932, when the Great Depression began to change allegiances in almost all major cities, Republicans ruled St. Louis. After Democrat Rolla Wells vacated the office of mayor in 1909, Republicans took possession of it until 1933. One mayor, Henry Kiel, served an unprecedented three terms, from 1913 to 1925. During this Republican ascendancy, issues of development and modernization had important places on the municipal agenda. However, the treatment of African Americans and their role in the city's political life formed both a beginning and an endpoint to these two decades of Republican rule.

The Segregation Ordinance of 1916

Merle Fainsod, in later life a Soviet scholar, wrote a master's thesis in 1929 about race and ethnicity in St. Louis politics. He described the attitude of white St. Louisans toward African Americans in the years prior to World War I "as a form of patient endurance toward an inferior but necessary creature."[1] St. Louis's black population grew slowly from 27,066 in 1890 to 43,960 in 1910, and blacks largely resided in only a few of the city's twenty-eight wards.[2] Nonetheless, white residents of areas bordering black neighborhoods worried increasingly about possible black expansion into their turf. As early as 1908, the *St. Louis Republic* reported on the fears of white residents of the West End: "North St. Louisans are fighting vigorously against the inroads of the blacks. The fight is not one of property owners alone but a concerted movement on the part of improvement associations and churches."[3] A resident remarked that the Twenty-sixth Ward Improvement Association "organized for no other purpose than to keep the negroes out of the neighborhood."[4] Two Catholic pastors made statements in support of their parishioners' attempts to maintain property values by keeping their neighborhoods for whites alone.[5] Father Peter O'Rourke of St. Mark's Catholic Church remarked, "I feel that it is not divine intention that the white and black races should affiliate."[6]

By 1911, the St. Louis Real Estate Exchange had decided that a municipal ordinance would be necessary to keep blacks from encroaching on previously all-white areas. According to the Exchange, "the ordinance will be patterned after the one now in force in Baltimore, and similar to ones in effect in Eastern and Southern cities."[7] Interestingly, in Baltimore, various improvement associations that championed the segregation ordinance had formed originally to fight for improved city services.[8] In St. Louis, on the contrary, white residents formed neighborhood improvement or protective associations after the turn of the century solely for the stated purpose of repelling and removing blacks from white neighborhoods.[9] Baltimore and St. Louis and other border-state cities were in the forefront of efforts to prohibit residential integration.

Also in 1911, the various improvement associations in St. Louis formed an umbrella group, the United Welfare Association. The following year, the Real Estate Exchange appointed a special committee to work with the Association on the issue of segregation.[10] In 1913, a bill designed to implement residential segregation was introduced into the city's Municipal Assembly. However, at this time, Republican politicians "consistently blocked segregation legislation because they feared to alienate black voters."[11]

Throughout the campaign for a segregation ordinance, the *St. Louis Post-Dispatch* opposed it consistently. The *St. Louis Republic* opposed it initially but tempered its stand as time passed. Mayor Henry W. Kiel was also a constant opponent, as was his fellow Republican, Congressman L. C. Dyer, who had a sizable black constituency in his district.[12] Other newspapers and politicians failed to follow their lead when the extent of sentiment for an ordinance among the general public became obvious.

The Real Estate Exchange, working in tandem with the United Welfare Association, used scare tactics to garner support for the ordinance its members favored and also linked support for municipal improvements to neighborhood segregation. According to a letter from a Real Estate Exchange officer, a central parkway, an integral feature of city plans dating from 1908, would displace "some 15,000 negroes." The letter continued, "Some of them may move next door to you."[13]

Frustrated legislatively, the United Welfare Association became the first group to take advantage of a key reform mechanism contained in the 1914 charter: the initiative. The association successfully obtained the signatures of 10 percent of St. Louis's registered voters on a petition to put the issue of segregation directly before the voting public. A special election was scheduled for February 29, 1916. Mayor Kiel held fast in his opposition, and several other Republican leaders joined him. However, many of the Republican committeemen either did nothing about the issue or worked for passage of the initiative.[14]

Almost half of St. Louis's 140,010 registered voters went to the polls on that February date. They easily adopted the segregation ordinance by a vote of 52,220 to 27,877. Since only 9,846 blacks were registered, some whites must have opposed the measure as well. Only three of the city's twenty-eight wards cast a majority of their votes against the ordinance, and each of these had a substantial African American population.[15]

St. Louis's adoption of a segregation ordinance was indicative of the tensions between whites and blacks in a number of cities in the early years of the twentieth century. Black migration from the South had begun in earnest and put pressure on existing ghetto boundaries. It also demonstrated the importance of the African American vote to elected officials and, in St. Louis's case, Republicans. Certain prominent politicians did not bow to popular sentiment but, rather, recognized the ongoing need for black support when taking a position on the measure. The black vote would be pivotal at a number of points in St. Louis's political history, and white politicians continued to court it, even while consciously or unconsciously denying blacks genuine equality in government or in everyday life.

The U.S. Supreme Court ruled that Baltimore's segregation ordinance was legally unenforceable in 1918. Hence, St. Louis's version was never put into effect. However, realtors and white homeowner associations in St. Louis continued to use restrictive covenants to prevent neighborhood integration. In addition, the St. Louis Real Estate Exchange sanctioned sales practices designed to hem in the black population to a limited section of the city.[16]

A Circumscribed Sphere: African American Participation in the Early Twentieth Century

The traditions of both North and South contributed to the opportunities for and limitations on African American residents of St. Louis in the early twentieth century. Not until *Brown v. Board of Education* and the passage of civil-rights legislation in the 1960s did the playing field significantly alter. Fainsod described the situation in 1929:

> Black and white attend separate schools, yet they use the same library facilities. The Negro is excluded from the gilded movie palaces, yet he can attend the more substantial legitimate shows provided he is willing to crane his neck from an obscure corner of the uppermost peanut gallery. He is excluded from white hostelries, eating places, barber shops, and dance halls, yet there is no objection to his crowding into the same department store elevator with whites and he is not put in a separate portion of the street car when he rides to and from work.[17]

The Missouri constitution of 1904 allowed segregation in education at all levels, and that is what occurred, from kindergartens on up to, and including, public and private universities. A distinct color line marked public accommodations and housing, which were kept as segregated as possible. St. Louis differed from many northern cities in that much of its segregation was de jure rather than de facto.

When it came to race and electoral politics, St. Louis most resembled other unreformed cities in the Midwest and the Northeast. African Americans were never denied the franchise in these cities and became part of various electoral coalitions. Not unlike Chicago, St. Louis elected African Americans to office early on. Charles Turpin, a Republican, ran successfully for the office of constable in 1918. The city was divided then into a number of districts for the purpose of electing magistrates (justices of the peace) and constables. Combined with a concentrated black population, this allowed African Americans a chance in district contests.

The Republican Party supported African American Crittenden Clark in his unsuccessful bid to be elected justice of the peace in

1924. "In view of the increasing importance of the Negro population of the city the organization simply could not offend the Negro vote. As a result full machine support was given to Crittenden Clark."[18] White politicians followed a limited quid pro quo pattern in seeking black support. Fainsod, writing almost three-quarters of a century ago, makes that explicit:

> It is clear that in politics the Negro in St. Louis will get only what must be given to him and not a bit more. Demands of expediency may occasionally force the candidate who appeals to the colored voter to show a generous front, but generally it may be taken for granted that the local party organizations are none too philanthropic toward the colored people; their attitude reflects the prejudices which have become sanctified by the customary community attitude toward the Negro.[19]

Despite prevailing sentiments in the white population, district elections permitted the election of black candidates to the positions of justice of the peace and state representative not long after Turpin's path-breaking victory. An African American also achieved the more powerful position of Republican ward committeeman in 1922. Although denied many rights, African Americans could use the franchise to gain some form of political representation and some share of the lower-level patronage jobs available to those supporting the successful party. African Americans in St. Louis had to live with some of the Jim Crow laws characteristic of the American South. But they could gain political office in the first quarter of the century because of district elections—part and parcel of the locality's machine-style system. Certain white Republican officials of that era did not overlook black residents; blacks represented a share of the vote and had proven unfailingly loyal to the party of Lincoln.

Henry W. Kiel and Republican Rule

St. Louis's 1914 charter had been designed to preserve the businesslike management of Democratic mayor Rolla Wells.[20] Nonetheless, supporters of the charter realized that the at-large provision for aldermanic elections "would guarantee a Republican majority of the council, especially with the influx of blacks to the city."[21] Despite Wells's eight-year tenure, the city had a strong Republican predisposition, based on the loyalty of the large German population. The city's African American residents also felt quite tied

Henry Kiel, mayor from 1913 to 1925, shown here in 1915. MHS Photograph and Print Collection.

to the Republican party. Many of the machine excesses of St. Louis politics at the turn of the century came under the city's Republican stewardship.

To a writer in a national reform journal in 1921, Republican mayor Henry W. Kiel (1913–1925) was the leader of a corrupt machine, "the best entrenched municipal machine in the country."[22] Kiel's personal electoral success—he was the city's first three-term mayor—made him a principal player in politics and government. However, his control was not hierarchical; instead, it was based on some critical alliances. Kiel worked very closely with county officeholders, who were led by clerk of the circuit court Nat Goldstein, and also with John Schnoll, chair of the city Republican committee.[23] Not unlike St. Louis's machine-style politicians of an earlier era, Kiel relied on the support of the "financial and utility combine known as the 'Big Cinch.'"[24] His secret dealings with the street railway franchise, the United Railway Company, almost ended his third-term hopes. He had to survive significant primary opposition and a serious Democratic opponent. Four of the five daily newspapers did not endorse him. Such serious primary opposition would have been less likely if a more hierarchical party structure existed. Kiel also was helped by the fact that many of the "civic-minded reformers" felt that the Irish-dominated Democrats presented no real alternative to Kiel's machine-style operations. Louis F. Budenz, the reformer and writer, spoke of "the doubt in many minds that the Democratic city committee would improve the situation, but rather make it worse. Its hitherto hopelessly minority character has caused it to fall into the hands of elements which seek generally to be lesser partners of the opposing machine and dependents of the same financial-utility combine which dictates to the Republican organization."[25]

In fact, the quid pro quo nature of St. Louis politics extended to both parties, and members of each depended on shifting alliances to maintain their position. Budenz's reform commentary was not the first nor the last to speak of a "machine" dominating St. Louis politics. Budenz failed to recognize that power was built on a series of deals rather than hierarchical arrangements. In fact, when Kiel, that powerful leader, sought his party's nomination as mayor in 1929, after only a four-year absence from the office, he was unsuccessful. In addition, in his three successful elections as mayor, Kiel had only "one plurality exceeding 10,000 votes."[26]

Machine or machine-style, reformed or unreformed, many of America's cities pursued similar development policies in the teens and twenties, embarking on numerous public works projects.[27] St. Louis was no exception to this trend. In 1923, Mayor Kiel and civic leaders saw the successful passage of twenty of twenty-one bond issues for various projects, including some originally conceived of by City Beautiful planners early in the century.[28] The money was meant for the erection of public edifices, a plaza and fountain, enclosure of the River Des Peres (often a floating sewer), and the building of a public hospital in the Ville, the traditionally black area of the city. River enclosure and construction of the downtown edifices began soon after the bond issues passed. Construction of a black public hospital, however, remained a dream deferred. African American voters did not forget this omission. They overwhelmingly had given their support to the bond issue and then failed to receive their due. Parenthetically, St. Louis's bonded debt was the lowest of any major city in the United States before passage of these twenty bond issues.[29] The low-tax, low-spend approach of Missouri and its southern neighbors also characterized St. Louis government in this era.

St. Louis's Critical Election

Republicanism had deep roots in St. Louis. However, a variety of circumstances changed the city into an arena of two-party competition for two decades. After the adoption of the 1914 charter, which instituted at-large selection of aldermen, each of whom represented one of the city's twenty-eight wards, no Democrat was elected to that office for eighteen years. Nor was a Democrat seated on the board of estimate and apportionment (mayor, comptroller, president of the board of aldermen) for nineteen years. Primary races sometimes were spirited contests though, and three-term mayor Henry W. Kiel did not always control his flock. Certainly, his opposition to the segregation ordinance failed to carry over to the rank and file.

St. Louis was not the only city to enjoy a strong Republican presence in the 1920s. In the presidential elections of 1920 and 1924, the twelve largest cities in the United States favored the Republican tickets by far more than a million votes.[30] Al Smith's 1928 candidacy changed this equation somewhat. Smith had been a progressive governor of New York state, and his origins were very urban. He was a product of New York City's lower East Side and had risen through the ranks in Tammany Hall. He also opposed Prohibition, and he was Catholic. The times were not ripe for his candidacy nationwide, but the voters in the twelve largest cities awarded him a 200,000-vote plurality, reversing the previous Republican edge. St. Louis voters, however, did not show signs of straying from the Republican fold in 1928, nor did they in the 1929 or 1931 local elections.

St. Louis's one-time rival for supremacy in the Middle West, Chicago, also experienced Republican stewardship during the early decades of the twentieth century. Bill Thompson, a Republican, served as mayor there in the 1920s. Questionable dealings and extravagances marked his administration. A Republican organization also ran Philadelphia.

By 1932, the enormity of the Great Depression finally separated St. Louis voters from their Republican identification, at least for a time. With many out of work, banks failing, the number of evictions rising, and private purveyors of assistance clearly unable to meet an unprecedented need, St. Louisans cast presidential ballots for another New York governor, Franklin D. Roosevelt, on November 8, 1932. Of 344,122 votes, 222,643 were for Roosevelt—65 percent of the vote. Every Democratic candidate on the ballot enjoyed similar margins, including five men seeking judgeships, six running for county offices, and two running in special elections for seats on the board of aldermen.[31] In addition, Democrats elected nineteen state representatives from the city and three state senators. Roosevelt was the first Democratic presidential candidate to carry the city since Woodrow Wilson in 1912.[32]

The 1932 results would predict the political near future. Locally, the 1933 mayoral contest would be key to the breakdown of Republican domination. In the Democratic primary, the clear favorite was Bernard F. Dickmann, president of the St. Louis Real Estate Exchange and a Marine veteran. He was a second-generation politician; his father had served three terms as sheriff, including a term during the World's Fair.[33] In his mayoral race, his first attempt at elected office, Dickmann enjoyed the support of the city Democratic committee.[34] He had been treasurer of the state Democratic committee.[35] Dickmann was an overwhelming winner in the primary. He then faced Republican Walter J. G. Neun, the president of the board of aldermen, in the April general election. The portents for the Democrats were excellent: In the primary, Dickmann had received 123,989 votes, "a greater number...than was received by any candidate of either party for Mayor in an April election."[36]

In the March primary, Dickmann also received a larger vote total than Neun in all the majority black wards, save one, the Sixth.[37]

Mayor Bernard Dickmann in 1934. Photograph by Gerhard Sisters, MHS Photograph and Print Collection.

The *St. Louis Post-Dispatch* noted that "Dickmann has made an appeal to the Negroes, and Negro clubs have been formed in his support."[38] The move of black voters to the Democratic column was a significant one. David Grant, a lawyer and political figure for several decades, addressed the question in a 1970 oral history:

> The Republican Party was quick to seize upon...it being the party of freedom, it had freed the slaves.... Blacks were brainwashed, and they were emotionally attracted to the Republican Party, and here in St. Louis, you could probably have counted the Democrats in 1930, black Democrats, on your hands and toes. In fact it was worse in 1930 to be black and a Democrat than it was today to be a card-carrying Communist.[39]

Blacks occupied a secondary position in the Republican ranks and sought to enlarge their role. After Charles Turpin's election as constable in 1918, he joined attorneys Homer G. Phillips, George Vaughn, and Joseph Mitchell in organizing the Citizens Liberty League. The League was designed to mobilize black voters within the Republican Party.[40]

By 1928, an increased demand for participation and services by blacks in the Republican Party emerged in the wake of African American Joseph McLemore's unsuccessful bid for a Republican congressional nomination. Blacks, such as David Grant, realized the importance of the black vote to Republicans and the little they received for it:

> It was the black vote that was keeping the Republican Party in power in the City of St. Louis. They had no white collar jobs; they had all the slop wagons with the mules; they had all of the mops and slop buckets, and that's all they had. They had one assistant city counselor.... These office-holders would make their black employees do work at their homes such as cutting their grass and being their butler.[41]

In 1932 and 1933, David Grant and George Vaughn worked to convince black voters to switch to the Democratic Party.[42] The leading black political figure in St. Louis for three decades, Jordan "Pop" Chambers, joined them. Chambers operated a funeral home and also owned a nightclub. Many felt that Chambers "led the 1930s exodus of blacks from the Republican Party into the Democratic ranks."[43]

Jordan "Pop" Chambers, shown here in 1962, helped convince many African Americans to switch from the Republican to the Democratic Party in the early 1930s. The St. Louis Mercantile Library at the University of Missouri—St. Louis.

Given a growing disillusionment with the paltry fruits of Republican participation, Chambers "and others believed that black St. Louisans would obtain more patronage and more political progress in a different party."[44] Chambers had the unique ability to command the respect of both black voters and white power brokers. According to David Grant, Jordan Chambers "came over" just after Roosevelt won in 1932.[45] Grant described Chambers as "unschooled" but added "he was a natural organizer. He was of this odd brand.... it takes an odd brand of human being to be a committeeman, a political committeeman.... A very wise man...who had the respect of the entire political family of St. Louis, principally because he kept his word at all times."[46] Saying that a politician keeps his word was the highest compliment that could be paid in St. Louis. It referred, among other things, to continuing with one's promised support for a candidate even if conditions changed drastically and the fellow was going to lose badly.

Chambers's role in the black community was that of a traditional machine politician who used services and jobs to win people's

However, because of the city's division of administrative authority, Dickmann had to share budgetary and contractual authority with Louis Nolte, the Republican comptroller, and Walter Neun, the Republican president of the board of aldermen, for at least two more years. Dickmann assumed overall control over at least seven thousand city employees. (The figure varies between seven and nine thousand in the various newspaper accounts.) The mayor could make a dozen direct appointments, and he could also appoint 189 employees in unclassified service. For other employees, the city charter said, "they cannot be reduced or discharged because of political opinions or affiliations."[53] But they could be terminated without cause. The *Globe-Democrat* noted that "When Mayor [Victor] Miller came into office [in 1929], although he was continuing the Republican regime at the City Hall, there was a rather general turnover in employees. Despite all provisions of the Board, means have been found continually to appoint or remove any employee at the will of administration heads."[54] Dickmann could use jobs to cement his authority, but the city's weak-mayor form would prevent him from completely centralizing control. Many at the time considered him a boss, and indeed he may have been the most powerful twentieth-century Democrat, but for only a brief period. His tenure lasted only eight years—two terms—and threats to his position of eminence in the Democratic Party were continuous.

Despite efforts of many whites to establish legal barriers to integrated neighborhoods, African Americans nonetheless occupied a pivotal position first in the Republican hegemony and then in the new Democratic ascendancy. African American leaders, no less than whites, focused their attention on patronage. The long-sought black public hospital was not just pork-barrel politics, although it would provide numerous jobs to nonwhite constituents. Named for the late attorney Homer G. Phillips, the hospital built by the Dickmann administration became a symbol to the black community, akin to the first black high school built in St. Louis. It was considered essential for the provision of health care to blacks in a mostly segregated city.[55] The facility also provided residencies and internships for black physicians and training for other black medical personnel available in only a couple locations in the United States. The movement of black St. Louisans to Dickmann's candidacy and support for the Democratic ticket combined machine-style elements with a deep desire for greater equality. That combination would prove emblematic of black St. Louis politics in the decades to follow.

Chapter 3

The Dickmann-Hannegan Years, 1933–1941

Almost a Political Machine

The incredible suffering brought about by the Great Depression led many in urban America to support Franklin Roosevelt and the Democratic Party. In turn, the Democrats began to enjoy significant success in municipal elections in cities such as Pittsburgh, Chicago, and St. Louis. This chapter depicts the formation of the Democratic style of governing in St. Louis and a short-lived effort to centralize power. In the end, ward factionalism maintained its hold on St. Louis's political operations.

Although Republican electoral successes at the local level ended in 1933, Democratic dominance of local contests did not become a virtual certainty until the mid-1970s. A Republican sat on the board of estimate and apportionment until 1975. After that, only one or two aldermen were Republicans. However, during the 1930s, it seemed for a time as if Democratic mayor Bernard Dickmann (better known as Barney) and his organization had created a centralized political machine that would dominate local elections. That dominance, however, proved transient. Dickmann never was free from challenges from fellow Democrats, often coming from county officeholders. He and his allies never could achieve the political consolidation that occurred under Democratic leaders in Pittsburgh and Chicago in the same period.

After being elected mayor in 1933, Dickmann strove to turn his victory into an era of Democratic supremacy. To accomplish this, he had to address a number of elements, including cementing his coalition, continuing the courtship of new allies, using jobs as a prime building block of support, and manipulating other governmental layers to augment his reward system. Dickmann found time to deal with substantive issues as well, including downtown redevelopment. During the latter part of his tenure, two major reforms to the political rules of the game began to move their way toward adoption. One was civil service for city employees, and the other was the election of aldermen by voters in their own wards rather than citywide. These reforms changed operations to a degree but not to the extent needed to fundamentally transform the political system.

Material Incentives

Jobs traditionally have been the most important building blocks of machine politics in St. Louis and many other cities. Given the city's factional nature, when Victor Miller replaced fellow Republican Kiel as mayor in 1927, a general turnover occurred among city employees.[1] In 1933, without even a trace of civil-service protection for incumbents, the city's approximately seven thousand jobs offered Democratic loyalists, out of favor for so many years, their first major rewards. By virtue of his ability to appoint the president of the board of public service, four city directors, the city counselor, supply commissioner, and city marshall, a new mayor readily could change the city work force through wholesale replacement.[2]

A veteran political actor noted that the Republicans had had incredible organizational strength prior to Dickmann's victory, chiefly because of their patronage opportunities. In the heart of the Depression, that advantage now fell to Mayor Dickmann and the Democrats, and they made full use of it. The political veteran also remarked that "some Republicans hung themselves" when the Democratic victors assumed control of the spoils. The value of a patronage job clearly increased during the Depression, and Republicans now found themselves on the outside looking in.

Dickmann realized that material incentives were key to cementing the support of various St. Louis ethnic groups. The largely German south-side wards gave the Republicans their heaviest support. On the other hand, the Irish of north St. Louis were longtime Democrats. (See Figure 3.) Dickmann, of German heritage himself, formed a key alliance with Robert Hannegan, an Irishman, who became the committeeman of the twenty-first ward in north St. Louis in 1933. Hannegan seemingly came from nowhere to capture that committee slot. At first, according to a longtime ward heeler,

> the ward regulars, who punched the doorbells and licked the envelopes and took voters to the polls did not take a liking to this handsome, dynamic Democrat who was a fresh face to almost everybody in the 21st Ward Organization, and a man who, appar-

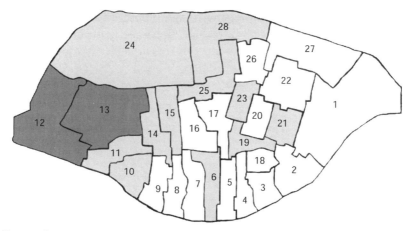

FIGURE 3: *Party Voting by Ward, Mayoral Contests: 1933-1941. Dark gray—all Republican, light gray—predominantly Republican, white—all or mostly Democratic. Illustrated by Ann Owens.*

ently, had not paid his dues. Hannegan was the most remarkable leader I have ever known. He simply took over with a charm and gusto that no one was prepared for. The organization men who envied him taking the post of Committeeman in the ward quickly forgot their animosity when Hannegan went into action.[3]

Hannegan's political skills led him quickly to the chairmanship of the city Democratic committee. In this post, he served as Dickmann's key political strategist and engineered a number of electoral victories. From City Hall, Hannegan moved on to become chairman of the national Democratic Party and is credited by some with making possible Harry Truman's selection as Roosevelt's vice-presidential running mate in 1944.[4] Some who lived through this period regarded Dickmann as rather a showman and Hannegan as the political brains of the pair.

During the 1930s, the growing list of Democratic officeholders came to include a large number of Irish names. Other ethnic groups began to provide pivotal support to the Democrats as well. The Lebanese, centered in the seventh ward, started to run successfully for office in the 1930s. The Depression and Roosevelt's policies turned that lower-income ward into a Democratic bastion. Anthony Webbe, elected a state representative in 1934, built the Democratic organization in the seventh ward, and patronage was his tool. He also gave away coal and Christmas baskets to needy residents. Webbe had the neighborhood churches furnish the names of possible recipients whom he would draw into his net. Informal social services were a key building block but, as someone who grew up in the seventh-ward organization noted, "The best thing we did was get people a job."

Blacks proved a significant element in Dickmann's winning coalition in 1933. An unnamed "political observer" contributed a chapter to a 1937 book about black St. Louis and maintained that the Democrats had supplied a few more top positions to blacks than Republicans had, including several legal positions.[5] For that observer, however, the door to real political power would open with the election of black Democratic committeemen and a commensurate share of the patronage committeemen had to dole out. For example, committeemen referred potential employees from their wards to positions at city offices, county offices, the board of education, the state of Missouri, and nearby industries. If a committeeman had supported winners in municipal or state elections, his ability to reward his constituents with jobs grew appreciably. Jordan Chambers, who led blacks to the Democratic fold in 1933, was

The dedication of Homer G. Phillips Hospital for Colored in 1936. St. Louis Post-Dispatch, 1936.

St. Louis Politics

seated as nineteenth-ward committeeman in 1938, the first black to hold that powerful post. (He was the only one for a number of years.) Chambers had sought the post unsuccessfully in the 1936 primary. (Committee people are elected in partisan primaries in August of presidential election years). He sought redress in the courts because he believed he had been unfairly deprived of the post. "The St. Louis Circuit Court ruled in January 1937 that Chambers had indeed been defrauded."[6] According to Harrison, Chambers's selection as committeeman in 1938 coincided with a majority of black St. Louisans becoming supporters of the New Deal.[7]

Mayor Dickmann also oversaw the building of a public hospital for the black community, which opened in 1936. Homer G. Phillips Hospital for Colored, as it first was called, was named in memory of a lawyer active in the struggle for black rights in St. Louis. An unknown assailant murdered Phillips in 1929. The new hospital had 670 beds. Promised to the black community in exchange for their support for the 1923 bond issue, it had not been built from those proceeds. As the only major item not built from the bond issue, this failure rankled many in the black community. That certainly was one reason that blacks turned to Dickmann and the Democrats in 1932. Of course, they also had hopes for greater patronage opportunities generally. Dickmann used the building of the hospital and his appointments in appeals for the support of African Americans in subsequent elections.[8]

During the 1930s, Italian immigrants residing on "the Hill" in south St. Louis also became an increasingly important part of the Democratic coalition. In the 1920s, L. Jean Gualdoni began to help his fellow émigrés to become U.S. citizens and solid supporters of the Democratic Party.[9] Patronage solidified this relationship after 1933. As a historian of this community noted, "The Hill's heavily working-class constituency gratefully accepted many menial city jobs in the 1930s and 1940s."[10] Gualdoni's chosen successor, Louis "Midge" Berra, helped stoke Democratic loyalties on the Hill through personal services and job provision for many years.

Another legendary ward boss who got his start in the 1930s was Anton Sestric. Of Croatian descent, he was first elected justice of the peace in 1932. Someone who knew Sestric well noted in an interview that politics in those days were very ethnic. Sestric's constituency was principally Slavic and Lebanese. With considerable industry located in his eighth ward, Sestric solidified his political base by getting jobs for people at private companies—thousands, according to this source. "A guy would tell Sestric that he was going to leave his job at a private company that Sestric had originally gotten for him and explain why. Sestric would then call the company, inform them that they [would] have a vacancy, and that he [would] have someone else for them."

The Depression made job provision for constituents even more critical than usual. Those relatively new to party politics, especially Democratic politics, worked within their communities to ensure support by providing economic lifelines. Federal work relief programs, especially the Works Progress Administration (WPA), provided valuable additional job placements. In Missouri, as in other states, political operators oversaw the distribution of these jobs. The federal government lacked the bureaucratic structure to administer these emergency programs and became dependent on city bosses.[11] Tom Pendergast, Kansas City's Democratic boss, supported Roosevelt early and reaped the reward. He gained "complete control of nearly all federal patronage in Missouri."[12] After 1935, that amounted to eighty to ninety thousand jobs.[13] Dickmann's relationship with Pendergast was not always positive. Politicians in Missouri's two largest cities frequently competed then over various elective offices. The city of St. Louis did receive some of the WPA jobs from the state, but Dickmann also acted to ensure that the city had its own supply. Dickmann lobbied Washington heavily for $6.75 million of WPA funds to be earmarked for the beginning of the Jefferson National Expansion Memorial on the banks of the Mississippi River. Forty-one city blocks would be cleared of old stores and warehouses to form eventually the national park now graced by Eero Saarinen's magnificent Gateway Arch. Upon receipt of these federal funds, Dickmann successfully urged city voters to pass a $7.5 million bond issue for this riverfront project.[14] These monies together permitted the hiring of many St. Louisans, no doubt in the usual partisan manner.

New Deal programs, and particularly the WPA, were a boon to some big city machines. "For the bosses, the WPA represented a unique public works grants-in-aid—a federally financed, locally picked labor supply for machine-initiated neighborhood projects."[15] WPA jobs fueled the growth of incipient political machines in Pittsburgh and Chicago.[16] Similarly, such jobs strengthened Dickmann's hand in St. Louis, but he did have to depend, at least in part, on the Pendergast forces for a share of the largesse coming through the state. A rivalry with the Kansas City organization, which included even contention over some local St. Louis offices, prevented full realization of the WPA potential, at least until the successful federal prosecution of Tom Pendergast for tax evasion in 1938 and the demise of his machine shortly thereafter.

Issue Politics in the Dickmann Era

Although control of the quid pro quo relationships that produced jobs and services in exchange for ballot support was a paramount concern to Dickmann, his mayoralty produced several major program initiatives. Notably, Dickmann prepared the way for a national park on the St. Louis riverfront, a park that today is the most visited of any in the United States. This project foreshadowed urban renewal, sacrificing a decaying area to create a tourist attraction.

Dickmann also pushed a major environmental initiative, and again he was ahead of his time. The widespread burning of soft coal in the city had created a significant air-pollution problem. Mornings often resembled nights because of a dense haze caused by the burning coal. Dickmann assigned his secretary (chief of staff in today's parlance), Raymond Tucker, to deal with the smoke problem. Tucker had come to Dickmann's staff from Washington University, where he was a professor of mechanical engineering. Tucker recommended the washing of coal "to reduce the ash and sulfur content of the smoke."[17] Members of the coal industry vehemently opposed any smoke-control measures. In fact, Illinois' Coal Operators Association threatened a commercial boycott of St. Louis if a strong ordinance were approved.[18] Much of the coal burned in St. Louis then came from Illinois.

After naming Tucker smoke commissioner in 1937, Dickmann pushed for standards that outlawed the burning of soft coal from Illinois.[19] Black Tuesday, November 28, 1939, was critical to that effort. The coal smoke "was so thick that day that the street lights had to be turned on from 9 A.M. until noon and then again at 4 P.M. so people could see to drive home. That dark day convinced people that St. Louis' problem was serious, and Mayor Bernard Dickmann and Smoke Commissioner Raymond Tucker received broad emergency powers to clean up the city's air."[20] Higher quality coal had to be used, and other energy sources were developed. The severity of the problem had been made clear, and opposition became muted. Tucker remained smoke commissioner until 1950. Pittsburgh later used the abatement program Tucker designed as a model and, by 1941, eighty-two other cities had examined St. Louis's program.[21] Although air quality improved greatly, this program also had its downside. In still difficult economic times, many working-class residents resented the increased costs they were forced to pay when Illinois' inexpensive coal was no longer available.

Forging a Political Machine

No doubt, Bernard Dickmann and Robert Hannegan tried to exert control over St. Louis elections and ensure that as many officeholders as possible owed their loyalty to them. Between 1933 and 1940, they met with considerable success but never achieved complete control. And they were challenged at every turn. By the 1941 mayoral election, their ballot-box potency had disintegrated.

Control was difficult to achieve in large part because of the very number of elected officials St. Louis voters selected. To gain full control, a faction would have to win a large number of elections, repeatedly. Table 3 illustrates the magnitude of the problem.

While Dickmann and Hannegan held sway in St. Louis, a Democratic machine in Chicago began to consolidate its authority. Although Windy City residents selected fifty aldermen from districts, they chose neither a comptroller nor an aldermanic president; aldermen often doubled as committeemen; and Chicago could not parallel St. Louis's twelve county offices, elected on a citywide basis.[22] Chicago voters were part of Cook County and participated in elections for county officeholders, but, in this period, their number of officeholders was far shy of St. Louis's 164. The sheer number of officeholders and the fragmentation they represented made St. Louis's institutional framework much less conducive to consolidation. Dickmann's attempts to centralize authority were more successful than perhaps those of any other St. Louis mayor, but just for a brief period.

Attempting Electoral Domination

Dickmann swept into office accompanied by fourteen Democratic aldermen, giving the Democrats control of the municipal legislature for the first time since the adoption of the 1914 charter. Two Democrats already had been elected to finish out remaining terms in 1932. The 1932 election, which marked Franklin Roosevelt's initial triumph in city and nation, also saw Democrats gaining the county offices at stake at that time—sheriff, circuit attorney, coroner, city treasurer, public administrator—and circuit judgeships.

In 1934, Democrats added significantly to their number of officeholders. They elected nine additional circuit judges, for a total of fourteen, as well as the probate judge. They also swept the remaining county offices. To represent the city in the state legislature, three

TABLE 3

St. Louis's Partisan Elected Officials
(Municipal and County) circa 1935

Office	Method of Selection
Mayor	At large
Comptroller	At large
President, Board of Aldermen	At large
28 Aldermen	At large representing districts
28 Committeemen	District
28 Committeewomen	District
19 State Representatives	Several from each of 4 districts
5 State Senators	District
9 Constables	District
9 Magistrates (Justices of the Peace)	District
Judge of Court of Criminal Causes	At large
Judge of Court of Criminal Correction	At large
Judge of Probate Court	At large
19 Circuit Court Judges	At large
Judge, St. Louis Court of Appeals	At large
Prosecuting Attorney	At large
Circuit Attorney	At large
Circuit Clerk	At large
Clerk of Court of Criminal Causes	At large
Clerk of Court of Criminal Correction	At large
Collector (of Revenue)	At large
License Collector	At large
Treasurer	At large
Sheriff	At large
Coroner	At large
Public Administrator	At large
Recorder of Deeds	At large

The city of St. Louis elected 164 officials during this period.

Democratic state senators and fifteen representatives were chosen by voters. The city also elected two Democrats to Congress and aided the election of a third member, whose district covered parts of both the city and adjoining St. Louis County. There had not been as many Democrats in office since 1904.[23] However, the sweep was not total: Republican candidates for justice of the peace in the fourth court district near downtown were successful, as were two candidates for constable in that area. Both of the successful constabulary candidates were black, as was one of the justices of the peace, indicating that the black move to the Democratic party was not yet complete. In addition, another Republican was elected constable from the first district on the south side.

The *St. Louis Post-Dispatch* attributed Democratic good fortunes in 1932 and 1933 to a shift in the black vote and to the Democratic Party's stance on the repeal of Prohibition.[24] Certainly ending Prohibition was popular in a city noted for its breweries and for its non-teetotaling immigrant population. According to the *Post*, Democrats urged the "wets" in 1934 not to abandon the party that had lived up to its pledge and said, "St. Louis had been helped through revival of the brewing business."[25]

Although three black Republicans were elected to office with black votes in 1934, many black voters selected Democratic candidates. "In holding the Negroes, the Democrats were helped by the fact that many of that race have received public relief, for which the Democrats have claimed and have received credit."[26]

The more conservative St. Louis daily, the *Globe-Democrat*, called the 1934 results a rout that "continued the work of Republican annihilation."[27] The *Globe* particularly noted the defeats of Republicans Edward Koeln as revenue collector and John Schmoll as circuit clerk. These two county officeholders "have been largely responsible for the local success of the Republicans at the polls during the last 25 years."[28] The county offices and their substantial patronage had been a key to Republican political power.[29] A description of Koeln offered by the *Globe-Democrat* succinctly illustrates the St. Louis system of individual rewards practiced by Republican and Democrat alike. "Campaign opponents have referred to him as the Big Boss, ward manipulator, exponent of machine politics, often enough during his career. But he has been called Mr. Eddie by many a poor devil, enfranchised or not, who needed a dollar, a job or a square meal."[30]

Dickmann's control over the Democratic Party in St. Louis became evident by the time of the 1935 aldermanic contests. He was successful everywhere in the March primary and had put together his own fourteen-member aldermanic slate. According to the *Globe-Democrat*, "Mayor Dickmann's slate of aldermanic candidates overrode all opposition in yesterday's primary election and with the unofficial tabulation of the ballots complete, had won in every race in the Democratic voting by overwhelming majorities, in no case having even a close contest."[31] In the rout, a Democratic incumbent who had alienated the mayor, Paul J. Hennerich of the tenth ward, lost his seat. In the general election that April, all Democratic aldermanic candidates won by almost a two-to-one margin, as did William L. Mason, Democratic candidate for aldermanic president. Dickmann now enjoyed a Democratic majority of two to one on the board of estimate and apportionment as well as a huge majority on the board of aldermen.

Despite this 1935 triumph, Dickmann still faced opposition in the city Democratic committee. Nominations for committeemen and committeewomen presented a greater challenge to the mayor in the 1930s than those for aldermanic seats. Voters in each of the city's twenty-eight wards selected their own representatives to their party's central committee, while aldermen, although ostensibly representing individual wards, were elected at large and often were less tied to the ward organizations. But the committeemen were clearly the more powerful players at this time. They controlled substantial amounts of patronage and often held county or state offices as well as their committee seats. Various factions at the ward level, both Republican and Democratic, had tried to control St. Louis politics for years, generally without much long-term success. Bernard Dickmann had more good fortune in this regard than other leaders, but his success was certainly temporal as well.

Democratic Party chairman John P. English, the recorder of deeds, led the opposition to the mayor. In fact, English unseated Hannegan as chair of the city Democratic committee in June 1935. Those aligning against the Dickmann faction had a majority on the central committee at that time. In response, Dickmann and his lieutenants tried to form their own organization, possibly to rival the existing ward clubs.[32] The Dickmann-sponsored Public Employees' Welfare Association set monthly dues of 1 percent of each member's salary. Although the association called the dues voluntary, it was expected that most city employees join Dickmann's association and pay this "lug," St. Louis's term for political dues. Ward organizations traditionally had supported themselves with the lugs they assessed on constituents placed in jobs. The new Welfare Association could undermine the financial underpinnings of the ward clubs.

Election of Democratic committeemen and women in the August 1936 primary was expected to be an important test of strength between Dickmann and his opponents. Dickmann indicated that he would carry the battle to every ward in the city.[33] A letter from city Democratic committee treasurer Harry J. Cantwell to Dickmann indicated the tenor of the fight:

> Do you not feel, being possessed of the political sagacity, mental capacity and physical embonpoint that you are, that regard should be given to the torrid heat wave now upon us and that for benefit of the city, the party and yourself that you devote your activities in the few remaining months of your term to the office in which a remorseful majority of the citizens of St. Louis unfortunately elected you?[34]

That this sentiment emanated from a fellow Democrat illustrates the nature of factional infighting in St. Louis.

The anti-administration faction (now led by William L. Igoe, the president of the board of police commissioners; Jimmy Miller, boss of the fourth ward and justice of the peace; and William J. Brennan, Democratic state committeeman) had begun to look for a strong candidate to run against Dickmann in the 1937 mayoral contest.[35] In turn, Dickmann sponsored candidates for the city Democratic committee in 1936 "in wards where incumbents opposed him so that he could gain control of the committee and its mayoral endorsement."[36] Of the fifty-six members of the committee, a majority of thirty-two were considered in opposition to the mayor before the 1936 balloting.[37]

Dickmann's strategy regarding the 1936 committeemen races has to be regarded as a successful one. He reestablished a majority on the city Democratic committee. One of his leading opponents, John English, lost his own seat as twenty-fourth-ward committeeman to the mayor's friend, L. Jean Gualdoni, from the Italian Hill. Other supporters of the mayor, such as John J. Dwyer and Charlotte Corcoran Lee in the twentieth ward, James Burke in the twenty-second, and William Walsh in the twenty-fifth, also won at the polls. (Dwyer took over leadership of the party after Dickmann left office.) Dickmann's triumph in 1936 was not complete, however. His candidate in the twelfth ward failed to unseat a leading opponent, James Miller. Nevertheless, the mayor did win far more than he lost,[38] and Robert Hannegan was able to resume his role as the chairman of the city Democratic committee.

President Roosevelt's November 1936 landslide victory again aided city Democrats, who captured every office on the ballot at that election. The results left only five Republicans holding either a municipal or a county office: Comptroller Louis Nolte, a judge of the court of appeals, a magistrate, and two constables.[39]

In assessing Dickmann's first term in office, the *St. Louis Post-Dispatch* remarked on the considerable party infighting both in the committee and on the board of aldermen. The *Post* found that Dickmann had "fared well in these contests."[40] Patronage, not surprisingly, was at the core of the disagreements. "Patronage, handled on a larger scale than ever before in St. Louis' municipal history, was the weapon with which he fought back, rewarding his friends and supporters, ruthlessly punishing his enemies and non-supporters."[41] The success of these endeavors can be measured by the results of the 1937 municipal elections.

In 1937, only two Democratic aldermanic nominations were closely contested. Four years before, there had been "sharp fights in all the wards."[42] This time around, every Democratic ward organization endorsed Dickmann for reelection, and the aldermanic slate he and Hannegan supported had little difficulty. The mayor had allowed the ward organizations input regarding the candidates that would represent their wards. Of course, mayoral opponents in several wards were targeted. In the Democratic primary on March 12, Dickmann carried every ward in the city, and his aldermanic slate, save one person, was victorious. In the first ward, Thomas V. Walsh bested the mayor's man, incumbent John A. Gentleman, by nine thousand votes. Four aldermanic incumbents who had opposed the mayor's legislative agenda went down to defeat by overwhelming margins.[43]

Dickmann easily won the April general election. He carried all but three wards. By record plurality figures, the voters also selected all fourteen Democratic nominees for aldermanic posts. The only discordant note was the reelection of the Republican comptroller, Louis Nolte, although his margin was less than six thousand votes.

The 1936 and 1937 elections certainly produced heartening results for Democratic stalwarts and lent credence to the existence of a Dickmann-Hannegan machine. Yet no election went by without some primary challenge to the mayor's supporters. The alternate center of power clearly appeared to be the county offices, with their independent sources of patronage and contracts. Those offices presented a considerable impediment to the development of a hierarchical machine in St. Louis. In cities that unified more easily, such offices were more limited or could be controlled by the

Dickmann and Hannegan, realized the benefits of maintaining a Democrat at the helm in Jefferson City.

McDaniel refused to concede, and Democratic leaders hoped an official canvass would tighten the race.[54] However, the canvass failed to do so and, in fact, tacked a few more votes on to Donnell's margin of victory. McDaniel again declined to concede.[55] Democratic leaders met at a number of conferences to determine their strategy. Directly involved were Robert Hannegan, chairman of the city Democratic committee, and Mayor Dickmann.[56]

The new year dawned without a certified governor and with the Democrats holding a majority of fifty-two seats in the combined senate and house. The chairman of the state Democratic Party, C. M. Hulen, visibly supported a Democratic petition to seat McDaniel instead of Donnell.[57] St. Louis's mayor clearly was tied to those seeking to block Donnell's accession. Dickmann nonetheless protested, "I am getting tired of charges that the St. Louis City Hall machine is trying to steal the election. If there is an investigation I would like to see every ballot box in the state, including St. Louis, opened."[58] Outgoing governor Lloyd C. Stark, a Democrat, threw a wrench into Democratic hopes when he vetoed the creation of a legislative investigation into the gubernatorial election.[59] Donnell then filed a writ of mandamus at the Missouri Supreme Court stipulating that he should be seated as governor. The Supreme Court halted the work of the legislative investigative committee, preventing that body from "opening, recanvassing and recounting the ballots in the November gubernatorial election."[60]

Dickmann's ties to those trying to seat McDaniel were recognized widely. At the annual Gridiron Dinner, he and Hannegan were roasted in a skit called "Bar the Bar"—"Dickmann-Hannegan-Waechtler Bar - Open All Hours - Don't Seat Nobody."[61] Meanwhile, the elaborate machinations of Democrats and Republicans continued until, on February 19, the Missouri Supreme Court ordered the General Assembly finally to seat Donnell, the Republican.[62] Donnell took the oath of office several days later.

Dickmann's Last Hurrah

The lengthy struggle to keep Donnell from becoming governor took its toll on the St. Louis mayor. "All this came home to roost on Dickmann, who was then making a third mayoralty bid, and on his man, Hannegan. Both had attended a meeting at which the Democratic state chairman had received the go-ahead signal for his strong-arm tactics. St. Louis Republicans, who had controlled City Hall for twenty-four years before the New Deal, saw their chance to come back."[63] The Republicans nominated Judge William Dee Becker as their mayoral candidate. In the March 1941 primary, for the first time since Roosevelt's impressive 1932 victory, those choosing a Republican ballot outnumbered Democratic primary voters.[64] Becker ran a hard race with solid Republican support, "united opposition...necessary to crush the Pendergast-Dickmann-Hannegan machine."[65] The *Globe-Democrat* noted that Republicans were using "the widespread criticism of Democratic insiders for having kept Republican Gov. Forrest C. Donnell out of office for 44 days."[66]

Although often at odds with the Kansas City boss, Tom Pendergast, Dickmann nonetheless was linked to him in this campaign and to corrupt machine politics in general. Judge Becker urged St. Louis voters to "beat the threat of boss rule which broods over St. Louis now as it once hung over the Kansas City of Pendergast days."[67] Becker refused to let up on his charges and used the Kansas City analogy for all it was worth:

> "Lugs" were put on jobholders in both places to build up the machines' war chests, city employees were kept under machine domination with no genuine merit system, crime increased, city finances got more in arrears, vote frauds became matters of national record, constructive opposition within the machines' own parties were shouted down, and both bosses sought to dominate state affairs. But even Boss Tom Pendergast never had the gall to try and steal a governorship outright.[68]

Dickmann, in fact, in the fall of 1940, had proposed amending the city charter to provide for civil service. His opponents stymied this reform. Fred W. Evers, chairman of the city Republican committee, called it "a Dickmann scheme to perpetuate his machine in the City Hall.... He wants to continue his power by keeping the 6500 Democratic officeholders on their jobs when the Republicans regain control of the city."[69]

Dickmann himself felt that his smoke abatement measures, which prohibited the use of inexpensive Illinois coal, contributed to his unpopularity with voters.[70] Whether it was due to the price of coal or the "governorship steal," it became evident that Dickmann had exceeded his welcome at City Hall. Judge Becker defeated Dickmann by thirty-five thousand votes, while all Republican candidates for aldermen, elected from wards on an at-large basis, were swept in as

Mayor Bernard Dickmann, circuit clerk H. Sam Priest, and city Democratic committee chair Robert Hannegan at a 1941 election rally. St. Louis Post-Dispatch, 1941.

well. Dickmann carried only four wards, not including his own. However, he did carry Webbe's seventh and Sestric's eighth. Comptroller Louis Nolte, long the only Republican beachhead in city government, again was reelected. In fact, his Democratic opponent withdrew shortly before Election Day.[71] Michael J. Hart, also a Republican, became president of the board of aldermen.

Although the Republicans had decried the machine practices of Dickmann and associates, they prepared to take over the spoils of office, including the more than seven thousand city jobs. Their modus operandi prior to 1933 had included ward-based politics with patronage at the core. However, the seeds sown in the mayoral campaign and the Donnell-McDaniel fiasco opened the possibility of change to some of the basic practices of city government.

When Dickmann sought reelection in 1941, the tables had turned, and a Republican was returned to the mayor's chair. The Dickmann "City Hall machine" had lived for eight years. A fatal miscalculation rendered it obsolete, a fate not many would have

predicted only two years before. In addition, two forthcoming institutional changes would have a discernible impact on a future mayor's
potential power base. Never again would a mayoral organization
exert as much influence or see as many allies triumph at the polls.
Nor would St. Louis again come as close to achieving a hierarchical
political machine in the years to follow. The existing institutional predisposition to ward factionalism became stronger, and the political
behavior associated with that factionalism continued unabated.

Bernard Dickmann never headed a true hierarchical machine, but
he certainly gave it a run for the money. Countervailing power in the
county offices prevented his complete domination of city politics.
Changes coming in his wake saw to it that no mayor again would
assemble quite the power base he did, and these changes strengthened the ward base of St. Louis's unreformed politics.

Contrasts with Other Machine Cities

In Chicago and Pittsburgh, Democrats managed to construct
more unified political organizations during the 1930s. Both
structure and leadership contributed to their success. Democratic
organizations in both cities succeeded in preventing a Republican
comeback, unlike in St. Louis.

In Chicago, Anton Cermak has received the lion's share of the
credit for forging "the city's first truly multiethnic political
machine."[72] Paul Green found that Cermak and his Democratic
allies "were pulling their party together during the period between
1915 and 1933."[73] Cermak's task was made easier by the infusion
of a better-educated, more middle-class brand of party activist
during the 1920s.[74] In 1931, Cermak defeated the Republican
incumbent, Bill Thompson. Thompson's questionable activities and
shenanigans hurt his cause with the voters.[75] Cermak used
interward rivalry to build his own organization. He was well on his
way to building a political machine in Chicago when he fell victim
to an assassin's bullet in 1933.

Democratic Party centralization did not stop with Cermak's
death. Ed Kelly, who replaced Cermak as mayor, and Pat Nash, his
central committee chair, expanded the political machine. Roger Biles
concluded that, "To a great extent, the amazing resiliency of what
came to be known as the 'Daley machine' was nurtured, shaped, and
enlarged under Kelly's leadership."[76] Cermak, and later Kelly and
Nash, solidified the central control of patronage by the head of the
Cook County Democratic committee. As part of that process, Kelly

and Nash structured the African American submachine led by William Dawson.[77]

Cermak and his successors began working on molding Chicago's Democratic Party in the 1920s. They were not new to party affairs the way Dickmann and Hannegan were in 1933. In Chicago, party leaders could set up an apparatus that endured for decades. The Democrats had seized the Chicago mayor's office in 1931, before Roosevelt was elected president. Like Dickmann, Ed Kelly used federal programs to his party's advantage, but he did not have to compete with a rival machine across the state.

Pittsburgh's Democratic unification also benefited from strong leadership. David Lawrence worked diligently in the 1920s to build an opposition party from weak fragments. Lawrence used patronage as his key weapon. He became Allegheny County Democratic chairman and rewarded those loyal to him. He also used patronage "to prevent the development of any would-be opposition."[78] Lawrence, in addition, gained control over "all federal patronage appointments in western Pennsylvania."[79] Because Philadelphia remained under the domination of the Republicans for two more decades, Lawrence had no real rival for control of New Deal patronage in Pennsylvania. His organization was able to elect a Democratic mayor in Pittsburgh in 1933.

Lawrence's successful centralization became apparent when he reorganized the local Democratic Party in 1932. He purged "a number of ward chairmen who had performed below his expecta-tions...and eliminate[d] several who had sided with the disgruntled element in the party. He streamlined the executive committee, cutting it in size, and established new lines of command to the ward level."[80]

During the Depression, jobs were the best inducement for political leaders in unreformed cities. By placing patronage under the control of the party chairman, those holding that office could exert greater control over candidacies and ensure support in party councils.

Dickmann and Hannegan had not put in time in the party trenches like their counterparts in Chicago and Pittsburgh. Nor had they spent a decade trying to reshape their party. They had consid-erable electoral success in the 1930s, however. If they had more time, they might well have achieved more centralization. In any case, the freewheeling ward tradition in St. Louis and the long history of factionalism (characteristic of Republicans and Democrats) would work against attempts to establish hierarchy within the party. St. Louisans, as their reaction to the Big Cinch demonstrates, disliked concentrated power. With its large number of elected officials, St. Louis presented the greatest number of competing points of influence.

Aside from having to deal with the obstacles presented by culture and structure, Dickmann and Hannegan made a considerable tactical error with "the governorship steal." It was seen widely as an unjustified power grab that defied the wishes of the people. Hannegan and Dickmann clearly damaged their own cause. In addition, a number of St. Louis's working-class residents, already suffering from the effects of the Depression, resented the increased prices they paid for coal and blamed Mayor Dickmann.

After Dickmann left office, the city entered a brief period of genuine party competition. Democrats and Republicans adhered to the traditional ways of party operation, and neither political party centralized.

Chapter 4

Adjusting the Template, Not the Tenor

Civil Service and District Elections for Aldermen, 1941

On September 16, 1941, St. Louis voters decided the fate of two amendments to the city charter that changed some of the rules that governed party politics in the city. Voters replaced formerly weak language on hiring by merit with a full-fledged and rather strict civil-service system. They also reverted to ward election of their twenty-eight aldermen in place of the citywide method employed since 1914. These changes had some important implications for St. Louis's political life, although their effects appeared gradually. While personnel reform weakened the power of the ward committeemen who controlled patronage, district elections for aldermen strengthened the ward in the long term and kept it as the principal locus for service delivery and ombudsman activity. These reforms, unlike others adopted in Boston, Pittsburgh, or other machine cities, failed to strengthen the powers of the mayor.

Civil Service

Establishment of a civil service was an integral component of the Progressive reform movement that reshaped the governance of many American cities at the turn of the century. Industrialization, urbanization, and increased trade necessitated a public work force with enhanced abilities and skills. The awarding of jobs based on political loyalty did not necessarily coincide with the attraction of a skilled work force. A number of cities adopted civil service hand-in-glove with nonpartisan, at-large municipal council elections early in the twentieth century. This coupling frequently ended overt machine-style practices and, at least initially, kept recent immigrants off the city payroll.

Ward Organization Endorsements

Ward committeemen paid most of their attention to two matters: endorsements and turning out the vote. Candidates always sought the support of the city's ward organizations. Whom to take in any particular race might depend on past friendship, or it might be based on whose victory would mean the most for the organization and its leaders. Committeemen also wanted to pick winners, and to some that was a paramount concern.

A few politicians reminisced about endorsements at the dedication of a park to the longtime leader of the tenth ward, Louis "Uncle Louie" Buckowitz. They said that Uncle Louie's word was always good—but he always waited too long to give it. Reading the tea leaves correctly could lead to greater individual and organizational benefits for ward stalwarts. Until the late 1960s, the leaders of the ward decided on endorsements by themselves. Their membership had opportunities to meet the various candidates and comment on them, but the final say lay with the committee-man. Into the 1970s, certain wards—usually in more middle class areas—became open wards. Their membership began to proffer endorsements based on a balloting of those members eligible to participate. Once an endorsement was given, the ward had to honor its commitment. That meant sticking with candidates even if their defeat appeared certain. The code of behavior was clear. After Red Villa's death, longtime ward leader Joseph P. Roddy was quoted as saying, "His word was always good. You can't ask for much more than that."[1]

Wards endorsed in all local races and in state contests as well. Picking winners at the state level meant greater access to state jobs. Missouri never will be found in the ranks of reformed states. It always has maintained a significant number of patronage positions. In addition, politicians running for state office could use the lure of possible appointments to the board of police commissioners or the election board to titillate St. Louis organization regulars. In primary elections during the 1930s, wards chose between pro-Pendergast and anti-Pendergast candidates. By the 1950s, it became a question of whether a ward would support candidates that Shenker and Callanan had endorsed or a Democratic rival favored by the newspapers or other factions.

Historically, taking a candidate meant putting his or her name on the ward's sample ballot and in other literature. When a ward organization endorsed a candidate, the candidate would help fund the preparation of election material, the costs of mailings, and "walking around money" for poll workers. As an example, Table 1 contains a list of ward expenditures prepared for Jack Dwyer's review and payment in 1962. Table 2 demonstrates how the city Democratic committee disbursed funds prior to the August primary.

TABLE 1

List of Expenditures Dated June 26, 1962

Prepared for Jack Dwyer by Albert N. Wallace

Filing Fee	$5.00
Campaign cards	19.25
Newspaper ads and pictures	45.00
Cocktail party rental hall	10.00
Rental of glasses and bar	27.54
1 Case whiskey	9.90
Miscell. (soda)	6.50
Printing expenses	93.45
Outdoor precinct party	125.10
Worker canvas	90.00
TOTAL	**431.74**

SOURCE: Handwritten note, Papers of John J. Dwyer, Saint Louis University Archives.

TABLE 2

Receipts and Disbursements from Records Of Democratic
City Committee Chairman John Dwyer

	Receipts
John Inglish	$10,000.00
Burleigh Arnold	$5,000.00
Don Meyer (from T. Guilfoil)	$1,000.00
Fred Weathers (from T. Guilfoil add. For M.E. Morris)	$500.00
Fred Weathers (from T. Guilfoil)	$1,000.00
Jos. Glynn (personal donation)	$1,000.00
Loan from Bank (cra.)	$20,000.00
Jos. Glynn	$500.00
TOTAL	**$39,000.00**

	Expenses
5th Ward (Troupe)	$ 1,000.00
9th Ward (Luaders)	$1,000.00
10th & 13 Wards (AB.)	$2,000.00
11th Ward (McAteer)	$1,000.00
14th Ward (O'Toole & Butler)	$1,000.00
18th & 19th Wards (Don Meyer)	$2,000.00
6th Ward (Kav.)	$1,000.00
7th Ward (P. Simon)	$1,000.00
21st Ward (Weathers for Mitchell)	$1,000.00
28th Ward (Robt. D. & Blair)	$1,000.00
26th Ward (N. Seay)	$2,700.00
4th Ward	$1,000.00
17th Ward (Buschman)	$1,000.00
Weathers (Delivery of Paper)	$1,500.00
Dwyer (Delivery of Paper 4th Ward) 3 edit.	$300.00
Weathers (for cartoonist) Truth	$100.00
Expenses for man sent to Miss.	$200.00
Argus (Mitchell)	$1,000.00
Mirror (Chapman)	$750.00
Defender (Hawkins)	$1,250.00
12th Ward (Mr. & Mrs. E. Wahl)	$1,000.00
22nd Ward (Matt O'Neill)	$1,000.00
20th Ward (Leroy Tyus)	$1,000.00
Delivery of paper 7-19-64	$760.00
15th Ward (J. Schmitt)	$1,000.00
TOTAL	**$26,560.00**

SOURCE: The Papers of John J. Dwyer, Saint Louis University.

A ward organization especially wanted to ensure the success of the candidates it had taken—committee people, alderman, state representative—in the primaries. These candidates often were contested thanks to rivals within the ward itself or to opposing factions from other wards. Other factions might put in a candidate just to irritate the regulars in the ward, or the challenger could represent a serious threat to current ward leadership. Sometimes, bitter warfare within a ward resulted in split wards. There might be two or three contending organizations with one headed by the committeeman, another by the alderman, and perhaps a third by the committeewoman or some combination of these. St. Louis's political fragmentation could be found at a number of levels.

1. Tim O'Neil, "Red Villa Praised as Man Who Lived for His Ward," *St. Louis Post-Dispatch*, December 9, 1990, p. 1A.

New York City long has been a practitioner of machine politics in a fashion resembling St. Louis. It never has abandoned its partisan and district elections for city council, but it did adopt a civil service in 1914. Historically, New York has vacillated between reformed and unreformed administration. However, a reform mayor and a strong institutionalized reform movement in that city did change municipal personnel practices, making classification and testing hallmarks of the process. In St. Louis, on the other hand, reformers had considerably less success in changing the city's quid pro quo personnel transactions in those early years of the twentieth century.

Ward committeemen in St. Louis—the chief employment agents—relied heavily on job provision to garner electoral support and on the lug, a payment that those placed in jobs had to pay to finance ward undertakings. Committeemen had a wide variety of positions to fill in 1940: all the positions in city government, in the county offices, slots in state government, WPA jobs, nonteaching jobs at the board of education, and jobs at various manufacturing plants. Each ward claimed so many municipal and county jobs in each department or office. Wards representing lower-income areas of the city relied more heavily on this patronage as a political tool. About seven thousand city jobs were at stake in every mayoral election. A new mayor—even from the same party as his predecessor—would replace a significant share of the work force when he assumed office. Although committeemen referred constituents for these jobs, a mayor had enough leverage to fill these positions to his advantage. Bernard Dickmann certainly tried to strengthen his power base by having city employees join and pay dues to an organization of his creation, the United Welfare Association. A number of committeemen saw this as a threat to their ward organizations and to the lug they received from each employee they had placed.

The spoils approach to public personnel administration provided a continuing invitation to those of a reform bent, to civic leaders, and to St. Louis's daily newspapers to seek changes in the process. Mayor Dickmann proposed civil-service legislation himself in 1940, but, by this point, his own popularity was waning. His plan met with little success, and Republicans accused him of trying to grandfather his own supporters into their public jobs.[1] Dickmann's successor, William Dee Becker, a Republican, picked up the torch of reform and announced his support for a municipal merit system during his mayoral campaign. The League of Women Voters then led the drive to put on the ballot a charter amendment creating a civil service. Before the September 16, 1941, special election on the proposition,

Mayor Becker continued the long tradition of cleaning house at City Hall. During his first four months in office, he appointed eight hundred full-time employees, and turnover affected about a thousand others, principally unskilled laborers.[2] Just two weeks prior to the election dealing with civil service, the *Post-Dispatch* reported that 39.2 percent of city jobs had changed hands since Becker took office. The newspaper expected the pace to quicken as Election Day approached.[3]

As September 16 neared, St. Louis's highest circulating daily newspapers, the *Post-Dispatch* and the *Globe-Democrat*, provided strong support for this charter revision. They did not confine their support to their respective editorial pages, however. Instead, they each used their headlines and news columns to foment support for a genuine merit system. On the Sunday before the special election, the *Post-Dispatch* made its feelings clear in its front-page subheadings: "Amendment No. 3 Offers Way to Remove Public Service from Politics." "St. Louis Charter Change Would Abolish Present Ineffective Efficiency Board and Set Up in Its Place a Personnel Administration Based on Competency of Municipal Employees."[4] The *Globe-Democrat* was not subtle either. On Election Day, the *Globe* illustrated its front page with a large cartoon depicting a woman with a broom outside an office labeled "Spoils System." The caption read, "This office gets the works, TODAY!"[5]

Post-Dispatch reporter Carlos F. Hurd summed up the rationale for passage of the amendment by describing municipal administration in St. Louis in a way that would capture any reformer's heart. This appeared in a page-one news column:

> St. Louis voters, at Tuesday's special city election, will abolish or will continue the spoils system of municipal employment, under which twelve persons, thrown out of city jobs by the change of party control in 1933, killed themselves.
>
> City employees, down to floor scrubbers, must hand out a "lug" from their pay envelopes at election and primary times.
>
> City work stops on election and primary days, and city employees canvass their home neighborhoods for the administration party, giving that party an advantage which only a popular upheaval can overcome.
>
> Important duties of city departments are performed by men and women chosen primarily for their degree of political acquaintance

and party regularity, and secondarily, if at all, for knowledge or aptitude in the city's work.

Party committee members—19 at one time during the last administration—hold appointive city jobs, and help form the framework of a political machine. The machine, held together by patronage, forces unworthy candidates for judicial office, on the voters. St. Louis lags behind other major cities, the Federal Government, and large private businesses, which have built up effective modern personnel systems.[6]

Charter Amendment No. 3 contained several safeguards designed to separate municipal jobs from electoral politics. Civil-service commissioners would have to come from the ranks of those who had not held any public or party office in the previous four years. The director of personnel would have to have public personnel experience and could be recruited from outside St. Louis. The charter amendment also required that examinations be given for each and every position and that the rule of three be used in selecting a candidate for a vacancy. (Under the rule of three, a supervisor would have to choose from among the three top scorers on the eligibility list.) Temporary appointments—a tried and true technique to avoid the requirements of a merit system—could last no longer than sixty days.[7] A classification system that would rank positions and establish pay grades also would be a key part of the plan.

The League of Women Voters provided strong support for civil-service reform during the campaign. The dean of the Washington University law school chaired the committee supporting its passage, and Becker, the present mayor, as well as three former mayors (Wells, Kiel, and Dickmann) were honorary chairs. Prominent black St. Louisans, including the Urban League's John T. Clark and future Republican alderman Sidney Redmond, also endorsed this reform. Joseph L. McLemore, an African American attorney, noted that "From the standpoint of the Negro employees of St. Louis, the system would be a great safeguard against dismissal from his job as long as he is efficient. Any plan that classifies people on the basis of merit should appeal to Negroes who are seldom given the consideration they merit."[8]

Certainly the newspaper articles of the time made it clear that the city's establishment desired this major change to government employment practices. However, not all politicians—Democratic or Republican—supported civil service. The chairman of the city

Republican committee, Fred W. Evers, was quoted as expressing fear "that civil service would 'ruin the organization.' Without the incentive of patronage, distributed in the old-time partisan manner, he held, 'You can't get the people out to vote.'"[9]

Despite the divided sentiments of the city's party officials, voters adopted Amendment No. 3, albeit with not many votes to spare. A charter amendment requires at least a 60 percent vote in favor for approval to take place. Civil service received 62.5 percent—a winning margin of just 2,966 votes. (See Table 4 for the ward tally.) Heaviest support for the merit system occurred in wards at either the northern or southern extremes of the city. The so-called "river" wards with strong organizations, as well as areas with sizable black populations, showed little interest in civil service. Figure 4 illustrates the gradations of support using a ward map of the city.

Immediately after the votes were counted, Louis E. Miller, Republican committeeman from the seventeenth ward, filed a court suit challenging the amendment. Missouri's high court threw out the suit a year later, and civil service took effect in 1942. Many politicians continued to skirmish against the measure. The board of aldermen voted to reduce the salary of the first director of personnel, F. Elliott Scearce, and he, too, had to go to court to receive his agreed-upon compensation. Despite this unhappiness, tests became the norm for all municipal job seekers, and favoritism in hiring became less direct and less frequent for a while. Scearce, who served as personnel director until 1978, prided himself on allowing no politician to tell him whom to hire during his tenure.

Patronage, however, did not end in St. Louis. Ward committeemen had other placement outlets for their constituents. Hiring for the county office jobs remained political, although such jobs were far fewer in number than those on the regular city payroll. State and school system jobs were still available too. And, in time, elected officials learned how to combine merit with politics by recommending their choice among the high-scoring candidates.[10] Nonetheless, the advent of civil service contributed to a gradual decline in the potency of the ward organizations. As George Washington Plunkitt, the quintessential Tammany ward boss, once mused: "How are you goin' to interest our young men in their country if you have no offices to give them when they work for their party?"[11] The merit system produced no election workers, and fewer came out to Candidates' Nights in wards, where more than 125 people used to fill a backyard easily on such an occasion. Well-attended torch-light parades still preceded every major election throughout the forties.

Table 4

Electoral Support for Aldermanic Elections
by Ward and Civil Service

Ward	Amendment 1 (Aldermen Elected by Wards)		Amendment 3 (Civil Service)	
	Total Vote	% Yes	Total Vote	% Yes
1	6,641	68.2%	6,609	62.9%
2	3,140	48.2%	3,119	45.4%
3	2,320	50.7%	2,275	42.3%
4	1,755	44.6%	1,745	38.6%
5	2,028	28.4%	2,028	23.7%
6	1,944	61.2%	1,937	39.4%
7	2,485	45.3%	2,467	40.8%
8	3,109	59.0%	3,074	53.0%
9	2,372	64.8%	2,363	59.2%
10	3,068	71.6%	3,057	62.5%
11	4,339	70.7%	4,328	64.5%
12	4,751	69.5%	4,729	63.1%
13	9,481	75.2%	9,451	73.0%
14	4,155	74.6%	4,140	72.1%
15	4,562	78.4%	4,516	75.7%
16	2,815	60.8%	2,778	50.3%
17	2,998	67.6%	2,972	49.0%
18	2,530	50.9%	2,518	46.5%
19	3,189	57.1%	3,119	37.8%
20	3,162	59.1%	3,106	48.8%
21	3,948	60.2%	3,939	57.0%
22	5,850	62.4%	5,813	62.6%
23	2,990	65.8%	2,902	51.6%
24	12,364	75.9%	12,396	74.1%
25	5,212	79.4%	5,204	80.4%
26	4,488	75.0%	4,465	73.5%
27	5,792	73.0%	5,767	70.0%
28	5,994	78.7%	5,983	79.8%
CITYWIDE VOTE	117,482	67.4%	116,800	62.5%

SOURCE: "Vote by Wards," *St. Louis Globe-Democrat*, September 17, 1941.

But the surest incentive to political participation—a job—became a rarer commodity. Of course, the patronage that remained in St. Louis continued to be ward based.

Ward Elections for Aldermen

The 1914 charter, in accordance with state law, provided that aldermen represent wards but that they be elected at large. This electoral method almost always resulted in an aldermanic chamber made up of twenty-eight members of the same party between 1914 and 1941. In addition, the mayor and/or the city party chairman often had influence over the selection of aldermanic nominees. In fact, a number of aldermanic candidates lived outside the wards they purported to represent. Slates were assembled easily and frequently were quite successful.

In 1914, the drafters of St. Louis's charter had wanted to elect aldermen from wards. But state law specified that cities of a certain size had to have at least one legislative chamber elected at large. In 1933, Missouri asked its voters to eliminate this provision, and, in 1934, they did. Following this election, the Missouri Supreme Court ruled that St. Louis voters would have to vote to change their charter to have ward elections. This measure appeared on the same 1941 ballot as civil-service reform.

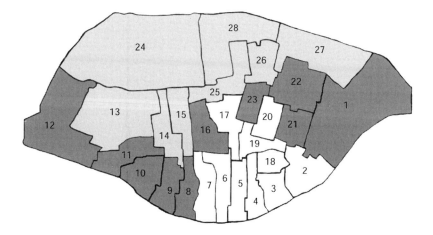

FIGURE 4. *Ward Vote for Civil Service, 1941. Dark gray—more than 70%, light gray—50%–69%, white—less than 50%.* Illustrated by Ann Owens.

Election Day and Ward Organizations

In the early decades of the twentieth century, ward organizations actively recruited voters. They would canvass every precinct to find newcomers and ascertain which party they supported. The son of a prominent St. Louis political family related that his mother climbed three flights of stairs in a number of buildings to see if a resident was registered and how he or she might vote. A precinct captain in Jordan Chambers's organization remembered going door to door as well. He knew just about everyone in his area by name, and people knew they could come to him with their problems.

Many organizations would prepare newspapers before electoral contests by stating the ward's endorsements and then hand-delivering them to voters. Some would have parades just before the election to whip up enthusiasm. On election day, poll workers were at each voting site, passing out handbills listing that ward's endorsed slate. In addition, "scratchers" would be stationed inside the polls, checking off the names of those who had voted. Registered voters who had not appeared at the polls by mid-afternoon and were presumed loyal to the ward would be contacted and brought to the polling place. A veteran politician told the story of his first trip to the polls at age twenty-one. A member of his ward's rather potent organization accompanied him into the voting booth to show him "how we vote the Democratic ticket."

Patronage workers did the election work. The ward had to deliver for its candidates, and the precinct captain had to deliver the precinct. Some precinct captains arranged to have family members who lived outside the city register in their precincts. Sometimes, other practices that also were not quite legitimate were used to ensure the proper result. A seasoned observer passed on a story about the vote count in a delivery ward. A ward regular helping with the count would have some carbon on his hands. If he saw a ballot marked for someone other than the candidate the organization supported, he would place an extra mark by another name on the ballot, thus invalidating the ballot. A committeeman also related that it was wise to have an influential friend represent you at the count to make sure the announced totals matched reality.

Ward organizations also paid considerable attention to absentee ballots. They were a good source of votes for the slate. A ward worker would bring the ballot by and ensure that votes were cast according to organizational preferences.

Majorities could be very lopsided in wards with strong organizations and poor populations. For example, the FBI and a federal grand jury investigated suspected primary election fraud in the fifth ward in 1944. Joseph L. "Bombie" Spicuzza, the ward's Republican committeeman, allegedly sponsored a "ballot blanket," which operated in the August primary election to give Spicuzza-endorsed candidates virtually unanimous votes."[1] Spicuzza countered by asking why the fifth-ward Democrats were not investigated; their totals were just as lopsided.[2]

1. "'Smear' Campaign Demoralized 5th Ward GOP, Spicuzza Says," *St. Louis Globe-Democrat*, November 9, 1944, p. 3A.
2. Ibid.

The city's newspapers offered the pros and cons of electing aldermen by voters of their own ward. The civil-service amendment garnered the lion's share of attention and support from the daily periodicals. Merit-system supporters did not necessarily back the election of aldermen by ward and strove to keep the two issues separate.[12] The *Post-Dispatch*'s analysis of a possible return to district elections reminded potential voters of the flagrant excesses of pre-1914 legislative behavior, when one chamber, the House of Delegates, was made up of district representatives. The *Post* noted that "shakedowns, sandbagging and vote-selling flourished until the resolute Circuit Attorney Joseph W. Folk intercepted a $75,000 franchise deal, for which the money had been placed in escrow, seized the money and used it in evidence against the combine men."[13] The *Post* continued at some length in this vein but ended by acknowledging that the council, elected at large, had also received considerable criticism. The newspaper mentioned that this charter change would not address the sizable inequality in ward population.[14] Opposition to ward elections has been part of a reform stance in many cities. The *Post*'s article did not create supporters for the charter change, but its coverage of this issue was less didactic than its articles on the benefits of civil-service reform.

Interestingly, the city Republican and Democratic committees "took no official position" on either measure, "but privately many of their members, especially in the river wards, were known to be in opposition."[15] Fred Evers, city Republican committee chairman, came out solidly against ward elections and civil service. The *Globe-Democrat* noted that "It is commonly reported that other Republican ward leaders, while making no public expressions, are privately lined up with the opposition. The Democrats are reluctant to talk, but informed leaders say the proponents of the measures can expect no assistance from organized Democratic sources."[16] In actuality, each party committee did little and, in effect, "'took a walk,' and apparently exerted no special efforts to defeat the proposal."[17] Accounts of old-timers note that many party regulars thought civil service would not pass. In fact, the general sentiment in the newspapers was that the merit system might go down to defeat while district elections might squeak through. In the end, both amendments were successful, thanks to a concentrated effort in the more affluent "residential" districts, offsetting opposition in the low-income "river wards." (See Table 4 for the ward totals.) District elections carried in twenty-four of the city's twenty-eight wards, losing only in several poorer wards bordering the Mississippi.

Reasons for opposition to aldermanic selection by wards were unclear. The change did represent decentralization in candidate selection, lessening the influence of the city committees and of a mayor like Dickmann, who had assembled aldermanic slates sympathetic to his purposes. Under the system put into effect in 1914, voters citywide chose all the aldermen. In both primaries and the general election, it was "possible for an aldermanic candidate to carry his own ward, but be defeated on the citywide vote, or to lose his own ward and be elected by the citywide vote."[18] If voters in a ward chose their own representative, that "would likely result in greater interest on the part of the Alderman in the affairs of his own ward."[19] Aldermen would also have to abide by a residency requirement. In addition, passage of the amendment would end any one-party monopoly in the board of aldermen.

A Day in the Political Life: Wards and Their Organizations

"You can't ever stop helping people with their problems."[1]

People came to their neighborhood politician with their problems. They knew him; they did not know the mayor. If an official returned their call, they remembered. Some of the city's political life still took place in saloons owned by elected officials. These saloons were places of recreation, but they also served as banks for some working people and as the site of ward meetings and strategy conferences. Loyalties were to people then, not to issues or ideas. Elected officials strove to keep their positions by being available for residents and helping them when misfortune struck.

A son of a prominent politician reminisced about a relative who was a magistrate. A young woman had come to his father's office in tears. She said, "You won't help me. I'm Serbian. You're Croatian." The magistrate told her we were all Americans now. She described her husband. He drank and gave her no money to buy food for the children. The magistrate asked where the husband worked and then arranged to receive his pay himself. He gave the woman the money she needed and the husband just a few dollars.

1. *St. Louis Post-Dispatch*, March 5, 1972; papers of A. J. Cervantes, Washington University Archives.

The newspapers made it clear that the most significant change brought about by ward election of aldermen was the possibility of obtaining African American representation on the board of aldermen.[20] The *Globe-Democrat* stressed that Amendment No. 1 "opens up the possibility that by 1943 the city will have two Negro Aldermen and that eventually four, or perhaps six, Negro members may be elected to the Board."[21] Minority residential concentration in St. Louis was pronounced, and, as in other cities with district elections such as Chicago or New York, African American representation on a city council would occur much earlier than in cities with council members chosen at large. In St. Louis, that political representation would come to pass while the accoutrements of segregation remained in many other areas of life. The prospect of black aldermen appeared not to be a significant deterrent to a "yes" vote.

The Failure to Centralize

Changes to the political rules of the game affect outcomes. The introduction of civil service lessened the role of jobs in cementing political alliances and diminished an easy way to ensure party workers. Committeemen had less to offer their potential supporters and allies. On the other hand, ward election of aldermen increased the importance of the ward as a political unit and tied the alderman more closely to his committeeman. Eventually, the alderman would assume the service function of the committeeman, negotiating for the citizen with the city bureaucracy.

Both charter changes in turn contributed to a decrease in the powers of the committeeman, but the diminution of his responsibilities occurred gradually. The sport of seeing "who was with whom"— the ward-organization endorsements—continued to matter to politicians and observers alike. Two-party competition remained a facet of St. Louis political life for some time, while class divisions among the wards became more marked. The advent of civil service did not fundamentally alter St. Louis's machine-style politics. The culture of exchange relationships did not change greatly. Although the amount of patronage was reduced, the ward unit continued to be the locus of political jobs. Eventually the aldermanic role increased in significance when municipal legislation gained in importance with the onset of federally funded redevelopment.

These reforms did not affect the city's considerable political fragmentation. Patronage and party affairs remained decentralized.

Ward elections for aldermen did nothing to enhance the power of the mayor and did not diminish the ward as the center of political activity. Reform in St. Louis again was partial at best.

In other cities where machine politics or its vestiges have not been eliminated completely, partisan power came to be centralized. For example, on being elected Boston's mayor in 1913, James Michael Curley stripped the ward bosses "of their ability to dispense patronage directly to their constituents...by making patronage his exclusive domain."[22] Boston's 1909 charter also provided for a nine-member city council elected at large on a nonpartisan ballot.[23] These provisions contributed to the growth of a strong-mayor system. Curley's continuing presence in local politics up to 1951 ensured the perpetuation of a machine style. The political culture looked back to its roots and emphasized "bread and butter issues such as jobs and basic services."[24] A more recent mayor, Kevin White, added to his support by using "his power over department heads...to implement policies to send municipal jobs and contracts to Boston residents and vendors."[25] In Boston, centralization permitted a relatively easy exercise of mayoral power, while tolerance of the old method of individual rewards remained as well. Even with reform, Boston's story is one of cultural continuity. Since St. Louis experienced far less centralization, its culture remained more openly based on quid pro quo transactions. St. Louis's citizens were accustomed to trading favors, and that practice continues today. Certainly the 1941 charter reforms did not temper that orientation to any significant degree. But, because there were fewer jobs to give, the likelihood of a voter promising support for a job declined.

At the height of the Depression, David Lawrence, chairman of the Alleghany County Democratic Party, also began to consolidate "his control over patronage."[26] The ward chairmen and the state legislators could not develop personal followings while Lawrence had his handle on local, state, and federal jobs.[27] At-large council elections, instituted just after the turn of the century, also facilitated the development of centralized power by denying ward interests a tie to legislative representation. As mayor in the 1940s, Lawrence had the power to become the unquestioned political father of the Pittsburgh Renaissance, a highly successful redevelopment alliance with the business community represented in the Allegheny Conference, which was led by Richard King Mellon.[28] Yet jobs and personal service have continued to remain part of Pittsburgh's culture in face of its significant centralization.

In Chicago, Anton Cermak began the building of a centralized machine apparatus in the early 1930s. Patrick Nash and Edward Kelly continued Cermak's work after his untimely death in 1933 and began the slating and job disbursement strategies that Richard J. Daley later would perfect. Although Chicago maintained the selection of its fifty aldermen by district, mayoral prerogatives generally were sufficient to keep the body in line, and they definitely were so after Daley's 1955 election. Chicago's mayor presided over the city council, and the mayor's vote could break a tie in that body. This may have been more of a headache than a benefit, but Chicago's mayor later received the power to appoint people to fill aldermanic vacancies, a power Mayor Richard M. Daley has used to his considerable benefit since 1989. In St. Louis, aldermanic vacancies are filled in special elections. The Democratic and Republican committeemen each nominate a candidate. Because the mayor in St. Louis cannot fill such vacancies, his power is more limited.

Thus, in other cities where machine-style politics reigned, institutional rules and changes to them aided, or at least did not impede, the development of strong executive power. Astute elected officials consolidated the rewards system as well as administrative power in their office. However, St. Louis's institutional array—especially the county offices with their power to collect taxes and fees—prevented a similar development. To this day, St. Louis's mayor continues to share power with the board of estimate and apportionment and county officials. While the charter changes of 1941 tempered certain machine practices, they failed to change the overall nature of the system. St. Louis's culture, based on individual rewards and service, was not radically different from that of Boston, Pittsburgh, or Chicago. St. Louis's structure and its rules, however, kept power drifting back toward the lowest political unit, the ward. Interestingly, no mayor serving after Dickmann achieved as much control over other elected offices. Dickmann saw many of his supporters elected to various offices during his eight-year mayoral tenure. The lack of centralized executive power later affected various forms of municipal policymaking. Certain mayors in more recent times were leaders in their own right. But competition from other officeholders, and by a culture that emphasized the ward as the pivotal political and legislative unit, eventually checked their leadership.

Chapter 5

Interregnum
From Party Competition to
Democratic Factions, 1941–1953

Republicans dominated municipal governance from 1914 to 1933. The Democrats then took charge for eight years. Victories for both parties, with neither dominant for the most part, marked the period 1941–1953. No matter which party held sway in the first half of the twentieth century, the politics were very similar. They centered on jobs and personal service. The St. Louis Democrats and Republicans both organized along ward lines. This structural decentralization helped keep the mayor and the city committees weaker than their counterparts in other cities. Both parties sometimes used the cloak of reform, but just as a device to gain political advantage.

In the 1940s, when neither party dominated at the polls, margins of victory frequently were not large. National contests affected state and county races in presidential years. During this transition period, little overt change occurred in municipal political life, despite the advent of civil service and the return to ward elections for aldermen. In the early part of this period, local politics took second seat to news from the battle zones around the globe, where many St. Louisans served their country during World War II. The war's end brought the soldiers home and swelled St. Louis's population to more than 850,000. However, by the early 1950s, the trends that affected so many major cities soon began to manifest themselves in St. Louis as well: significant suburbanization, freeway building, and a business-governmental alliance to restructure downtown. St. Louis's peculiar institutional and cultural setting would shape its particular responses to these trends.

St. Louis long had been a workingman's town, although the city certainly had pockets of considerable wealth. For many immigrant residents, politics were a path to mobility. Patronage enabled many to modestly support their families while the politicians wheeled and dealed and aligned. Today, many people describe St. Louis as a large small town. Among the political players, everyone knows everyone else, in addition to knowing whom they grew up with and whom they went to high school with—and so it always has been. And in this workingman's town, many have had ties with organized labor. Unions have participated in local politics on a regular basis. This intimacy of acquaintance also has extended to some involved with organized crime. Political, labor, familial, and other ties have overlapped often.

As in other unreformed cities, political participants in St. Louis usually would "go along to get along." They followed their own code. Loyalty was a paramount virtue, as were trust and steadfastness. Friendship mattered as well. Many not troubled by sleights of hand at the ballot box would be appalled at those "who did not go home from the dance with the guy who brung you." You never could switch horses in midstream. If someone was right with you, you might not worry about his other dealings.

St. Louis's unusual layers of governance and its plethora of elected officials certainly enabled the parochial political system to flourish. The war years and the immediate postwar period were the last times that issueless politics would hold sway. The specter of urban decay and subsequent calls for renewal altered the previous business-as-usual agenda. A corporate-sponsored program to rebuild the center of the city would take form as this period drew to a close, followed closely by a struggle for civil rights that would ruffle the political status quo.

During the years 1948–1952, an evident factional cleavage among Democrats arose. One elected official referred to it as "banks vs. unions." Portrayed by some (including the *Post-Dispatch* and the *Globe-Democrat*) as a contest between good and evil, this cleavage affected alignments for many years.

Horse Races

Following the ouster of mayoral incumbent Barney Dickmann in 1941, Republicans held many of the reins of municipal power, including all three seats on the board of estimate and apportionment. In 1941, they also succeeded in capturing all aldermanic seats at stake in the last citywide vote for aldermen. In the 1943 municipal elections, they continued their dominance. The Republican candidate for the aldermanic presidency, Aloys P. Kaufmann, polled 56.6 percent of the vote of an electorate truncated by the absence of

Republican mayor Aloys P. Kauffmann in 1947. MHS Photograph and Print Collection, Hangge Collection.

so many serving in the armed forces. The move to district elections of aldermen, however, prevented a Republican rout. Seven of the fifteen aldermen elected (those from even-numbered wards plus a special election in the third)[1] were Democrats. Interestingly, two Republican victories were historic. The first woman to be elected alderman, Clara Hempelmann, won in the twelfth ward. The board's first African American legislator, the Rev. Jasper C. Caston, carried the sixth ward. Black allegiance did not become solidly Democratic until the 1950s. Republicans were the first to draft African Americans as aldermanic candidates.

In July of 1943, Mayor Becker and other civic leaders perished in the crash of a glider plane. Aldermanic president Kaufmann became acting mayor. He had to run for the office in a special election held at the time of state and national contests in November 1944. In that contest, Kaufmann bested the Democratic nominee, Patrick J. Burke, a business agent for the American Federation of Labor Milk Wagon Drivers Union. Kaufmann received 53 percent of the vote and bucked the general Democratic tide that had city voters again favoring Franklin Roosevelt as well as various Democratic candidates for state office. Kaufmann ran forty-seven thousand votes ahead of Republican national standard-bearer Thomas E. Dewey. The *Globe* felt that the "immediate pressure of an organization," the PAC, formed by the Congress of Industrial Organizations (CIO), had helped turn the tide against Dewey.[2] The *Post-Dispatch* also felt that the CIO PAC had played a strong role in organizing and getting voters to the polls.[3]

St. Louis's newspapers continued to take an active part in influencing electoral outcomes in this decade, in both news columns and editorial pages. On the Saturday before the general election, the *Post-Dispatch* taught potential voters how to cast a split ticket, Democrats for Kaufmann or Republicans for Roosevelt.[4] The illustration accompanying the article showed a ballot clearly marked for both Kaufmann and FDR.

The April 1945 general election actually became the Republican high-water mark. The party never fared as well in subsequent municipal elections. Voters seemingly abandoned their independence of the preceding April and placed three Republicans on the board of estimate and apportionment. Mayor Kaufmann and Comptroller Louis Nolte convincingly won reelection, and Albert L. Schweitzer beat long-term alderman Walter Tobermann for the aldermanic presidency. The margins of victory were strikingly similar in all three contests. In addition, in the races for aldermen of odd-numbered wards, Republicans won thirteen of fourteen contests. Only Democrat Joseph R. Slay of the seventh ward won. A second African American Republican, Walter Lowe, was elected to the board from the nineteenth ward after beating black Democrat David Grant by 917 votes. Despite the Republican triumph, the board still had seven Democrats and twenty-one Republicans. The *Post-Dispatch* attributed the Republican rout to Democratic disorganization locally and to "the disclosure of the record of Sheriff John F. Dougherty and some of his deputies."[5] Sheriff Dougherty had hired deputies with criminal records, including some who had faced murder charges.

The 1947 elections presented more of a mixed bag. Charles Albanese, Republican alderman from the thirteenth ward, won the aldermanic presidency, and Republicans retained complete control of the board of estimate and apportionment. Democrats captured seven of the fourteen aldermanic seats at stake. A third African American Republican, Sidney Redmond, won a seat from the eighteenth ward.

Except for the wards electing black Republicans, the Democrats controlled the central part of the city. These geographic divisions had strong class overtones. The *Post-Dispatch* noted that "The Democratic wards largely coincide with the dwellings of many citizens who work with their hands while a considerable part of the clearly Republican territory of the South Side and North Side is inhabited by white collar groups and takes in the only districts where there has been much home building before and since the war."[6]

Some of these class distinctions proved rather ephemeral, however. Democratic territory soon extended toward the periphery of the city. But those at the core of Democratic Party ward organizations remained people with blue-collar backgrounds, "lunch pail" Democrats.

In 1949, the Democrats broke the grip of the Republicans on the board of estimate and apportionment. Joseph Darst, previously unsuccessful in citywide contests, bested Republican J. Edward Gragg in the contest for mayor. Darst, a realtor, had served as director of public welfare in the Dickmann administration. Fellow Democrat Milton Carpenter also succeeded in dislodging eight-term comptroller Louis Nolte. In addition, eight Democrats won aldermanic seats, while just six Republicans prevailed. Democrats assumed control of the board of aldermen, albeit by a one-vote margin, for the first time since Dickmann's defeat in 1941.

The realignment of African American voters became more evident in this election. Democrat DeWitte T. Lawson defeated the black Republican incumbent, Walter Lowe, in the nineteenth ward. Regarding the citywide contests, the *Post* reported, "to the Democrats went the Negro wards, the long eastern tier known as the river wards, a strip across the center of the town and the Hill area, south of Forest Park. All seven wards with an appreciable proportion of Negro voters went Democratic."[7] Democrats clearly had strengthened their grip on the blue-collar center of the city.

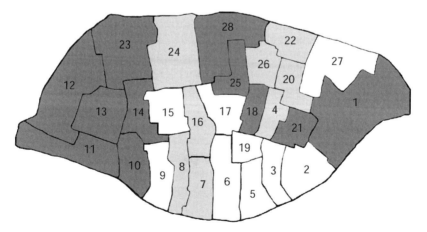

FIGURE 5. *Party affiliation on the board of aldermen, 1945–1951. Dark gray—Republican, light gray—Democratic, white—becoming Democratic.* Illustrated by Ann Owens.

fill a vacancy as circuit clerk, was the only incumbent. He was joined in the winner's circle by other veterans of ward politics: Del Bannister, collector of revenue; Joseph "Juggy" Hayden, license collector; Anthony Denny, recorder of deeds; William Geekie, prosecuting attorney; James McAteer, clerk of the court of criminal corrections; and James Patrick Lavin, clerk of the court of criminal causes. All except McAteer hailed from the growing Democratic heartland in north St. Louis. Table 5 shows the give and take in county office holding during this interregnum period. By 1952, the real contests for county office had moved to the Democratic primary and reflected the "banks and unions" cleavage more than a partisan divide.

TABLE 5

Democratic "County" Office Victories

	1940	1942	1944	1946	1948	1950
Circuit Clerk		H. Sam Priest		Rep.		Phelim O'Toole
Circuit Attorney	Franklin Miller		James Griffin		James Griffin	
Recorder of Deeds		Rep.		Rep.		Anthony Denny
Prosecuting Attorney		Rep.		Rep.		William Geekie
Sheriff	James Fitz-Simmons		John Dougherty		Thomas Callanan	
Collector of Revenue		Rep.		Rep.		Del Bannister
Treasurer	John Dwyer		John Dwyer		John Dwyer	
Coroner	Louis Padberg		Thomas Callanan		Patrick Taylor	
Public Administrator	Thomas Madden		John Cullinane		Thomas Brady	
License Collector		Rep.		Rep.		Joseph Hayden
Clerk, Ct. of Crim. Correction		Rep.		Rep.		James McAteer
Clerk, Ct. of Crim. Causes		Rep.		Rep.		James Patrick Lavin

Note: Rep. — Republican.
SOURCE: St. Louis Board of Elections.

Banks and Unions: Democratic Division

A relative youngster involved in St. Louis politics related that, for several decades, factional cleavages among Democratic politicians could be described as "the banks versus the unions." Although the reality appears to be more complicated than this simple characterization, it certainly provides a logical place to begin to look at the internal politics of the Democratic Party, soon to be overwhelmingly dominant in St. Louis politics. Although the banks-versus-unions distinction applied heavily to the traditional party politics of jobs and contracts, it came to affect major substantive issues as well.

In the postwar period, particularly after 1950, newspapers in many major cities were linked with the business community and pro-development elected officials who supported urban renewal.[9] St. Louis was no exception. However, the bias toward downtown development was subsumed by media coverage of potential union power, power that might be damaging to development plans. The principal dailies, the *Post-Dispatch* and the *Globe-Democrat*, were no strangers to the linking of fact and opinion. They fought for civil service in their news columns, and in 1944 the *Post* instructed voters on how to split tickets (to help Republican mayor Aloys P. Kaufmann when the still-popular FDR headed the Democratic ticket).

In the mid-1940s, the *Post* highlighted contributions that a CIO PAC made to various candidates and, in particular, the PAC's registration and get-out-the-vote efforts. The paper's depictions of this labor involvement in local politics appeared initially to have little effect at the polls. However, by the end of the decade, the daily newspapers had a new target: a machine, in their terms, heavily influenced by the Steamfitters (or Pipefitters)[10] union. Any mention of this purported machine in the columns of the city's most important newspapers carried strong negative connotations well into the 1960s.

A certain irony exists in the negativity attached by the fourth estate—journalists—to labor efforts to affect electoral outcomes. After all, much of St. Louis is and has been a blue-collar town. Workingmen there were always highly unionized. St. Louis's union members and local politicians worked together to prevent Missouri from becoming a right-to-work state, like many of its southern neighbors. Many politicians associated with the "banks" side of the equation were not aristocrats. Frequently, they too had been workingmen before choosing a life in politics. Goals were not dissimilar either: They all wanted to elect themselves and their friends to office, and, if contracts were to be let or development rights granted, they wanted their share.

The county officeholders who collected the city's various taxes and fees headed the banks faction. The custom then was for the treasurer or collector of revenue to place the money taxpayers remitted in non-interest-bearing accounts at various banks in the state. Bankers, grateful for the business these elected officials provided, saw in turn that they and their friends bought tickets to various fundraisers and helped bankroll campaigns. By and large, bank allies were sympathetic to the urban-renewal projects of the 1950s.

The lines between banks and unions sympathizers could be diffuse at times; some committeemen joined both teams at different intervals. Certain political alliances in St. Louis always have been transitory while others were rooted deeper—in friendship or enmity. In some electoral contests, the margin of victory could be narrow. An important goal for any committeeman was taking a winner. Those judged able to deliver their ward had opposing camps vying for their favor.

Jack Dwyer, city treasurer and longtime chairman of the city Democratic committee, epitomized the bank people. (The Democratic City Central Committee consists of the party committeemen and committeewomen from every ward.) Politics were Dwyer's life. Although treasurer for almost three decades, he spent most of his time on political matters and selected staff with a fiscal background to keep his office running smoothly. According to a number of sources, Dwyer was respected widely by his associates, both in and outside of politics. He also was credited with the ability to bring the party together for the general election, after its sometimes-bruising primaries. After his death, the *Post-Dispatch* said, "A generally soft-spoken man, Mr. Dwyer was an able organizer and a skillful director of city campaigns. He was a shrewd and resourceful politician who worked quietly and effectively behind the scenes and avoided the limelight as much as possible."[11] Dwyer also had the "ability to remain on friendly terms with those he opposed in battle."[12]

Dwyer was committeeman from the north side's fourth ward. Over the years, its population became predominantly African American. Yet Dwyer was reelected as committeeman every four years. He had the reputation of a man who took care of his people with jobs, food baskets, and whatever else might be required. Unlike the situation in neighboring wards, blacks would not gain committee posts in the fourth ward until after Dwyer's death in 1966. By that time, Dwyer no longer lived in the ward he represented, a practice not at all unusual then. Dwyer and his friends were St. Louis boosters, favoring downtown development in the 1950s.

A gathering of party leadership: Thomas Eagleton, John Dwyer (seated), Raymond Tucker, and Stuart Symington in 1958. The St. Louis Mercantile Library at the University of Missouri—St. Louis.

A note found among Dwyer's papers showed that banks in St. Louis had made loans to his organization prior to a primary election. He also received some individual donations. Dwyer used this money to print newspapers for distribution in his ward and also gave some of his fellow committeemen $1,000 to $2,000 for election expenses.[13] Dwyer was known as "the party's best solicitor of campaign funds."[14] In Dwyer's day, there were no campaign financial disclosure forms or campaign spending limits. Donations often were made in cash. In his memoirs, former U.S. speaker of the house and longtime congressman Tip O'Neill described a fundraising breakfast held for the Kennedy campaign in St. Louis in 1960:

> One of the most successful events we put together in Missouri was a fund-raising breakfast hosted by Augie Busch, who owned the brewery. Busch had invited thirty businessmen to meet with Jack Kennedy at a thousand dollars a head.
>
> Twenty-nine of them showed up at the meeting. Augie Busch collected the money, and then he and I and Kennedy excused ourselves and stepped into the men's room.

"How did we do?" said Kennedy.

"We raised twenty-nine thousand in cash and twelve thousand in checks."

..."Jeez," I said. "This business is no different if you're running for ward leader or president of the United States."

. . . When I first ran for Congress in 1952, I raised $52,000, and I don't recall seeing a single check. It was just the custom to give cash."[15]

Cash also left no tracks.

Dwyer and his fellow officeholders were comfortable allies for the bankers and business leaders. They were expert at the political game and made few waves. They provided some jobs and other benefits to those with few resources, but they did not challenge the status quo. They used the system they inherited without trying to change it. Dwyer in particular was a welcome figure to many bankers and businessmen. According to one old-timer, Dwyer could fit comfortably in a boardroom and was a member of the Missouri Athletic Club, making him a rarity among ward politicians in the 1940s and 1950s. In addition, Dwyer enjoyed a cordial relationship with Central Trust Bank, an out-state institution that played a leading role in state elections. One veteran of politics in the 1950s said that Central Trust actually handpicked statewide candidates.

Writing in the *St. Louis Business Journal* in 1991, Alfred Fleishman, founder and former head of the most prominent public relations firm in town, summed up Dwyer well. "When Jack Dwyer gave you his word, you never needed his signature.... You had to respect a guy like that. Businessmen respected him. Democrats respected him. Republicans respected him. That's about the best you can be in politics."[16] Fleishman pointed out the key to Dwyer's long success and highlighted St. Louis's dominant political value.

On the union side, the CIO PAC garnered some attention in the middle 1940s. This came less than a decade after the sit-down strikes at automobile plants and the violence that frequently took place when industrial unions tried to gain recognition in mining, steel, and automobile assembly.

Eventually the CIO would merge with the more established and conservative American Federation of Labor (AF of L). In St. Louis, the newspapers turned their attention from the PAC to the Shenker-

Callanan or Shenker-Callanan-Hogan machine and its attempts to win more local offices. There is no consensus among survivors of that period regarding the pluses and minuses of this group and of the Steamfitters, to whom they were closely connected. One longtime party regular remarked that all the players had the same interest: jobs. The Steamfitters wanted contracts given to companies that employed their membership. Building and redeveloping began in earnest after the war, and steam heat was only one option in the construction lexicon. Yet the connotation of something unlawful, corrupt, or even violent clung to the Fitters, a sentiment that set them outside the normal ebb and flow of machine politics, St. Louis style.

Larry Callanan headed the Fitters for most of the period from the 1940s until his death in 1971. His brother Thomas ran successfully for coroner in 1944 and sheriff in 1948. Their base of operations was the second ward, on the city's north side. Larry Callanan himself had had brushes with authority in his early life. He spent time at Bellefontaine Farms as a juvenile offender and, in 1927, received a five-year sentence in a state prison for armed robbery.[17]

Callanan's reputed ally at the end of the 1940s was Edward J. "Jellyroll" Hogan. Hogan was elected a state senator in 1944 and served in that post until 1960. In the early 1920s, Hogan had been the leader of an Irish gang bearing his name. Frequent fights with the rival Egan's Rats left more than a dozen dead.[18] Hogan also was a union agent. He represented the soft-drink workers for more than forty years. Although some who remember this period question placing Hogan at the same level as Callanan, the newspapers clearly did so in the early 1950s.

The third member of the "machine" triumvirate, Morris Shenker, immigrated to St. Louis from Russia as a child. He began his career as a lawyer to the poor and to African Americans. He was "one of the most successful trial lawyers St. Louis has ever seen."[19] Shenker represented various figures tied to organized crime during Senator Estes Kefauver's televised hearings in 1949, and many became familiar with his heavily accented speech. Shenker became active in ward politics in the 1930s and later served as committeeman of the twenty-fifth ward. Past history and present associations rendered Callanan, Shenker, and Hogan—all highly active politically—suspect in the eyes of many, including the major newspapers.

Sizable cash reserves made the Steamfitters powerful and feared. Fitters earned high wages for that time. The union automatically deducted a sizable chunk from each member's paycheck and put it into the Steamfitters' Voluntary Political, Educational, Legislative,

Lawrence Callanan of the Steamfitters with attorney Morris Shenker in 1953. Photograph by Buel White, MHS Photograph and Print Collection.

Charity, and Defense Fund. Larry Callanan and company thus had ample amounts of cash to funnel into electoral contests at all levels of government. Callanan also used his membership to get out the vote. Thus, the Fitters were far from inconsequential as an electoral threat.

For many, Steamfitters leaders skated at the edge of illegality, and they aroused a good bit of fear. There is some truth to that depiction. During the 1950s and 1960s, several federal indictments were filed against Larry Callanan. Earlier, in 1954, he was convicted of labor racketeering and spent several years in prison. Morris Shenker represented Jimmy Hoffa of the Teamsters Union during the 1950s and was his attorney when he was sentenced to federal prison. He also represented other labor leaders accused of corruption.

During these decades, the Fitters sought political allies from two other groups outside the party establishment. They looked to a new breed of black politicians tied to civil-rights activism and to the Lebanese faction centered in the seventh ward.

Although Thomas Callanan first was elected to citywide office in 1944, the newspapers did not identify him as the leader of a "machine" until 1950. In its coverage of the August primary of that year, the *Post-Dispatch* noted his growing importance. One of its election stories had the following secondary headline: "Organization

Slates Almost Entirely Successful—Democrats Backed by Callanan Win in Every Contest."[20] Callanan backed the winning Missouri senatorial candidate, Thomas Hennings; opposed a new charter that failed to gain adoption; and backed those who gained the Democratic nomination for the county offices. The *Post* continued to play up Callanan's pivotal political role in its coverage of the November 1950 general election. The headlines again touted Callanan's role and linked him to Morris Shenker, then twenty-fifth-ward committeeman.[21]

A few months later, the *Post-Dispatch* heralded a "sweeping defeat of Shenker-Callanan forces."[22] In the March 1951 municipal primary, city voters also had to select a successor to Congressman John B. Sullivan, who died in office. Republican Claude Bakewell opposed Democrat Harry Schendel for this seat, which had alternated between the two parties during the past decade. In his campaign, Bakewell linked his opponent, Schendel, to the Shenker-Callanan forces. Bakewell directed "attention of voters to the recent Kefauver crime committee hearings here, particularly the part played by Morris A. Shenker, a Democratic power in representing underworld figures called to testify."[23] On its editorial page, the *Post* complimented Schendel's record in the Missouri House of Representatives, where "he sponsored minimum-wage legislation and…voted to open the University of Missouri to all qualified students regardless of race," as well as his support of urban redevelopment.[24] However, the *Post* also noted that the Shenker-Callanan forces had supported Schendel over Sullivan's widow for the Democratic nomination.

> These rising party manipulators were in a position to control the choice of the Eleventh District Committee and control they did….Morris Shenker's role in the criminal practice of St. Louis is well known. At the two-day hearing held here by the Kefauver Crime Investigating Committee, Shenker was the lawyer for James Carroll, William Molasky and three other witnesses. The right of Mr. Shenker to represent these men and their right to have counsel are unquestioned. But it is a very fair question whether the Democratic Party needs to deliver itself to him in St. Louis—indeed, whether it even needs him as committeeman.

> The race between Mr. Bakewell and Mr. Schendel does more than send one man to sit among 435 in Washington. It helps decide how tight the Shenker-Callanan control is going to be in St. Louis.[25]

The newspapers, as well as the candidates, followed a similar tack in the contest for the aldermanic presidency decided in the April 1951 municipal general election. Republican Charles Albanese faced Mark Hennelly, the Democratic nominee and former legal associate of Morris Shenker. The battle lines were drawn even more clearly, and the result was the same: victory for the Republican candidate supported by the newspapers.

The *Post-Dispatch* said that the 1951 campaign for aldermanic president centered on the issue of "Shenkerism." The *Post* asked, "What has been the effect on the public of the television appearance of Morris A. Shenker...as a criminal attorney representing big gamblers at the Kefauver committee hearings? To what extent has control of the Democratic Party by Shenker and Sheriff Thomas F. Callanan (the so-called issue of "Shenkerism") alienated independent voters and some Democrats?"[26] The *Post* also discussed the failure of either the AF of L or CIO political committees to back Hennelly, which occurred allegedly because of Democratic attempts to dominate their ranks.[27] Noting that the political machines of both parties knew how to deliver votes, the *Globe-Democrat* urged independents to support Albanese to prevent one-party control of the board of estimate and apportionment. They also supported Albanese because "the Democratic candidate is allied by personal friendship and association, if nothing else, with the Shenker-Callanan political machine which seeks to control city affairs."[28]

A brief perusal of newspaper headlines throughout early 1951 reveals the general atmosphere and leads to a greater understanding of the attacks on "Shenkerism" by opposing candidates and the press. Beginning in 1949, Senator Estes Kefauver's hearings on organized crime received considerable attention and were carried live by the new medium of television. Depictions of associations between mobsters, certain union officials, and politicians captured a great deal of attention. The headlines of March 20, 1951, were typical of the era: "'Growing Empire of Crime' Pictured by O'Dwyer"; "Costello Due Back on Stand Today, Admits Ties with Tammany Hall."[29]

Corruption in urban politics is not novel. Tales of turn-of-the-century politicians focused on various kinds of graft and unseemly associations between machine politicians and various nefarious types. Such stories fueled the Progressive reform movement. The televised coverage of Kefauver's hearings made the allegations of corruption far more immediate. Television was a new entertainment phenomenon. Many new owners of TV sets tuned in to the hearings, and people stopped to watch the hearings on sets in department store showrooms.

In his major study of the media, David Halberstam noted that "Democrat Estes Kefauver had been catapulted into national prominence with his televised hearings on crime.... He had already angered the party officials by his investigation of gambling and rackets, which repeatedly embarrassed big-city Democratic administrations."[30]

With the stimulation of these hearings, some taking place in St. Louis, it is no wonder that the Shenker-Steamfitters alliance seemed threatening to many St. Louisans. It was part of the spirit of the times. How deep-seated a threat Shenker and Callanan actually posed is open to debate. What is clear is that charges of "Shenkerism" or being a tool of the "Shenker-Callanan machine" were used to defeat various political opponents and eventually to help elect a mayor sympathetic to the downtown development desired by civic elites. It might also be pointed out that this time in American political history was rife with accusations of guilt by association and the blacklisting of those Americans who appeared to have nontraditional political perspectives. "Shenkerism" clearly was a far cry from Communism, but an eerie similarity exists in some of the coverage. Today, survivors of that era acknowledge the political power of the Fitters but cannot or will not explain why that union was viewed with such dread fifty years ago.

In August of 1952, many candidates backed by the "Shenker-Callanan-Hogan machine" incurred defeat. Phil M. Donnelly, candidate for the Democratic gubernatorial nomination, spoke out against the "machine's influence."[31] The Shenker faction supported his opponent, Phil Welch. Donnelly said that the faction's chief purpose "is to gain control of the Election Board and the Police Board."[32] (The governor appoints members of those boards.) St. Louis's mayor, Democrat Joseph M. Darst, also called for voters to cast an "anti-Callanan ticket."[33]

St. Louis voters responded. They cast out Callanan as sheriff and rejected other candidates tied to his faction that August. The *Globe-Democrat* crowed, "The Callanan-Shenker Democratic machine went down to a crushing defeat early today under an avalanche of votes tossed into the ballot boxes by an aroused St. Louis citizenry. In what promises to be the most startling political upset here in years, Sheriff Thomas F. Callanan himself—the man who aspired to become political boss of the state—was defeated in his own race."[34] Edward Dowd, a former FBI agent, defeated the Shenker-Callanan candidate for circuit attorney. Donnelly also was successful; he became the Democratic gubernatorial nominee. Interestingly, Local 688 of the Warehouse and Distribution Workers Union, led by

Harold Gibbons—and with a membership of ten thousand—also opposed Donnelly.[35] As part of the Teamsters network, Gibbons himself soon played a leading role in St. Louis politics and provided another installment of the "banks versus unions" saga.

During the early years of the twentieth century, sharp lines were drawn between the business elite (the Big Cinch) and labor. That cleavage helped prevent significant reform to St. Louis's municipal government. It reappeared in the 1940s and 1950s when union power potentially could stifle plans for postwar urban renewal.

It was in this setting that a man who wished to transform the city emerged as its highest elected official. With some background in politics, he managed to initiate a number of development programs. However, when Raymond Tucker tried to change fundamentally the political structure of the city of St. Louis, he met with failure. Schisms that had affected charter writing in 1914 remained, and machine politics marked by ward factionalism had deep roots. Strong resistance to institutional change persisted in many areas of the city. St. Louis's structure, as well as its institutions and the culture and behavior it shaped, continued to put its stamp on major postwar initiatives.

Chapter 6

The Tucker Years, 1953–1965
Renewal, Reform, and Race

The post–World War II years present a watershed in the American urban experience. Swollen with returning GIs and their burgeoning families, many northern central cities reached their population peak in 1950. It was also the high point for many cities in the volume of manufacturing and the number of blue-collar workers employed in their factories. In the second half of the twentieth century, the huge movement to suburbia of people and businesses changed urban geography dramatically. Central cities increasingly became home to the poor and members of minority groups. With their aging infrastructures, these cities also had to confront declining revenues. Many municipal officials sought new roles for their cities to bolster the local economy.

Housing shortages after the war gave increased impetus to the suburban push that had begun years before. Little housing had been built during the Depression and the war itself. In *Crabgrass Frontier,* Kenneth T. Jackson highlighted various reasons for America's unique suburban phenomenon:

- available land
- balloon construction
- preference for detached dwellings and home ownership
- state laws impeding central city annexation and allowing formation of suburban municipalities
- federal programs.[1]

Of particular importance to St. Louis's history is the phenomenon whereby a number of federal programs actually helped empty central cities of both population and commerce. Federal programming also strengthened the economic and racial segregation already part and parcel of the urban landscape. Especially pernicious were the federal mortgage loan guarantee programs. Both the Federal Housing Administration (FHA) and the Veterans Administration (VA) made possible mortgage guarantees widely used after the war by eager homebuyers. Using criteria developed by the federal Home Owners Loan Corporation (HOLC) in the 1930s, FHA and VA redlined central cities on a vast scale, making it very difficult for purchasers to obtain mortgages for homes there. The federal government thereby encouraged development of brand-new suburban communities. Under the HOLC criteria, the best housing was found in "new and homogeneous" neighborhoods. "Homogeneous meant 'American business and professional men.'"[2] Areas with older housing stock and home to residents of less-favored ethnic groups (such as Jews) received a low rating. The lowest rating applied to areas settled with African Americans. As Jackson noted, "The Home Owners Loan Corporation did not initiate the idea of considering race and ethnicity in real-estate appraisal.... The HOLC simply applied these notions of ethnic and racial worth to real-estate appraising on an unprecedented scale."[3]

In the late 1940s and 1950s, government-guaranteed loans spurred suburban growth in the St. Louis area and elsewhere, making possible new homes for white professionals and workers. Older parts of the city, in turn, suffered from the inability of prospective homeowners to use FHA or VA loans with their low down payments and thirty-year terms.

Federally subsidized road building also damaged central city fortunes. Although civic leaders in St. Louis and elsewhere originally saw freeway building as a means to lure people back to downtown, the effect was just the opposite. Freeways cut into central cities, destroyed neighborhoods, and definitely encouraged the suburban exodus. Judd and Swanstrom found that these new expressways "took land off the tax rolls...damaged surrounding property and cut cities off from their waterfronts."[4] With funding from first the Highway Act of 1944 and then the 1956 National Defense Highway Act, major cities took the 90 percent federal match and the state's 10 percent and forever altered their urban fabric in an endless and fruitless quest to ease traffic congestion. The automobile and the ubiquity of automobile ownership in the U.S. also enabled extensive suburban growth and made the central city a less significant hub in the metropolitan area. Support for public transportation was anemic at best. In addition, the federal government began to locate military and other facilities in the sunbelt, and the federal tax code discouraged the renovation of production facilities inside central cities. Instead, tax policy aided and abetted the building of new plants in suburbs and in the southern and southwestern sectors of the country.

Just as American civic leaders looked to highway building as a key component of central city renewal in the 1940s and 1950s, so also did they embrace an urban renewal that involved massive tearing down and rebuilding. The federal government again was the enabler. The Federal Housing Act of 1949's Title I established a $1 billion loan fund to enable cities to plan redevelopment projects, acquire land, and clear properties.[5] The land could then be sold, at a loss, to redevelopers.[6]

Although the emphasis in the 1949 act was on the provision of low-cost housing, certain mayors and business leaders saw the opportunity to facilitate downtown development and remove slums from the city core. In the case of New Haven, Connecticut, Robert Dahl noted, "Urban redevelopment soon acquired a nonpartisan aura that continued to surround it throughout the next decade."[7] In his study of urban renewal in New York City, Joel Schwartz found a "broad consensus about the lengths the city had to go to rebuild itself. This included agreement on the removal of low-income groups to make room for the valued middle class.... Redevelopment gave legal authority and large public subsidies to private realtors to uproot low-income people."[8] A general belief in the premises of urban renewal extended beyond the East Coast. Many in St. Louis and other cities accepted the philosophy as well. The premises of urban renewal became standard operating procedure for a generation of planners, business leaders, realtors, developers, and public officials.

To carry out an urban-renewal program it became necessary to marry more formally private and public power. In many cities, in John H. Mollenkopf's terms, "a confluence of forces" occurred that included "a mobilized business community, a growth-oriented mayor willing to enlist that business support, [and] the establishment of new and more powerful development agencies."[9] Many scholars' works highlight the widespread support urban renewal initially enjoyed from across the political spectrum. Whether they were initiators or whether they were cajoled into participation, heads of major businesses were key players. Many unions joined in support of these programs because of the work they provided to their members. Those owning downtown real estate—department stores, utilities, banks, and newspapers—had a natural interest in the enhancement of the core city.

In St. Louis, the urban-renewal era coincided with the mayoralty of Raymond Tucker. He initiated or gave support to projects similar to those in other cities. He also helped create and mold an organization of top business leaders—Civic Progress—to make renewal possible.

The desire to physically remold the landscape accompanied a desire to streamline and modernize municipal government structure in St. Louis. Several plans were devised in this era, taken to the voters, and decisively defeated. These defeats demonstrate the resilience of politics based on ward factionalism and the endurance of the culture associated with those politics. Class divisions helped perpetuate this status quo, despite a strong mayor who had considerable business and newspaper support.

During the Tucker era, the civil-rights struggle also moved to the forefront. The governmental response to that movement did not differ greatly from that of other cities. St. Louis's history of de jure and de facto segregation compounded the city's adjustment to the struggle for equality. Its machine-style politics also shaped the struggle and the eventual outcomes. Control of jobs and of contracts lay beneath the surface of the discourse and affected attitudes toward public accommodations, schools, and housing.

This chapter will discuss how the structure of the city affected the course of the Tucker mayoralty in terms of urban renewal and government reform. Chapter 7 will address the struggle for equal opportunity that took place during Tucker's term in office. Events in St. Louis mirror those in other cities, but St. Louis's institutional structure and culture clearly affected the regime formed there as well as the city's general responses to urban change.

Raymond Tucker was one of only three individuals to serve as St. Louis's mayor for three terms. He left his mark on the city's physical landscape, although fundamental structural reform eluded him. He was part of a new breed of mayors emerging in the 1950s, determined to modernize their bailiwick, particularly the central business district. This era valued planning and expertise and exemplified a positive attitude. Mayors during this period believed they would make their cities bloom again and that they had the programs to do it.

Tucker's predecessor, Joseph Darst, was no different. He supported charter change and physical redevelopment, and he created a network of business elites to further these goals. In addition, he campaigned against candidates endorsed by Callanan and Shenker. Ill health prevented Darst from seeking a second term, but he already had anointed a successor—Raymond Tucker, a mechanical engineering professor—who, when part of the Dickmann administration, had eliminated the pollution caused by the burning of low-sulfur coal.

Tucker's First Mayoral Quest

Raymond Tucker ran for mayor in 1953 as Joseph Darst's heir apparent. He had the backing of the civic elite and the newspapers, although only a handful of wards endorsed him. Tucker's principal opponent in the Democratic primary, Mark Eagleton (father of Senator Thomas Eagleton), garnered most of the ward support. Eagleton and Tucker both had strong resumes.

Tucker most often was portrayed as an expert, a man above the political morass. He had spent most of his career as a professor of mechanical engineering at Washington University and had headed his department there. As smoke commissioner, he removed the sulphurous haze from the city by ending the use of soft Illinois coal. Experts from other cities, such as Pittsburgh, consulted him when they strove to clean their cities' air.[10]

Tucker also had participated in local politics. Before becoming smoke commissioner, he served as secretary to Mayor Barney Dickmann (a post later called chief of staff or deputy mayor) in a highly politicized administration. During this period, he also headed the Twelfth Ward Regular Democratic Organization, and in 1945 he chaired the Democratic Citizens Committee. Nonetheless, Tucker's academic qualifications distinguished him from many St. Louis politicians. Just before the election, the *Post* noted that "As an engineer, Tucker considers himself particularly qualified to tackle the problems that will confront the city in the next four years, particularly in regard to housing, slum-clearance, installation of docks and warehouses, and establishment of adequate airport facilities."[11]

Tucker's opponent, Mark Eagleton, also had impressive qualifications. A former Republican, Eagleton switched allegiances during FDR's fourth presidential campaign in 1944. Eagleton had served on the St. Louis School Board from 1937 to 1943. In that position, he fought for open meetings and opposed a superintendent with questionable financial dealings.[12] In 1945, Governor Donnelly named him to the St. Louis Board of Police Commissioners. He left that board in 1946 because he disagreed with its stand against unionization of police officers.[13] Eagleton also served briefly as a war-crimes prosecutor in Germany in late 1946. His mayoral campaign emphasized the need to alleviate traffic congestion in St. Louis.[14]

Differences on the issues were not the principal focus of the campaign, however. Instead, the Tucker-Eagleton contest was cut from the same cloth as other recent banks-vs.-unions contests in St. Louis. The race also could be described as "reform vs. regular."

Despite some political roots, Tucker ran as an expert above the fray. His "activity in helping write the civil service law and as head of the freeholders board, which drafted a charter considered inimical to patronage, did not serve to bolster his cause with many politicians."[15] In fact, Tucker supporters depended on a strong Republican crossover vote in the primary. The Republican contest was one-sided.[16] Tucker's advocacy of urban renewal and good government reached across St. Louis's traditional partisan lines.

Tucker's campaign actively portrayed Eagleton as a Callanan-Shenker ally and "charged that the Callanan-Shenker machine is out to regain its lost power by backing Eagleton."[17] The twentieth-ward organization, chaired by Thomas Callanan, had endorsed Eagleton, and this endorsement was used repeatedly against him. Robert G. Dowd, vice chairman of Tucker's speakers' bureau and a magistrate, stated that Tucker had not solicited Callanan's support. "It was suggested to Mr. Tucker by members of the Callanan-Shenker machine that he meet with their group. He refused to do this and has stated that he will not compromise his principles to gain the support of this political machine."[18] The *Globe-Democrat* also noted that Eagleton's law partner, James Waechter, played a significant role in Eagleton's campaign and that Waechter had represented the sheriff's office when Thomas Callanan was its head.[19]

On the eve of the primary, Eagleton vigorously denied the charges that he had solicited Shenker's and Callanan's support.[20] Eagleton also "filed a $200,000 damage suit against Tucker and four of his campaign leaders because of their allegations."[21] These charges hurt Eagleton, particularly when Thomas Callanan's home was bombed that February, just before the election, perhaps because of infighting among the Steamfitters.[22] No one was hurt, but this extra publicity about the Fitters made the charges of the Tucker camp resonate.

As a *Globe-Democrat* editorial acknowledged, Tucker and Eagleton did not differ on such matters as the earnings tax, slum clearance, new housing, or the new business organization Civic Progress.[23] Yet the newspapers clearly favored the Tucker candidacy. The *Globe* felt that "Eagleton would try to serve the city well but has no background in city administration."[24] The *Post-Dispatch* endorsed Tucker on multiple occasions. On March 12, the *Post*'s editorial called on independents and Republicans to cast their ballots for Tucker.[25] The *Post* said, "He will be defeated if the primary voting is dominated by machine politicians."[26] An accompanying cartoon (Figure 6) called for a "yes" vote on a bond issue also on the ballot,

FIGURE 6. *"Vote for the Bond Issue and Clear St. Louis's Front Yard."* A *political cartoon calling for a "yes" vote on an urban-renewal bond issue.* Illustrated by Daniel Fitzpatrick, © 1953, *St. Louis Post-Dispatch.* Reprinted with the permission of the *St. Louis Post-Dispatch,* 2002.

a bond issue that would facilitate urban renewal. The *Post* became more explicit the next day (March 13). It editorialized that "the leaders of a badly beaten machine, determined to make a come-back obviously are more afraid of Mr. Tucker than of his opponent."[27] Perceived associations were portrayed as critical to the election. Neither the *Post* nor Tucker's campaign staff mentioned that Eagleton enjoyed the support of Jack Dwyer and other commit-teemen not part of the Shenker-Callanan alliance.

Tucker won the primary but by a slim margin, only 1,679 votes.[28] Eagleton carried the north side with the exception of the twenty-sixth ward. Tucker dominated in the more Republican south. He carried every ward there except the twenty-fourth, with its strong Democratic organization based in the Italian Hill neighborhood. In the city's central corridor, the middle-class twenty-eighth and twenty-fifth wards went with Tucker, as did the more working-class seventeenth. It was a close election, and this contest was also a harbinger of future politics in the city. Class and racial distinctions were evident in the tally. Tucker's identification with reform and renewal helped in more affluent parts of St. Louis. His separation from regular ward politics also played better in these neighborhoods than in working-class sections of the city. Support for Tucker's programs would have a similar dual nature.

Tucker went on to beat his Republican opponent easily in the April general election. But the narrowness of the primary victory and the composition of his supporters reflected the city's past reform battles to some extent. They also provided clues to future contests. The presence of twenty-eight ward organizations, with class and race geography and ties to county officeholders, allowed Tucker to consolidate only so much power in his new office. He won a number of battles and pushed certain programs quite successfully, but he failed to change the playing field. Institutional reform eluded him, and St. Louis's quid pro quo political culture, nurtured for so long by decentralized patronage and changing alignments, continued to shape and hone physical and racial change.

Strong ward organizations still exchanged favors, and jobs and contracts remained the cement holding relationships together. Ward regulars looked not at the issues of the day when endorsing candidates but, instead, at the office-seeker liked by their committeeman and his friends. After a candidate was picked, the ward organization had to carry him on Election Day to ensure its reputation.

Regime Building St. Louis Style

American cities, although not powerless, possess neither the legal nor the fiscal ability to act independently in most matters. As Judd and Swanstrom note, "city politics in the United States arises from the intersection of governmental power and private resources...the growth of the public sector has not eclipsed the authority of private institutions to make critical decisions involving jobs, land use, and investment."[29]

The inherent limitations of municipal power have led to the formation of regimes in most cities. These regimes comprise public officials and the business elite. To Clarence N. Stone, the regime becomes "the informal arrangements that surround and complement the formal workings of governmental authority."[30] Regimes in various cities are not identical. They differ because of the nature of the business communities as well as distinctions in urban geography, demography, and government.

Regimes played perhaps their most conspicuous role during the urban renewal era, the 1950s through the mid-1960s. In major cities, the business community generally found favor with the idea of strengthening downtown, building expressways, and removing slums and blight. In some cities, bold mayors cajoled reluctant business leaders into active involvement with urban renewal. In other cities, business was a more forceful partner.[31] Regardless of which partner was the instigator, the effect was the same. The components of urban renewal were similar across the United States. Business and local officials shared a common view and a common approach.

In the 1950s, elite business organizations formed in many cities to focus on civic improvement.[32] St. Louis was no exception. Mayor Joseph Darst created Civic Progress in St. Louis just prior to leaving office in 1953. His successor, Raymond Tucker, expanded the organization and worked closely with it throughout his tenure. Howard F. Baer, no stranger to St. Louis's leading citizens and their community involvements, presented an interesting sketch of Civic Progress's founding in his memoir. Baer relied on a memo prepared by one of the original members, William A. McDonnell, of the aircraft corporation that bore his name:

> In 1953 the then Mayor Joe Darst had reason to be concerned about his city, that St. Louis had been sitting on its hands for 20 years while others had spent tens of millions to stimulate growth and activity....
>
> Now Darst had heard of an organization called the Allegheny Conference in Pittsburgh, where dynamic activity seemed to be under full steam; and he appointed eight men to consider the advisability of a similar effort for St. Louis. They were Sidney R. Baer of the department store, Arthur Blumeyer of the Bank of St. Louis, David R. Calhoun of St. Louis Union Trust Company, attorney James Douglas, Aloys Kaufmann, former mayor, J. W. McAfee of Union Electric, Powell McHaney of General American Life Insurance, and Ethan Shepley, attorney and Chancellor of Washington University. About then Ray Tucker succeeded Darst as mayor, and quickly there were added 10 other men, including August A. Busch, Edwin Clark, Donald Danforth, Morton D. May, William McDonnell, Sidney Maestre, Edgar Queeny, Edgar Rand, Tom K. Smith and Clarence Turley.[33]

The members of this new group journeyed to Pittsburgh to see how the Allegheny Conference worked. However, the method of operation these St. Louisans created differed a great deal from what they had observed in Pittsburgh. St. Louis business leaders chose not to have Civic Progress be inclusive of the wider community and not to have its own staff or offices, as the Allegheny Conference did. Instead, St. Louis's business leaders decided that Civic Progress should be a small group consisting entirely of the chief executive officers of the largest and most important companies. These top executives had to attend the monthly meetings in person. They could not send a representative. According to Baer, McDonnell noted that "the usual order of things in creating a new civic body is to make sure that all community elements are included…. By avoiding such an approach, the closely limited fraternity of capable executives, with corporate power behind them, could talk to each other in confidence, without bombast, or fear of press, and with the knowledge that their discussions would not be public property. And if they decided on a course of action requiring money, they could provide it from their own corporate treasuries."[34] There would be no professional staff to push the group into projects simply to justify its existence.[35] Instead, a senior person at the public relations firm of Fleishman-Hillard would work with Civic Progress and be its spokesperson. The purpose of Civic Progress would be to work closely with government officials, principally at the local level.

The Allegheny Conference had a larger number of members and a professional staff from the beginning. It also spawned subsidiary organizations to deal with housing and other community concerns. Its cadre of professionals provided independent information and technical assistance to city departments. Richard King Mellon, whose family's holdings crisscrossed many major Pittsburgh corporations, dominated the Conference originally. In turn, the Conference managed to work with a strong mayor who controlled Pittsburgh's political life, David Lawrence. Thus, the Steel City's regime took on a corporatist character almost from the get-go, and the Allegheny Conference came to be seen as a neutral, expert partner.[36]

In St. Louis, Civic Progress remained an elite group, removed from view. In the early Tucker years, the popular perception was not necessarily negative. However, over time, Civic Progress's aura of mystery contributed to perceptions that Civic Progress was similar to the Big Cinch, the business alliance active at the turn of the century. The sayings "Civic Progress runs this town" and "nothing happens unless Civic Progress wants it" have been repeated often by politicians, members of the fourth estate, and many citizens. In addition, lack of an office or staff limited the ability of the business group to generate independent programs or to provide expertise to local government. Baer's accounts of Civic Progress involvement in the design of Busch Stadium and other municipal projects depict the activities of a group of enthusiastic amateurs.

Civic Progress was at its most active during the Tucker mayoralty. Weekly meetings were held at the mayor's office, and the mayor's staff prepared the agenda. From interviews with participants at that time, the period apparently was marked by mutually shared concerns and mutually agreed-upon remedies. The business leaders making up Civic Progress sought support in Washington, D.C., for St. Louis's renewal efforts and wooed aldermen and other public officials at home. One former alderman remembered the receptions Civic Progress held and also his inclusion on a trip to the nation's capital. Tucker and the business leaders of Civic Progress shared a mindset then and considerable empathy. The mayor fit into their gatherings and shared many of their values. Although not as removed from the political realm as some thought, Tucker had a strong professional résumé and executive experience. He fit in the boardroom as few St. Louis mayors could. However, the weak institutionalization of Civic Progress would contribute over time to a more loosely coupled regime. The fragmentation of political power in the city and the region also brought about a regime lacking cohesion after Tucker left the mayor's office.

Urban Renewal

St. Louis's 1947 City Plan has been the base-planning document for the city since it was adopted.[37] The plan was prepared under the aegis of nationally known engineer and planner Harland Bartholomew, who had prepared a number of St. Louis plans since his first in 1908. The purpose of the 1947 City Plan was to "wipe out the obsolescent blighted areas and costly decaying slums."[38] The plan found much of the heart of the city, including a number of historic neighborhoods, blighted. As Mary Bartley noted, "The 1947 plan is a product of post-World War II thinking, and it reflects that era's popular notion that limitless access for automobiles was desirable.... The mindset of the era was to look forward, to get rid of the old, and to ignore the past. There is no mention of urban fabric or context, much less preservation."[39]

These ideas regarding the obsolescence of the downtown, the city streetscape, and much housing were commonplace then in the United States. St. Louis's renewal efforts under Mayor Tucker were not unique, but they were thoroughgoing and, in some instances, created difficult problems for succeeding generations of residents and officials.

St. Louis, by 1958, had received $999,190 in urban renewal capital grants.[40] City voters augmented this allotment when they approved bond issues totaling $110.6 million in May of 1955. (Voters had turned down a similar measure two years before.) Bond approval made possible the construction of three freeways—Highway 40, later to be Interstate 64; Interstate 70; and Interstate 44. I-70 was allowed to pass through the downtown, separating major buildings from what soon became the national park housing Eero Saarinen's soaring Gateway Arch and from the Mississippi River. I-44 sliced through the Hill neighborhood, dividing the traditional Italian enclave, and I-55 split the Soulard neighborhood. The city authorized a $10 million allocation for slum clearance, and other monies were earmarked for improvements to the infrastructure.[41] The Land Clearance for Redevelopment Authority (LCRA) handled St. Louis's urban-renewal programs. It was headed by Charles Farris, whom some have likened to M. Justin Herman, San Francisco's redevelopment czar, a mini Robert Moses.

The major urban renewal site in St. Louis was the Mill Creek valley, close to downtown and City Hall. In 1954, a LCRA survey found that "99 percent of the residential buildings (in Mill Creek) were in need of major repair, 80 percent were without private bath and toilet facilities, and 67 percent lacked running water."[42] The residents of Mill Creek were mainly African American. Demolition began there in 1959 and displaced 1,772 families and 610 individuals.[43] Some of those displaced moved to public housing. Most crowded into the northern half of the city on either side of Grand Boulevard and triggered a significant white flight to the northern part of St. Louis County.

In the 1950s, these plans for renewal and for freeways had many proponents. Their long-term effects were not known, nor were they predicted, except by a rare few. It might be added that until 1961, Tucker seemed very much in control. The development he favored was quite popular, except with those whose immediate environs were affected.

Redevelopment of the downtown was a principal feature of central city renewal. In St. Louis, this necessitated the completion of the national park on the Mississippi River, begun during the Dickmann administration and soon to be home to the Gateway Arch, a formidable piece of public art. Congressman Leonor K. Sullivan secured new federal monies to move the project along in the 1950s.[44] Planners and officials also viewed the Mill Creek project as a boon to downtown, because it removed deteriorated dwellings and a large minority population from the periphery of the central business district. Mayor Darst had pushed for the construction of several high-rise public-housing projects, including the infamous Pruitt-Igoe, to absorb the city's growing number of low-income families. With work on these projects planned or underway, attention turned to the core of the business district.

In 1958, LCRA director Charles Farris proposed that a stadium be built downtown[45] to replace Sportsmen's Park in north St. Louis. Civic Progress member James Hickok led a major fundraising effort for the proposed stadium. In his St. Louis history, Ernest Kirschten discussed the construction of the stadium and the role played by Anheuser-Busch executive August Busch, Jr.:

> Naturally, this is more than a baseball matter. The redevelopment also involves new office buildings, ample parking garages, and a large motel. It is intended to replace more than twenty-five blocks of rather squalid lofts and parking lots, to beef up the downtown shopping district, and to extend the rehabilitation of the city. Yet the stadium would be out of the question without the Cardinals as chief tenants. So Gussie Busch has agreed to move in and put up a large share of the needed capital too. He figures that what is good for St. Louis is good for the brewery.[46]

Busch exemplified the first generation of Civic Progress members. He and his initial cohorts were St. Louis natives likely to tie their success to the city's, as business leaders in other major cities did at that time. St. Louis's business leaders joined Tucker in believing that redevelopment represented progress and a means to restore a central city to its past glory.

Elections and the Tucker Influence

The municipal elections of 1955 provided evidence of Mayor Tucker's increased popularity. During Tucker's first two years in office, the board of aldermen had weakened the city's "master traffic control plan" and had delayed action on a bill to set up another board of freeholders to draft a new city charter.[47] The mayor played a major role in the 1955 municipal elections to select aldermen from even-numbered wards and an aldermanic president. Tucker actively supported Donald Gunn, formerly the U.S. internal revenue collector in St. Louis, for president of the board. A. J. Cervantes, alderman from the fifteenth ward, opposed Gunn in the Democratic primary.

A reporter for the *Post-Dispatch* noted that Gunn "supported civic betterment,...the proposed bond issue, expressways, and hospital improvements. He spoke out strongly against abuses of 'aldermanic courtesy,' and spot-zoning, and in favor of the election of a board of freeholders."[48]

St. Louis's governmental system of divided power and its ward-based politics combined to promote the tradition of aldermanic courtesy: the board of aldermen did not approve a project in any alderman's ward unless that alderman supported it. In other words, there was a code of mutual noninterference that strengthened the aldermanic role while inhibiting citywide planning. Aldermanic courtesy also could inhibit projects that spanned ward boundaries. In the 1950s, those supporting renewal—Tucker's administration, Farris, the business elite, and the newspapers—deplored spot zoning. Aldermen often had pushed to change the zoning of a particular parcel to accommodate a certain business. For the advocates of renewal, such an approach contradicted the need for comprehensive

Mayor Raymond Tucker (center) in 1957, shown here with Alderman Anton Niemeyer, aldermanic president Donald Gunn, Alderman T. H. Mayberry, and Alderman Fred Haag. Photograph by Jack January, St. Louis Post-Dispatch, 1957.

city plans prepared by experts, and it reflected the parochial concerns of ward-based politics.

In its editorial endorsement of Tucker's ally, Donald Gunn, for aldermanic president, the *Post-Dispatch* stressed its support for Tucker's redevelopment agenda.[49] The newspaper applauded Gunn's support of the upcoming bond issue and of a board of freeholders to create a new charter, as well as his advocacy of slum clearance and expressways. On the other hand, the *Post* found that "Mr. Cervantes since 1951 voted forty-eight times to override mayoral vetoes of the evil spot-zoning ordinances."[50] Gunn won the primary by thirty-one thousand votes. He went on to defeat the incumbent president, Republican Charles Albanese, by a two-to-one margin. It was a Democratic rout; of the fourteen aldermanic seats at stake, Democrats won twelve.

In 1957, Tucker sought reelection. Thomas Callanan opposed him belatedly in the Democratic primary. Callanan, defeated in his bid for reelection as sheriff in 1952, had been a leader of a strong faction dominated by the Steamfitters Union. Tucker's successful bid for a second term illustrated his popularity. He defeated Callanan by garnering 68,479 votes to only 16,625 for his opponent. He carried twenty-six of the twenty-eight wards, losing only the fifth and the nineteenth, each having a large African American population. In the general election, he trounced his Republican opponent by an even more impressive margin. Democrats again took twelve of the fourteen aldermanic seats at stake and elected Democrat John Poelker, a former FBI agent, as comptroller.[51]

Until this time, the ward committeeman played the leading role in ward affairs. He aided constituents and organized Thanksgiving and Christmas baskets for needy families as well as staged various ward functions. The committeeman held the allocation of jobs in his hands and attempted to control whomever served in the legislature or on the board of aldermen from his bailiwick. The board of aldermen's statutory powers are relatively weak. For example, the board cannot vote increases to the city budget. But as the furor over spot zoning demonstrates, aldermanic votes had become increasingly important to the renewal agenda. Aldermen, not committeemen, were wined and dined by Civic Progress, anxious for their support of redevelopment. An alderman's say about what went on in his or her ward made the urban legislator a more important player. It was the alderman who began to deal with neighborhood groups on a regular basis. Most important in terms of political arrangements, the alderman gradually replaced the committeeman as the person to call about municipal service.

Turkeys and Christmas Baskets

Ward organizations continued to perform recreational and charitable functions. The infamous "Christmas basket"—a couple of chickens, bread, onions, and potatoes—was a standard feature of ward life, as was the Thanksgiving turkey. Even predominantly affluent wards, such as the twenty-eighth, continued to prepare these baskets each year until the early 1990s. City Democratic committee chairman Jack Dwyer helped to assemble and deliver such baskets to his constituents in the fourth ward every year. In the tenth ward, Louis Buckowitz, who served as alderman or committeeman for many years, began organizing an Easter egg hunt for a large number of children in 1936. This famous egg hunt endured for more than fifty years.

Louis Buckowitz at the Easter egg hunt he organized for fifty years. The St. Louis Mercantile Library at the University of Missouri–St. Louis.

At the same time, many manufacturing enterprises in the city began to shut their doors or move outside the city limits, diminishing the pool of blue-collar jobs to which committeemen long had referred their constituents. Civil service had taken its toll on city patronage, and the school board moved haltingly to substitute merit for political pull in the hiring of its nonteaching staff at its building and maintenance division. Legislation enacted at City Hall became more important, while the traditional providers of jobs had fewer positions to give out. Interestingly, strong ward organization leaders such as Joe Roddy, Albert "Red" Villa, and Ray Leisure chose to become aldermen, not committeemen, in the 1950s. Political activity shifted, and aldermen became more pivotal players. Despite Mayor Tucker's popularity and the adoption of his initiatives, politics remained centered in the wards. It was a question of who in the ward had the most juice. (During this period, it also became more common to have divided ward organizations. Occasionally a committeeman headed one group and a committeewoman another. The alderman might be with either of them or have his or her own group.)

Callanan's poor performance against Tucker seemingly demonstrated a significant decline in Steamfitter clout. (One political veteran claimed that Callanan knew that his belated candidacy would be unsuccessful. He ran just to ensure that there would be some opposition to Tucker.) Although the Fitters failed to achieve high municipal office in St. Louis, their hefty political bank account brought them a number of allies across the country. In discussing the ill-fated design of Pruitt-Igoe, a large high-rise public housing complex near downtown, James Neal Primm noted that "Because of the economic and political power of the Steamfitters, virtually the only item that was not pared down was an elaborate and expensive steam-heating system."[52] Elevators may have stopped only on every third floor in that housing project, but there was steam heat. Lambert described Steamfitters Local 562 as a union of just one thousand members that controlled a political fund that grew by $11,000 every week.[53] Campaign contributions from the Fitters flowed to members of Congress from Tennessee, Michigan, Minnesota, Oklahoma, and Wisconsin as well as Missouri. Edward Long, a U.S. senator from Missouri, particularly benefited from Fitter contributions. Long had the heating system at the federally financed Blumeyer housing project "changed from electricity to gas—a system that would employ Steamfitters in its construction. The change of the system reportedly held up construction of the project a year."[54]

While the Steamfitters' presence in St. Louis politics subsided to some extent, another union became active in municipal affairs. Its activism resembled that of a social movement as much as a political group. The Teamsters and their local leader, Harold Gibbons, sought to organize communities to fight for improved conditions. One prominent issue they addressed was rat control. Teamsters Local 688, warehouse and distribution workers, set up a "Community Action Stewards Assembly," an "attempt to use 'shop level' mechanics on the ward and township level."[55] Community stewards, present in each ward that had more than twenty-five members of Local 688 residing there, heard neighborhood grievances at organized meetings and worked with public officials for solutions. The stewards,

---

Red Villa

In the eleventh ward, the Carondolet area, Alderman Albert "Red" Villa represented his working-class constituency in a traditional manner. He and Committeeman James McAteer toured their ward each week to look for problems to report to the proper agency. Villa also held court for about ten hours a day in his south St. Louis tavern.

In this workingman's saloon where women and fancy drinkers are rare, Villa talks to his people about streets that need fixing, trees that need trimming, personal property taxes that have to be paid, traffic tickets that have to be disposed of, city stickers that need to be bought and the hundred other problems people bring.[1]

The *Post*'s obituary of Villa described his traditional method of operation. "His kind of politics meant doing favors for constituents, lining up patronage jobs and getting his slate elected—not thinking up clever 'sound bites' for news cameras or hiring pollsters."[2]

1. John Angelides, "Red Villa, a Man of Contradiction," *St. Louis Globe-Democrat*, August 16, 1969.
2. Tim O'Neil, "Red Villa Praised as Man Who Lived for His Ward," *St. Louis Post-Dispatch*, December 9, 1990, p. 1A.

numbering about fifty, also held monthly meetings themselves at Teamster headquarters. Steven Brill cited an explanation of the stewards' work given by Local 688's head, Harold Gibbons: "If, let's say, we needed a playground in that neighborhood, we'd have the steward get all our members together and start raising hell. We'd call a meeting, and you know when you're talking about a playground it isn't just for Teamster members. So our guys would get every goddam neighbor to go to the meeting, too. In the 24th Ward, which was our best ward, we'd have 1,500 or 2,000 people, when the ward committeeman might get 150 to his meeting. He'd die. And you know they'd listen to us."[56]

The Teamsters' community organizing effort challenged St. Louis's ward politicians.[57] The Teamsters also enjoyed good relationships with the African American community. Ernest Calloway, an African American and a longtime activist, worked for the Teamsters. They seemed quite potent in the 1950s. However, their power in local politics also was relatively short-lived. As the 1960s began, Teamster political activity in St. Louis began to wane. Ten years later, the stewards were but a memory. Gibbons's activity had shifted to the national Teamsters office. Similar to the Steamfitters, the Teamsters had tried to exercise union influence on city officials. But the Teamsters also provided a model for the neighborhood organizations that began to spring up in the sixties and offered alternatives to the regime's downtown-centered agenda.

The Attempts at Political Reform

Raymond Tucker's first involvement in attempts to reform St. Louis's political structure actually occurred four years before he became mayor. His predecessor in office, Joseph Darst, asked him to shepherd charter revision. Darst originally had been a Democratic Party regular who tried for citywide office twice in the 1940s before finally being elected mayor in 1949. He had not been part of the county-office crowd, however. Darst had served as public welfare administrator for the city under Dickmann and had been a colleague of Tucker's. He supported Tucker's election in 1949 to a board of freeholders[58] that would draft a new city charter. The freeholders were selected on April 5, 1949, the day Darst was elected mayor. The slate placed before the voters, which included Tucker, had business and newspaper support and backing from the Council on Civic Needs. The League of Women Voters actually put it forward. Both the Democratic and the Republican Party organizations

- increase the authority of the mayor in budgetary and fiscal matters
- alter the board of aldermen by substituting a combination of at-large and district seats for the current board elected from twenty-eight wards. Called the 7-7-1 plan, it would create seven new wards each electing its own alderman, seven elected at large, and the president of the board, elected citywide as well
- reorganize a number of city departments
- create a new bureau of traffic engineering with the power to initiate rules and regulations that could not be repealed by the board of aldermen for six months
- increase the salary of the mayor to $25,000 per year.[68]

This proposed charter was a threat to the sitting aldermen and to their ward organizations. At least half the aldermen would lose their jobs if the charter passed. African American politicians, just beginning to increase their hold on city offices, also would lose representation. There would be fewer wards for them to represent, and election to at-large aldermanic seats would be unlikely at that time. St. Louis had not yet elected a nonwhite in any citywide election. The wary aldermen set August 6, 1957, as the date for the charter vote and specified that, to cast a vote for the new charter, the voter had to place an X over the word "no" on the ballot.[69] Since no offices were at stake in August 1957, the turnout would be lighter in less-organized sections of the city. Clearly, this method of casting a vote was intended to deter voting.

Opposition to the charter came from a number of sources. Some ward organizations and their leaders, particularly in less affluent areas, urged a "no" vote. Committeemen Anton Sestric, Louis Buckowitz, Matt O'Neill, and Midge Berra made their opposition known. Aldermen Joe Roddy and A. J. Cervantes joined them. In addition, African American politicians strongly advocated a "no" vote, among them Jordan Chambers, the "dean" of black elected officials. Neighborhood businesses of various types also expressed displeasure with the 7-7-1 formula. These smaller businesses felt that the proposal would give power to the "'money interests,' as it was alleged that the latter would be able to control city-wide elections through superior access to mass media and related forms of exercising influence."[70] In addition, the AFL and the CIO councils and the Teamsters opposed the charter. The Teamsters used "the charter campaign as a means of strengthening their program for local political participation."[71] Proponents of the new charter, including the mayor, saw the 7-7-1 formula as a means of diminishing aldermanic courtesy—not challenging an alderman on projects within his or her ward—and spot zoning, adjusting zoning of an individual property.[72] These proponents, not surprisingly, included the League of Women Voters and the Chamber of Commerce. Mayor Tucker, of course, was the most prominent sponsor, and former Republican mayor Aloys P. Kaufmann joined him in his endorsement. Tucker's allies on the estimate and apportionment board, comptroller John Poelker and aldermanic president Donald Gunn, voiced their support of the charter. Jack Dwyer, Democratic committee chair and now a staunch Tucker supporter, was the only ward organization figure to advocate for the proposed charter.[73]

St. Louisans had grown accustomed to their wards and their accessibility to their representatives. The charter vote showed that this was true particularly in blue-collar and low-income areas of the city. The charter failed by a vote of 108,618 to 72,160. The charter carried in only five wards. Each of these five—the twelfth, the fifteenth, the sixteenth, the twenty-fifth, and the twenty-eighth— were clearly middle-class, professional bastions. The margin in the fifteenth was very close however; the charter carried there by only 58 votes.

Although Raymond Tucker had been reelected handily only a few months before the 1957 charter vote, he had little support with regard to this reform measure. His principal backers from business and the newspapers stood with him, but the majority of St. Louisans, working people by and large, did not. They were comfortable with the system they had, the only one they knew. One former elected official maintained that the charter would have been adopted if the majority of aldermen were to be elected from wards. Even so, a number of people would lose their elected positions, and the city would have had a stronger chief executive. A popular sentiment then and now is to prevent one person from having all the power. Further, opponents called it a loss of democracy to have fewer elective offices. Echoes of the ordinary people pitted against the Big Cinch appeared again in this campaign. Many voters apparently saw the charter as something that would diminish their political efficacy. And they appeared to like what they knew. The city vote divided clearly along income lines.

A second effort at governmental reform occurred shortly after the 1957 charter defeat. It was pushed not by Mayor Tucker but by an alderman frequently in opposition to the mayor's proposals. This alderman, Democrat A. J. Cervantes of the fifteenth ward, had lost to Tucker's candidate in the election for president of the board of aldermen in 1955. In that same year, after his defeat, Cervantes began to seek support for a board of freeholders from both St. Louis City and St. Louis County to address the separation that resulted from the 1876 divorce. Cervantes hoped for a plan that would create one metropolitan city or bring the city into the county again as another municipality.[74] Another possible scenario would involve the creation of metropolitan districts to administer services in both city and county.[75]

Mayor Tucker originally denounced Cervantes' actions as "politically premature."[76] During the mid-1950s, the Metropolitan Sewer District (MSD) was created to serve both city and county. Cervantes subsequently began to work with Saint Louis University and Washington University on his own plans for modernization. The universities applied successfully for a grant of $50,000 to conduct the Metropolitan St. Louis survey. As a result of this study, a recommendation was put forward to create "a multifunctional special district...for the St. Louis City-St. Louis County area. No existing local governmental unit, whether a municipality or a school district, would lose its legal autonomy" under this proposal.[77]

Pursuant to state law, to create this special district, a board of freeholders had to be assembled after the requisite number of signatures from voters in the city and county were obtained, submitted, and approved. Mayor Tucker appointed the city representatives, the St. Louis county executive did likewise for the county, and the governor selected an out-of-state representative. In their year's work, the freeholders settled on a plan to create the multifunctional special district. The district would have a legislature of fourteen members, twelve elected and one each appointed by the St. Louis mayor and the county executive. City voters would choose three representatives at large, as would county voters. The other six would be elected from districts. The combined vote of the city and the county would elect the president. These elections all would be nonpartisan.[78]

For many in the city, proposals such as this appeared to diminish sovereignty. Government would be removed further from the people, and existing governmental patterns would change. City politicians—with the exception of Cervantes—found little to like in the freeholders' proposal. It would change fundamentally the city's political standard operating procedures and further weaken its ward organizations. Labor-union representatives joined ward officials in opposing this plan.

As a reform document designed to increase economy and efficiency, the plan's natural allies were the business elite as well as the daily newspapers and good government groups. Again in these reform efforts, the lineup resembled the Big Cinch versus the hoi polloi. As Robert H. Salisbury succinctly noted, St. Louis politics—at least in terms of structural reform—divided along class lines.[79] In this particular referendum, the dichotomy of class was compounded when Mayor Tucker joined the opposition. Tucker had been silent during the board of freeholders' deliberations and for a time after the board concluded its work. The mayor finally spoke out on October 3, 1959, just a month prior to the election. He "objected to the omission of many metropolitan-type functions, the failure to reduce the number of governmental units," and the failure to bring the city back into the county.[80] Schmandt, Steinricker, and Wendel noted that "Tucker's opposition was damaging to the plan even among county voters who were more influenced by his position than by the views of their own elected officials. In attacking the proposal the mayor chose to disagree with those most closely identified with him and his projects."[81] Schmandt and his colleagues felt that the mayor decided as he did because he probably believed "that political merger is the only satisfactory solution to the metropolitan problem and lesser remedies will only weaken the position of the core city and dilute its powers."[82] County voters rejected the freeholders' plan. Not surprisingly, city voters did likewise. Heaviest opposition came from Jordan Chambers's nineteenth ward, where the plan failed by a nineteen-to-one margin.

During the 1950s, voters approved a large bond issue and reinstituted the city earnings tax at a rate of 1 percent. Voters both rich and poor bought into some part of the fight for municipal progress. When that fight involved structural change, however, the critical support vanished. Working-class residents, their representatives, and labor allies seemingly had scant trouble with paying for bricks and mortar to implement physical progress. But they clearly did not want to give the growth coalition more opportunity to make decisions. This was especially evident in the African American community, which had elected its first alderman only little more than a decade earlier. African Americans wanted to maintain the opportunity to obtain more offices.

Just two years after this defeat, in November 1961, a stalwart contingent of reformers recommended a "Borough Plan to Revitalize St. Louis." Proponents of this plan favored the most radical change possible: the creation of a single new political subdivision encompassing both city and county. All existing governmental bodies would be consolidated.[83] The plan called for twenty-two boroughs to be created within the new combined jurisdiction, eight in the city and seven in the county, with an additional seven spanning the boundary between the two. After supporters collected thousands of signatures, this plan went before city and county voters in November 1962. Few prominent St. Louisans joined the bandwagon for the borough plan. County businesses and elected officials supplied much of the opposition to it.[84] Many city residents clearly opposed any changes to the status quo that might dilute their political efficacy. On Election Day, the borough plan went down in ignominious defeat. In the city of St. Louis, 74 percent of those voting opposed it. In the county, the rejection figure was 79 percent. Not one city precinct favored the plan; only two in St. Louis County produced a favorable margin. There was no class bias in this vote; members of every possible group found their way into the opposition.

Thus, in a thirteen-year period, St. Louis City voters examined four structural changes of greater and lesser magnitude. They rejected them all. The city's elected officials varied in their support for these efforts. In the end, Mayor Tucker found that he could not alter political structure the way he changed the downtown landscape. In two of the cases, he himself opposed the changes. The outcomes maintained the status quo: a fragmented environment, city vs. county, and county divided into ninety municipalities. Segregation by class and race went hand in glove with the jurisdictional divisions. St. Louis City residents demonstrated a strong degree of comfort with the familiar and a stout opposition to any change that might disadvantage their place in the political sphere (or what they were told would disadvantage it).

In the same decade that Raymond Tucker and his business and newspaper allies failed to achieve governmental reform, centralization did take place in other major machine-politics cities. Philadelphia and Chicago—by different means and for different reasons—each managed to strengthen the position of mayor. In Philadelphia, the Republican Party dominated city politics. By 1950, the Republicans were tainted by corruption and showed a lack of competence. Business leaders, the newspapers, and the reform wing of the local Democratic Party combined to push adoption of a new charter in 1951 that strengthened the office of mayor and weakened traditional party politics. In addition, ward and precinct lines—political boundaries—no longer were identical to council districts.

In Chicago, in 1955, Democratic politicians moved to replace an ineffectual, quasi-reform mayor with one of their own, Richard J.

Daley, the party chairman. Daley understood power, understood where to get it, and assembled a political machine like no one else had. Daley successfully combined his mayoral role with his political one. However, Milton Rakove, a noted chronicler of the Daley era, stated succinctly, "A lot of people call it the Richard J. Daley machine, but the machine was there a quarter century before Daley."[85] Gary Rivlin, a Chicago journalist, made the same point. According to Rivlin, "Daley did not invent the Chicago machine; he perfected it."[86]

Daley first cemented his power by taking "City government away from the ward committeeman."[87] Daley himself became the central focus of the machine. He also became the focus of government by increasing his control of the budget. He had "jobs and money, which are the two things that really count in the machine."[88] Daley moved the allocation of patronage to the top of the party hierarchy.

In St. Louis, Raymond Tucker always depended on a reform constituency. That constituency, along with nationwide sentiment for urban renewal, kept him in office for three terms. But he failed to garner the support he needed to augment his organizational position. Skepticism about power, authority, and money in St. Louis prevented significant structural or behavioral changes, as did the content of the specific proposals. In St. Louis, many continued to cling to the notion that more elected officials equaled more democracy and provided more influence to those of modest means.

Tucker and the Politicians

Although not a political novice, Raymond Tucker's orientation veered toward expertise and professionalism in government, and his natural allies were members of the city's burgeoning growth coalition, especially the men of Civic Progress and the publishers of the city's newspapers. He had little ward support in his first race for mayor but picked up a great deal more when he faced only the belated, tarnished candidate Thomas Callanan the second time around. Some ward-organization people became his allies. Joe Roddy, leader of the seventeenth-ward organization, endorsed him three times. Jack Dwyer did not back him the first time out but became a loyal ally thereafter. Fred Weathers, the widely respected African American committeeman of the eighteenth ward, was also in the Tucker camp.

The mayor had a mixed relationship with the board of aldermen. A majority supported many of his urban-renewal initiatives, bond issues, and the reinstitution of the earnings tax. On more localized items, mutual appreciation dissipated. According to a contemporary chronicler, Ernest Kirschten, the "lack of ward-heeler support bolstered Tucker's independence."[89] But it also led to difficulty with "organization" aldermen who regularly overrode his vetoes in his first term.[90] Kirschten concluded that the mayor and the aldermen had to learn more about each other. By his second term, Tucker began to defend his legislative colleagues. "They are now co-operative on major issues. [Tucker] says they are jealous only where minor matters are concerned. The placing of a 'Stop' sign is an important detail in their relations with their constituents. So is a 'spot' zoning ordinance. Tucker believes that citizens have a right to seek such favors. He feels they will yield whenever they are convinced of the overriding importance of the general welfare. When they and their aldermen persist in having their way, the mayor believes there has been a 'failure of communication.'"[91] These platitudes were uttered after the mayor received a sizable reelection

Mayor Tucker and the board of aldermen, half of whom are shown here taking the oath of office in 1953, did not always agree on the issues. St. Louis Post-Dispatch, 1953.

margin in his quest for a second term. Also evident in various readings and interviews is the notion that Tucker had a firm belief in the rightness of his approach. To him, aldermanic concerns were parochial by nature.[92] His reform efforts certainly underscored those sentiments.

The Tucker papers at the Washington University archives contain a number of communications in which Tucker used the aldermen as whipping boys, referring to them as people who inhibited progress. A 1957 press release from his office conveyed this sentiment.

> The Aldermanic refusal to even bring to a vote the proposed ordinance establishing the Ozark Expressway route is a dramatic current example of aldermanic courtesy which has so often thwarted progress in our city.... No small group of legislators should have life-or-death control over important pieces of legislation such as the Ozark bill.... The opposition of some south side residents whose homes would have to be demolished for the expressway is certainly understandable but experience on other highways here indicates they will be amply paid by the state for their property.[93]

The Ozark expressway, I-44, cut the Hill neighborhood in half. The Hill represented one of the few intact ethnic enclaves in St. Louis. Populated by immigrants originally from Lombardy and then Sicily, and their descendents, the Hill community fought the freeway vigorously and enjoyed the help of two of their brethren in doing so, the alderman and the parish prelate. Tucker's attitude on this matter, however, was far from unique. He represented the views of many who favored renewal in central cities. Expressways represented positive growth; saving the integrity of aging neighborhoods did not.

The various aldermen who opposed Tucker on freeways or spending bills operated from selfish interests as well. But it is probably not too far a stretch of the imagination to say that the growth politics of the 1950s were more inimical, in at least certain aspects, to a system of ward-based factionalism than they would be to a more reformed system. The expressways eventually were built and neighborhoods demolished in St. Louis, just as they were in so many cities. But in St. Louis, there was never complete acquiescence. On more than one occasion, Tucker appealed to a larger audience for support when some aldermen questioned his strategy. Some politicians were with him, some clearly were not, and others shifted as time passed.

Later Elections

Political scientist Robert Salisbury wrote about the class cleavage in St. Louis politics. There was, to his way of thinking, a mayor's faction and a county office faction, with many aldermen allied with the latter.[94] Salisbury also felt that there were two types of wards: delivery wards and newspaper wards. Delivery wards had strong organizations, and ward endorsements mattered to constituents. Low-income families frequently populated these wards. On the other hand, newspaper wards were more affluent, and their voters more independent. Residents there were more likely to pay attention to a *Post* or a *Globe* endorsement than to a ward organization's sample ballot.

These dichotomies do not, however, explain the bulk of St. Louis voting. Salisbury's work was published in 1961 and applied to Darst's term and Tucker's first two. The dichotomies fit some elections of that era better than others. The votes on a new charter in both 1950 and 1957 followed the newspaper-delivery division. However, the voting for mayor in 1961 and 1965 did not.

Tucker was the quintessential newspaper candidate. A civil engineer, he was perceived as an expert and a professional. His non-involvement in most ward intrigue and his endorsement of the urban renewal agenda earned him repeated plaudits and support from St. Louis's dailies. Yet he lost support in the "newspaper" wards between his second election in 1957 and his third in 1961. He slipped even further in his unsuccessful bid for an unprecedented fourth term in 1965. Of course, his longevity in office may have been a factor in that last race. But the effects of his policies could have hurt his popularity as well in St. Louis, a city of neighborhoods.

Many felt that Tucker would coast to a third term. Surprisingly, however, he won the critical Democratic primary by only 1,272 votes. His opponent, Mark R. Holloran, did well in north St. Louis and carried a few central and southern wards as well. Tucker won the twenty-eighth ward, a newspaper ward, by only forty-one votes. Holloran was the Democratic national committeeman from Missouri and campaigned actively only in the few weeks just before the primary. He was able to field a large number of canvassers and election workers, however.[95] Holloran attacked Tucker for his preoccupation with downtown development and neglect of other areas of the city.[96]

A. J. Cervantes opposed Tucker in the Democratic primary in 1965. Cervantes, instigator of greater ties with the county, had served as president of the board of aldermen from 1959 to 1963. The candidacy of strong Tucker supporter Donald Gunn stymied his

Mayor Tucker and his campaign chairman, Vincent McMahon, examine a Tucker reelection poster in early 1965. Tucker lost the election to alderman A. J. Cervantes. Photograph by Renyold Ferguson, St. Louis Post-Dispatch, 1965.

bid for reelection. Gunn had defeated Cervantes for this post once before, in 1955, but had not run in 1959. In 1963, Gunn, an attorney, overcame incumbent Cervantes, owner of an insurance agency and a taxicab company, by only 125 votes.

Cervantes and Tucker had been at odds over a number of issues during Tucker's mayoral tenure. In his 1965 reelection campaign, Tucker again portrayed himself as the expert above the fray and his opponent as just the opposite. Tucker said, "I do not believe a majority of the citizens want to take a chance by turning control of City Hall over to the politicians...he (Cervantes) will have the burden of keeping the promises he has made to the ward politicians in return for their support. A motley crew of ambitious ward politicians has flocked to my opponent's banner. This is not surprising. I have always been opposed by those among the ward politicians who are unwilling to put the broad interests of their city ahead of the narrow interests of their ward."[97] Cervantes campaigned on the obligation to address the needs of the general St. Louis business community, not just the downtown interests. He also spoke against the demolition of neighborhoods.

When the ballots from the March 9 Democratic primary were counted, it was clear that St. Louis would have a new mayor, a mayor more obviously a politician and someone who would not fit in as comfortably in the boardrooms of Civic Progress CEOs. Cervantes also would not enjoy the newspaper support that Tucker had. This mayoral vote was an especially heavy one, and Cervantes won by 14,442 votes. Tucker carried three clearly newspaper wards, but his margins almost everywhere were reduced.

Table 6 depicts the voting in some of the newspaper and delivery wards in several elections from the Tucker era. The sharpest split between these two groupings is evident in the vote for a new charter in 1957. Not one ward with a strong organization cast a majority of votes for the charter. The "yes" votes accumulated in wards with more middle-income residents. Similarly, the so-called newspaper wards endorsed the charter. The strongest support came from the twenty-fifth and twenty-eighth wards in the center of the city, home to many of St. Louis's wealthiest families.

The dichotomy between newspaper and delivery ward does not carry over as neatly when candidates are involved. Salisbury, writing in 1960, postulated that there was a mayor's party and a county-office party within the Democratic fold. Yet the vote tallies from wards with strong organizations demonstrate that some organization leaders allied with Tucker, all or part of the time, and some did not. Sestric, Dwyer, and Roddy were Tucker allies more often than not, as was Fred Weathers, the African American committeeman of the eighteenth ward. However, these leaders did not always carry their candidate. Their varying levels of support show up in the totals. Two wards that never supported Tucker, the seventh and the nineteenth, also demonstrate some variation.

It would be erroneous to presume that organizations had little effect on the votes of their constituents. Delivery wards still could deliver. But it also would be erroneous to presume that delivery wards always went in the opposite direction of newspaper wards or that the latter always were uniform in the same direction. Salisbury is accurate in seeing a Tucker party and a politicians' party during a good part of the Tucker mayoralty. Yet some politicians were with Tucker. And some of the middle-income, independent voters abandoned him in 1961 and/or 1965. When A. J. Cervantes became mayor, the distinction between mayor's party and politicians' party dissipated. Tucker was an anomaly in St. Louis, although not among other big-city mayors of his era.

TABLE 6

Selected Election Results by Ward Type

Ward Description	% for Tucker 1953*	% for Tucker 1961*	% for Tucker 1965*	% for 1957 Charter
Delivery wards				
1 White, m.c.	47.3%	62.4%	60.0%	46.9%
2 White, w.c., Fitters	32.9%	24.3%	34.9%	31.5%
3 White, w.c.	36.2%	53.9%	36.7%	28.3%
4 Black,Dwyer	25.2%	46.4%	51.8%	37.2%
5 Black, poor	32.4%	45.5%	28.7%	25.8%
6 Mixed, poor	65.8%	76.8%	74.2%	22.0%
7 Lebanese, poor	29.4%	41.6%	22.6%	18.3%
8 White, mixed income, Sestric	72.4%	55.5%	31.3%	27.7%
9 White, w.c., Aboussie	54.8%	4.9%	29.4%	25.5%
10 White, w.c., Buckowitz	59.5%	28.0%	31.6%	28.4%
11 White, w.c., Villa	62.8%	55.4%	44.0%	33.2%
17 White, w.c., Roddy	58.2%	34.6%	39.8%	39.5%
18 Black, Weathers	30.7%	58.6%	53.1%	16.8%
19 Black, Chambers	16.9%	19.0%	53.1%	15.6%
24 White w.c, some m.c., Hill	42.4%	71.0%	44.9%	45.6%
Newspaper wards				
12 White, m.c., Republican	72.5%	58.3%	57.7%	50.8%
23 White, m.c.	72.3%	67.6%	60.8%	61.5%
25 White, m.c. to upper	76.9%	67.5%	67.9%	79.6%
28 White, m.c.	71.2%	51.0%	54.8%	76.4%

note: m.c.—middle class, w.c.—working class.
*Vote percentages are from the Democratic primary.

Because of his background and the programs he espoused, Tucker was not a natural favorite of the various St. Louis factions. Dickmann moved more naturally in both the political and civic worlds. A couple of retired politicians active in the Tucker years complained that he rarely appeared at ward events, even Candidates' Night. The wards were not the linchpins of his support. Instead, Tucker criticized the politicians and made politics seem like a dirty word. He was a precursor to some of today's politicians in that regard, but he also clearly resembled the turn-of-the-century Progressives in his lack of expressed appreciation of politics or politicians.

Salisbury is accurate when he notes that organization strength relates to income. However, it should be noted that only a *few* wards ever supported structural change that would dilute ward power. Three referenda on such change showed that a clear majority of residents—except the best off—were not disposed to major change to their political system. Further, in wards with strong organizations, the charter vote does not necessarily correlate with the vote for Tucker, who espoused the reform agenda. Each mayoral election was a finite event that reflected resident sentiment and political alignments at that point in time. Class, and race in some cases, indicates the predisposition of a ward but is not always a clear predictor, except on referenda on structural change. These data also show that alignments in St. Louis are not necessarily durable and may relate to a certain time, to specific issues, and possibly to perceived wrongs.

Salisbury accounted for the broadest differences among St. Louis voters. These differences had been present during the charter reform elections of 1941. When there are candidates on the ballot, particularly for the city's highest office, other factors besides organization or socioeconomic status come into play. Media is important, and, at this time, television became an influence. Voters developed views of incumbents because of perceptions derived from events, speeches, and contacts. Finally, in St. Louis, all of the old-time ward leaders were never on the same side.

The number of true newspaper wards was small. Principally members of the working or lower-middle class populated most areas of St. Louis even in the 1950s. Many looked to ward leaders for guidance instead of to the daily papers, but some did not. The widespread use of television advertising soon would provide alternate cues for many voters as the Tucker era came to a close. Ward influence dissipated in some areas, and a struggle between black and white Democrats lay ahead. The dichotomy of race simplifies electoral choices; it became a more significant vote divider than class in St. Louis, as it did nationally.[98] In St. Louis, and also to some extent in Cleveland and New York City, the lack of centralization of political and administrative power also perpetuated factions as political loci, in both African American and non-African American sections of the city.

Tucker and Renewal and Reform

During Raymond Tucker's three-term mayoralty, federal funding became a critical factor driving local action. The beginning of highway building and slum demolition changed the cityscape and made local legislators more critical. Tucker was a reformer who set himself out as a nonpolitician. Yet he strengthened and used a coalition with the leading members of St. Louis's business community to push a renewal agenda and stymie other elected officials. He tried to reform local institutions both as private citizen and as mayor, in a way that would have aided his agenda. In this, he failed.

What is most evident perhaps is that St. Louis's peculiar brand of politics—with its unusually high number of elected officials, especially those chosen citywide—did not change in form, despite Tucker's ardent hope. Although the power of certain actors shifted, the normal activity regarding alliances and patronage continued. The political motions going back to the nineteenth century remained. William Clay's decision to become a committeeman helped to marry civil rights and ward politics and gave an additional boost to perpetuating the system, as chapter 7 will show.

In later years, the city's economic position would become dire, as the exodus of residents and businesses continued. The optimism of the Tucker period faded, while the negative aftereffects of his physical reconstruction of St. Louis became apparent. An urban geographer noted that "St. Louis destroyed too much, and by the 1960s the downtown was separated from the rest of the city.... There are still few connections with the city beyond."[99]

St. Louis's wards continued to have organizations, make endorsements, and seek friendships. The county offices remained, still interrelated to the ward system. Aldermen increased their power legislatively and began to show signs of eclipsing their committeemen in importance. Most important, however, power remained diffuse, and the fragmented structure endured, which continued to affect how issues were addressed and how officials performed. The concept of ordinary people, who identified with their wards, versus a Big Cinch helped maintain fragmentation and factionalism in St. Louis.

Chapter 7

St. Louis and the Civil-Rights Struggle

The struggle for civil rights in St. Louis was shaped by the city's history of segregation and by activities occurring elsewhere in the United States. The struggle was not easy in St. Louis, although white resistance certainly was not massive or violent. In fact, it was subtle more than anything else. But political paternalism continued to mark the city's course. After the halcyon days of the civil-rights movement, African Americans in St. Louis, following their leaders' example, began to marry cries for justice with cries for political spoils. Unlike in Baltimore or Chicago, black voices outside machine politics did not assert themselves on the political stage. St. Louis's fragmentation and the ward-centered nature of its local politics contributed to that outcome.

Political integration, albeit only to a certain degree, occurred in St. Louis before equality of opportunity in other areas of life. St. Louis's use of electoral districts helped African American candidates win the offices of alderman, committeeman, constable, and state representative years before an African American could dine in the same restaurant as a white person or try on clothes at a department store. Nonetheless, election of African American candidates did not signify equality at the political bargaining table. The major newspapers printed the words "a Negro" when mentioning the name of any nonwhite—including officeholders—in any story they printed. White politicians made certain deals with their black counterparts, but the white committeemen clearly continued to call the shots. Jack Dwyer and other white committeemen on the north side of the city remained in their offices long after their ward populations became predominantly African American. Dwyer and his counterparts offered their constituents certain jobs and other favors but only reluctantly brought them into their ward organizations on anything even approaching equal footing. A number of these committeemen also lived outside the wards they represented. In Chicago, similar wards were known as "plantation" wards.[1]

The Plantation Wards

In August of 1964, the longtime chairman of the Democratic Party, John J. "Jack" Dwyer, sought reelection as fourth-ward committeeman, a post he had held for almost three decades. Dwyer no longer lived in this ward himself, and the ward had become predominantly black. African American Arthur Kennedy challenged him in this election. Kennedy received support from members of CORE and from Young Turks who were not part of the traditional black power structure. Kennedy had been involved for quite some time with the NAACP.[1] The tenor of Kennedy's campaign can be glimpsed in excerpts from the *Defender*, a black newspaper:

> Old time Negro politicians who have set beside the table of white committeemen and office-holders to catch the crumbs that fell, now find themselves faced with the possibility of being rejected by the Negro voters. In each of the predominant Negro population wards opposition has developed against those who advocated a "go slow" policy of integration. Many of the conservative Negro leaders are now looked down on as puppets and parrots for Dwyer and Mayor Tucker....

> In their zeal to retain Jack Dwyer in control of the all Negro ward...they are trying to sell the voters on the idea that we Need Uncle Jack. What they are saying in effect is that a Negro is not qualified to represent Negro people.[2]

Established black leaders countered Kennedy's supporters by stressing that Dwyer was the Democratic Party's "chief patronage distributor."[3] In an article in another black newspaper, the *Argus*, Buddy Lonesome made the case for Dwyer:

> In the 4th Ward, heavily populated by Negroes, I find myself in the unique position of supporting the incumbent committeeman, Jack Dwyer, who happens to be white, against Arthur Kennedy. The fact remains that Jack Dwyer

in addition to being the 4th Ward Committeeman, is also chairman of the Democratic City Central Committee. The position carries with it a great deal of prestige and influence. As a consequence, the 4th Ward has a heavy share of FAT jobs, being held by Negroes. Jack Dwyer…has also dispensed patronage liberally among his Negro constituents…. In order to continue to obtain our Fair Share of municipal jobs, Jack Dwyer must be retained.[4]

This election took place at the height of the civil-rights movement. Yet Dwyer won handily, receiving 3,239 votes out of 5,251 cast. Dwyer had spent his career dispensing jobs and favors. He reminded the fourth-ward voters of that fact by distributing newspapers filled with photographs of ward people and places benefiting from his connections or his largesse.

1. Ernestine Patterson, "The Impact of the Black Struggle on Representative Government in St. Louis, Missouri" (Ph.D. diss., St. Louis University, 1968), 180, 187.
2. *Defender*, May 5, 1964, cited by Patterson in *Impact of the Black Struggle*, 188-89.
3. Patterson, *Impact of the Black Struggle*, 190.
4. Buddy Lonesome, *Argus*, July 31, 1964, p. 7B, cited by Patterson, *Impact of the Black Struggle*, 192-93.

Some political veterans expressed considerable displeasure at part of Massachusetts congressman Tip O'Neill's account of a fundraising trip to St. Louis during the 1960 Kennedy presidential campaign. Kennedy's people wanted to increase registration in African American sections of St. Louis. According to O'Neill, party chairman Jack Dwyer and others were troubled with this plan because increased black registration could threaten their power base.[2] Given the changed population of some north St. Louis wards still represented by white committeemen, O'Neill's depiction appears plausible.

The white establishment in St. Louis—politicians and business leaders—was not highly confrontational. But its members were far from quick to accede to demands for equal rights. Beginning early in the twentieth century, St. Louis's black community campaigned for both civil rights and a greater role in the city's political process. Since the politics were ward based and machine style, that meant a share of the patronage jobs and a seat at the table when deals were cut.

TABLE 7

St. Louis's African American Population

Year	Total Population	Percent Black	Black Population
1900	575,238	6.2%	35,516
1910	687,029	6.5%	44,541
1920	772,897	9.1%	70,282
1930	821,960	11.5%	94,261
1940	816,048	13.4%	109,254
1950	856,796	18.0%	154,160
1960	750,026	28.6%	214,507
1970	622,236	40.9%	254,495
1980	453,085	45.5%	206,154
1990	396,685	47.5%	188,408

SOURCE: Statistical Abstracts of the United States and Census of Population, U.S. Census, 1990.

In 1919, a number of young blacks met at Pythian Hall in St. Louis and came forward with a list of demands addressed to the city's Republican Party, which they had supported overwhelmingly. Their demands, as reported by William L. Clay, Sr., were:

- A Negro to be elected congressman
- A Negro to be elected as a judge
- A Negro to be elected constable
- A Negro to be elected ward committeeman
- A Negro to be elected ward committeewoman (when women received the right to vote)
- A Negro to be appointed superintendent of garbage collection.
- Negroes to serve on grand juries
- Negroes to serve on petit juries
- A Negro city undertaker
- Negro uniformed policemen
- A Negro on the board of education
- A Negro fire department
- A city hospital staffed entirely by Negro doctors, nurses, and orderlies.[3]

The strong linkage between jobs and representation and between political and economic interests is clear from these demands.

A number of the demands were met during the next decade: An African American constable (Republican) took office, a Republican committeeman was selected, blacks began to serve on grand juries, blacks were made trash-collection supervisors, a black undertaker was hired to bury black paupers, and in black areas two fire stations staffed by blacks were established.[4] Homer G. Phillips Hospital, a public facility for blacks, opened a few years later, after Bernard Dickmann became mayor. However, it would take five decades before a black was elected to Congress and almost as long to ensure equal access to public facilities and accommodations.

In the 1920s, St. Louis's black population, soon to begin the move to the Democratic Party, developed its own political avenues, using church groups and civil-rights organizations. These African Americans worked at times apart from the partisan process and at times within it, choosing whichever method increased their political power and basic civil rights. Political power by itself did not imply a basic restructuring of existing civic institutions. Instead, it meant a greater role for blacks in the system that already existed.

Beginning with the 1919 manifesto, African Americans began to set conditions on their support for candidates and for referenda. The failure of Republicans to honor their promise made in the 1920s of a black public hospital certainly helped the black movement move toward the Democratic Party. Ironically, the first black committeeman and the first three black aldermen elected in St. Louis were Republicans. Neither political party was sympathetic however—in the 1920s, 1930s, or 1940s—to an agenda of political, legal, and social equality for nonwhites. The electoral system in St. Louis allowed some degree of African American representation because of its small geographical districts but offered no real seat at the table.

In his study of black and white politics in Los Angeles, Raphael Sonenshein noted that northern and midwestern communities with substantial black populations were more politicized than their counterparts in western cities. Cities such as St. Louis, Chicago, Milwaukee, and Detroit had "strong competing ethnic communities, remnants of party organizations, and high levels of white racial animosity."[5] The struggle for patronage exacerbated feelings aroused by the national civil-rights movement. Schools and residential areas became sites of struggle in cities with sizable black populations.

St. Louis's black population (see Table 7) was quite small at the turn of the century. World War I opened many factory jobs to blacks who came up from the South in, then, record numbers. In 1943, deployment of mechanized agriculture spelled the end of the share-cropper system and caused a great migration of more than 4 million blacks to the north. These events are reflected in St. Louis's changing population, although, because of its southern character, the city was a less-desirable destination for those fleeing the South. Along with other border state cities, St. Louis had adopted a segregation ordinance in 1916, later found to be constitutionally unenforceable. Restrictive covenants and realtor practices combined to carry out the intent of that ordinance, however, and the redlining sanctioned by the federal government created a growing ghetto area.

Many northern cities tried to exclude blacks from housing in white areas. In addition, many employment opportunities, access to good schools, and the right to be served at hotels and restaurants all were denied to those of color. In St. Louis, the exclusion was all encompassing. The state constitution provided for segregated schools, and institutions at all levels—private and public—separated the races. However, integration in private higher education occurred earlier in St. Louis than in southern cities. Jesuit Saint Louis University began to admit blacks in 1947, and Washington University, a private school, followed suit in 1949. The St. Louis archdiocese integrated all its schools in 1952. After the Supreme Court ruled that separate schools were not equal in 1954, the St. Louis Board of Education adopted a strategy of tacit compliance. De jure segregation was phased out beginning that fall, although residential patterns continued to ensure that most schools were either all white or all black. Black schools, often in need of considerable repair, continued to receive less funding and had fewer resources than their white counterparts.

In 1948, the Supreme Court had outlawed restrictive covenants. The case in point, *Shelley v. Kraemer,* emanated from a neighborhood in north St. Louis where blacks wanted to move. In his biography of civil-rights activist Ivory Perry, George Lipsitz elaborated on the struggle over housing:

> The magnitude of black migration to St. Louis created an enormous demand for housing. In the 1950s the area of the city open to black residents increased from 500 to 650 square blocks, but all 150 of these new blocks had already been designated as deteriorating or blighted by the City Plan Commission before blacks moved in. Loan agencies refused to extend credit to whites for purchases in those areas, further encouraging white flight. Unscrupulous realtors exploited the black demand for housing (as well as hostility to blacks) by "blockbusting"—frightening white homeowners about declining property values in order to panic them into selling houses at low prices that realtors could then resell to blacks at inflated prices.[6]

Pressures were building in St. Louis's black community over schools, housing, and employment.

The charter reform commission that Raymond Tucker had chaired in 1949 did not include a public-accommodations section, lobbied for by the local NAACP and other black groups. City voters overwhelmingly chose not to adopt that charter. "Its worst beating" came in seven low-income wards, six of which had a sizable black population.[7] The *Post-Dispatch* noted that black voters "were strongly opposed to the charter for its failure to include a civil rights plank."[8] Of course, the fear of higher taxes was also a major contributor to the defeat of the proposed charter.

In the 1957 vote on a later attempt by Mayor Tucker to replace the city charter, many blacks opposed the 7-7-1 formula, which would have reduced the number of aldermen elected from wards and increased at-large representation. According to Salisbury, "Negroes saw 7-7-1 as a means to reduce the number of Negro aldermen, both present and prospective. Thereby, the representation of Negro interests, the recruitment of Negro leadership, and encouragement of Negro political participation and self-consciousness would all be hindered. Any Negroes who might be elected at large—something which had never happened in St. Louis as of 1957—would be 'Uncle Toms,' or so felt many Negro leaders."[9] Salisbury questioned the rationale for this black rejection of the 1957 charter: "Under 28-1 Negroes made little progress toward these objectives until 1961, and the main white support for them has come from the city administration and from Aldermen representing middle-class wards, all staunch 'Progress' supporters."[10] By "Progress," Salisbury meant the Tucker agenda of urban renewal and structural reform. In fact, all black leaders did not oppose the new charter in 1957. Ward politicians certainly did, but two black newspapers urged a "yes" vote. Their logic was that if there could not be a public-accommodations bill under the present arrangements, why oppose different ones? This entreaty garnered little support at the polls, however.

Whether Mayor Tucker was a strong supporter of civil rights and a public-accommodations bill is an open question. He was certainly a man of his time, but his position evolved to a certain extent. St. Louis had a council on human relations established in the early 1950s. One of its members was Harry Pope, owner of a chain of strictly segregated cafeterias. Tucker reappointed Pope to the human-relations council in 1956, despite opposition from the local NAACP.[11] Tucker also refused to pay the expenses of an aide to travel to Jefferson City to testify in favor of the creation of a state human-rights commission.[12]

Minutes of an October 1955 meeting of the St. Louis human-rights body capture the mentality of that time, even among well-meaning individuals. In this meeting, the board members discussed the hiring of a new executive director. Harry Pope, the cafeteria owner, said, "We should avoid considering any one who has been active in organizations such as The Urban League, NAACP or CORE [Congress of Racial Equality], as these people might have trouble adopting a patient attitude toward the problems which are not met by the Council." Fellow members joined the discussion. Walter Eberhart remarked, "I believe we must look for a person who is familiar with community problems.... For the good of the Council, I don't believe we can afford to consider a Negro because much of our work deals in negotiation with white people, trying to get them to grant concessions to the Negro, and to eliminate discrimination in whatever places of business it might be." Mrs. Edward Smiley added, "There are a lot of Negroes who could qualify and also pass for a white person." Pope concluded, "We might just as well face it—the places and problems that have to be attacked deal with white people. Now the question is, 'Will a white person speak as freely to a Negro person about these problems or would they be embarrassed and hold back and not express themselves?'"[13] Not surprisingly, a white director was hired.

Tucker did appoint a few African Americans to commissions and named the first black department head in 1961. He offered verbal support to a public-accommodations measure. A number of attempts to pass such a bill at the board of aldermen failed before the board finally adopted the measure on May 19, 1961. By that time, civil-rights activity in the United States had increased considerably, and freedom riders set out throughout the South to challenge segregation in public transportation.

The 1961 aldermanic vote on public accommodations was twenty to four. The four opposing aldermen were from the twenty-fourth ward (the Hill), the eighth, the second, and the first—all organization wards. The latter two wards were located in north St. Louis and had just begun to undergo population change. A white alderman from north St. Louis, A. Barney Mueller of the twenty-first ward, refrained from voting. Raymond Leisure, part of the strong seventh-ward Lebanese organization, was noticeably absent. Leisure had opposed a similar measure in 1959, as had Mueller. Ironically, the leadership of the seventh ward formed ties with leading black politicians during the next two decades. The seventh ward also had a sizable minority population residing in the public-housing projects built there in the 1950s.

The 1961 public-accommodations vote represented a change for certain aldermen who had opposed a similar bill in February of 1959. Those whose vote changed included Louis Aboussie, ninth ward; Joseph Roddy, seventeenth ward; John Sartorious, twenty-third ward; and Albert "Red" Villa, eleventh ward. Reasons for the earlier opposition seem varied. One aldermanic old-timer mentioned that businesses in his ward—particularly taverns—opposed such a law because they felt they would lose customers. A. J. Cervantes, who had considerable black support when he defeated Tucker in 1965, voted "yes" on both occasions. In his memoir, Cervantes noted that after he was first elected an alderman in 1949 from the fifteenth ward in south St. Louis, he voted against a public-accommodations bill.

> My constituents of the Fifteenth Ward didn't think much of the lofty liberalism of the downtown civic leaders or the professional educators.... The black community, at that time not very numerous in St. Louis—about 18 percent—was unorganized and carried little political weight. So I felt no compunction, political or moral, about voting against public accommodations.[14]

After his vote, Cervantes' older brother as well as one of his high school teachers, both priests, inveighed him to shift his position. When the next vote occurred, he did. Cervantes wrote that after that vote, his "phone at home rang constantly for days," and callers were vituperative and abusive.[15] At that time in St. Louis, a white politician's support for civil rights carried a political price.

The 1961 bill defined public accommodations as "places or businesses offering or holding out to the general public services or facilities for the peace, comfort, health, welfare and safety of such general public, including but not limited to public places providing food, shelter, recreation or amusement."[16] The law did not extend to establishments "in which a landlord-tenant relationship exists, such as flats, apartments and rooming houses."[17] Tucker signed the new ordinance with alacrity, saying, "We cannot remove overnight the difficulties created by past patterns of social action. We must, however, fix a firm program toward the elimination of these difficulties and vigorously pursue that program."[18]

It took eight attempts between 1954 and 1961 to pass a public-accommodations bill. By 1961, the massive and often brutal resistance to civil-rights demonstrators in the South affected the climate of opinion. On the local level, the Missouri Restaurant Owners Association had ended its strong opposition to such an ordinance

William L. Clay and Louis Ford as CORE protesters in 1963. The St. Louis Mercantile Library at the University of Missouri–St. Louis.

nine months prior to the bill's passage and had begun to work with the local NAACP and CORE on a voluntary desegregation program.[19] Picketers had stationed themselves at the White Castle on north Kingshighway, the Parkmoor, and Howard Johnson's as well as other popular eateries. According to someone close to Tucker, the mayor saw that no action was taken to remove the picketers. Tucker later refused to mention his actions during his 1965 reelection campaign, although friends urged him to do so.

Tucker's record on civil rights is not a clear one, and certainly many of the aldermen sent out mixed signals as well. In 1962, the board of aldermen succeeded in adopting an ordinance that banned bias in employment. The aldermen from the ninth, second, and twenty-fourth wards were absent, and the aldermen from the tenth and twenty-second wards left the chamber before the vote was cast.

The election of William L. Clay, Sr., to the board of aldermen in 1959 placed a strong proponent of civil rights on the city's legislative body. Clay had worked for the NAACP and also was active in CORE. Passage of civil-rights legislation was an integral part of his platform during his campaign. Clay and several others active in CORE worked with some of the ward organizations in African

American areas.[20] For CORE strategists, the issue of equal access to jobs was most salient. They felt that "Mayor Tucker's Committee on Human Relations (was) only a buffer between Negroes and Employers…. The history of committees is to delay action."[21]

In 1963, CORE decided to target financial institutions that welcomed black depositors but not black employees. CORE had negotiated with St. Louis banks for eighteen months and could document the absence of black employees from nonclerical positions at these financial institutions.[22] The Jefferson Bank on Market Street became a principal target of the demonstrations. The bank in turn sought a restraining order to stop them. The *Post-Dispatch* cautioned against "unjustified direct action."[23] The *Globe-Democrat* was more explicit: "The efforts of this infinitesimally small but boisterous segment of the St. Louis community will disgust and revolt all of those who—like this newspaper—have been trying so long to open new opportunities to Negroes to improve the status of the race."[24] The white establishment definitely felt discomfort when tactics associated with protest in the South appeared in their city.

On August 30, 1963, circuit court judge Michael J. Scott issued a restraining order restricting demonstrations at the Jefferson Bank. At four o'clock that afternoon, about one hundred picketers arrived at the bank, having decided to defy the restraining order. "In the hours and days that followed, nine CORE leaders were seized and either jailed or released on bond."[25] Among those arrested was Alderman Clay of the twenty-sixth ward. Picketing outside the bank continued for quite some time afterward but within the confines of the injunction prohibiting demonstrators inside.

Nine people were tried for "indirect" criminal contempt, because they disobeyed a court order at the Jefferson Bank. Five received jail terms. Alderman Clay's sentence was 270 days or 9 months in jail. Mayor Tucker's reaction to the arrests at the bank represented that of many prominent St. Louisans. He said that:

> Such methods, as used in Friday's spectacle at the Jefferson Bank, reflect no credit upon the civil rights movement. They debase the serious principles involved. Civil rights leaders should adapt their tactics to the specific local situation. Methods which are necessary in some localities where community leadership is opposed to their goals are surely not appropriate for St. Louis.[26]

Tucker's reaction, a lack of comprehension, was not an uncommon one among northern whites. Many white leaders failed to understand the problems closer to home that encompassed inequalities perhaps not as visible nor as violently enforced as those in the former Confederacy.

Tucker's words brought him no additional friends in St. Louis's African American community. Clay and his compatriots quickly became heroes to a black population that had known considerable discrimination, both blatant and subtle, over many years. While serving his sentence in the city jail, Clay had to miss aldermanic meetings. The board of aldermen refused to excuse his absences and fined him for each meeting that he could not attend.[27]

During his stay in jail, Clay decided to alter his political path in a decision that had important ramifications for black politics in St. Louis. From his third-floor cell, Clay opted to leave the board of aldermen and instead seek the position of twenty-sixth-ward commit-teeman. Someone close to Bill Clay pointed out that Clay felt that real political power resided with the committeemen, not the aldermen. In addition to his civil-rights background, Clay also had known and assisted Jordan Chambers. That background helped explain his choice. In the August 1964 primary, Clay defeated the incumbent, Norman Seay, a fellow demonstrator at the Jefferson Bank who also had spent time in jail on that account.

Clay held the post of committeeman for a number of years. When Clay first decided to run for that office, Frederick Weathers, leader of an older pro-administration (pro-Tucker) group of blacks, apparently said that Clay was "exploiting civil rights in an effort to gain control of the party organizations before the gubernatorial elections and the 1965 city election when Cervantes is expected to run for mayor."[28] Clay indeed did support Cervantes vigorously when he upset Tucker, and he did try to influence endorsements in that race and many others.

Clay was a young rebel. He challenged the black old guard as well as the Tucker administration and its allies. In a further act of defiance, Clay took a paid position as a business agent of the Steamfitters in 1965 and helped some blacks enter apprenticeship programs with that previously segregated union.

Clay, with the air of civil-rights hero, became an important part of St. Louis's ward-based factional politics. His election as commit-teeman changed his emphasis from legislation to patronage and contracts. Although he was elected to Congress in 1968, he main-tained that emphasis when dealing with St. Louis politics, something he did often. And he remained a committeeman for more than a decade. Clay's respect among African American voters made him a

Bill Clay and supporters on election night, 1968. Photograph by Fred Sweets, *St. Louis Post-Dispatch,* 1968.

powerful ally to both white and black politicians. Structural reform was never a concern of his. Like many other St. Louis politicians before him, he sought to put people loyal to him in places of influence. Patronage concerns were also never far from his mind. His voting record in Congress always received stellar marks from many liberal groups. Clay was pro-labor, opposed the death penalty, and was routinely against involving the United States in limited struggles abroad. At home, however, he was a product of St. Louis's political culture and behavior. When he sought the office of committeeman, he further meshed civil rights and the city's regular politics. Ironically, Clay made this career shift at a time when committee people had begun to lose the power they once had. For Clay, the existing structure and its concomitant political culture helped set the parameters for African American political involvement. Clay's activities were a guide for many African Americans in St. Louis, as Chambers's had been earlier.

Other veterans of the Jefferson Bank demonstrations followed Clay's immersion in ward politics and its factional infighting. Soon, there was no civil-rights movement independent of the political organizations. Black politics in St. Louis became unequivocally machine-style politics, and individual rewards remained more important than systemic change. This turn of events strengthened the prevailing political culture based on individualized rewards, factional loyalty, and other quid pro quo transactions.

African American Leaders in Other Cities

The political route chosen by African Americans in St. Louis—working within the machine-politics milieu—resembles that of other cities to some extent. But some key differences exist as well. For example, Baltimore's system of government is similar to St. Louis's. The position of mayor is stronger there, but Baltimore also has an independently elected city-council president and comptroller and a city council chosen from districts. However, there are only six districts; each elects three members to the council.[29] According to Marion Orr and also to Kevin O'Keefe,[30] Baltimore's black incorporation differed from St. Louis's. In Baltimore, black residents lived either in east or west Baltimore. The east siders practiced machine politics and were generally lower income. Clarence "DuBro" Burns led the east-side faction. He worked for white bosses and carried his precincts for them.[31] More affluent African Americans lived on the west side and were involved in civil rights. Their most famous product was Congressman Parren Mitchell. This split between machine politics and civil rights continued into the 1980s. Kurt Schmoke, Baltimore's first African American mayor, had a more west-side orientation, given his Harvard and Yale education and background as a prosecutor. Machine politics and civil rights did not remain separate in St. Louis, however, as they did in Baltimore.

African American political participation in Chicago also provides interesting comparisons. In Chicago, Mayor Edward Kelly, who took office in 1933, quickly "cast about for a means to cement his alliance with the strongest Negro leaders."[32] Kelly aided William Dawson's switch to the Democratic Party. Dawson had been involved in civil-rights activism but then became a creature of the machine and its incentive structure. Under Kelly, Dawson functioned in a similar manner to St. Louis's Jordan Chambers. In both cities, the black organizations were issueless.[33] In his first mayoral race, Richard J. Daley profited greatly from the support of Chicago's black community. After a few years, however, Daley changed his relationship with then-Congressman Dawson. Daley began to deal directly with black committeemen, undercutting Dawson's position. Dawson became "little more than the ceremonial leader of the black wards."[34]

James Q. Wilson feels that black political development in Chicago was a product of the city's machine. "Negro politics reflect the politics of the city as a whole."[35] To Wilson, black leadership was not at the forefront of a fight for social change "because of the nature of the political organization itself."[36]

In St. Louis, Jordan Chambers was a cohesive leader of the only African American faction. His focus, similar to Dawson's, was on traditional machine activity. William Clay enmeshed himself in party operations; despite his civil-rights background, he followed a traditional path. Dawson left civil-rights activism behind to become a party man, a loyal soldier. After Chambers died in 1962, divisions sprouted up among black elected officials, in a manner Wilson would say reflected the city's political makeup.[37]

In Chicago, that city's first black mayor, Harold Washington, ran against the machine he personally had exited a number of years before. Chicago has been home to very successful black business people, the Nation of Islam, and the Reverend Jesse Jackson's Operation Push. There were allegiances outside the machine structure, although they initially were not competitive with it. However, St. Louis lacked the African American affluence and presence of a sizable number of large African American businesses. In St. Louis, politics seemed the clear path to mobility, and they were attuned to the political culture of the larger society.

TABLE 8-1

Demographic Decline

Year	Population	Percent Decline from 1950
1950	856,796	—
1960	750,026	12.5%
1970	622,236	27.4%
1980	453,085	47.1%

SOURCE: U.S. Bureau of the Census, Censuses of Population. Washington, D.C.: U.S. Government Printing Office, 1950, 1960, 1970, 1980.

the decades that followed in tandem with the relocation of countless businesses and industries from the urban core. The American arsenals of democracy lost their status as linchpins of manufacturing. Cities used urban renewal and freeway building to reverse these patterns, but mostly to no avail.

The central city of St. Louis was a striking victim of these demographic and economic changes. As Table 8-1 illustrates, the city lost almost half its population between 1950 and 1980.

During the same period, St. Louis City became a less significant portion of its metropolitan area. Limited to the sixty-one square miles imposed by its 1876 divorce from St. Louis County, St. Louis fell from 61.2 percent of the area's population in 1950 to just 19.2 percent in 1980.[1]

This demographic decline also led to a loss of political clout in Washington, D.C., and in Jefferson City. The Supreme Court's one-person-one-vote decisions in the early 1960s mandated congressional, state legislative, and city council districts of roughly equal size. To wit, St. Louis lost seats in the U.S. Congress and in Missouri's General Assembly and Senate after 1962. Missouri's legislators generally had not been St. Louis's best friends. With the city's delegation shrinking in size and no ready coalition partners in the offing, St. Louis's chances for possible assistance declined further. St. Louis's twenty-eight wards also had to be refashioned so that they were similar in population. Prior to the establishment of new boundaries in 1965, population had varied widely between the river wards, which had few residents, and wards such as the twenty-fourth, which had five times as many people.

Central cities all saw an increase in minority residents in the years after World War II. St. Louis's African American population more than doubled to 46.4 percent[2] between 1950 and 1980. This shift implied that an increasing number of African Americans would seek and hold political office in the city. To many white city residents and suburbanites, St. Louis became a black enclave, marked by poverty and crime. Howard Baer noted this phenomenon in describing changes to the central corridor in his memoir:

> There are dozens—no scores, well, maybe even hundreds of blocks north of Olive and Lindell and west of 12th that are full of windowless houses, ransacked apartments, littered streets; if not quite so abandoned as these whole neighborhoods, there are areas farther west and north which are not far from blight. Motorists will do well to avoid some of this area even in daylight, and blight and decay seem perilously close to the best of streets, even into Portland, Pershing, Kingsbury, and Lindell.[3]

Between sections of the city and between the city and many of its neighbors in St. Louis County, a significant chasm based on poverty and race had developed. Baer again offered a telling description:

> It was all too apparent that they feared the blacks as harmful to their physical safety, to their property values and to their children's schools. Many of them have, with no little effort, moved to the county from the city, believing they were insuring their families better education, more stable housing, less chance of being victimized or vandalized.[4]

In 1970, 41.5 percent of all children in the city grew up in poverty, and 14.4 percent of all families had incomes below the poverty level.[5]

Researchers have discovered a strong link between crime and unemployment. For example, Carol W. Kohfeld and John Sprague found that the number of unemployed males aged eighteen to twenty-five in St. Louis neighborhoods was associated with the number of crimes committed in that area.[6] Table 8-2 highlights a notable decline in manufacturing jobs in St. Louis. The jobs that had traditionally furnished a livelihood and eventual mobility to immigrant families disappeared to suburbia and beyond, at the time that more and more African Americans relocated to central cities. Some of those trapped inside the city, with inadequate transportation and few marketable skills, turned to public assistance or to illegal jobs.

TABLE 8-2

Manufacturing Decline in St. Louis

Year	# of Manufacturing Establishments in St. Louis City	# of Employees in Manufacturing in St. Louis City	% of St. Louis City Civilian Work Force in Manufacturing
1960	—	—	31.2%
1963	1,970	129,069	—
1970	—	—	27.8%
1980	—	—	21.6%
1982	1,107	68,900	—

SOURCE: U.S. Bureau of the Census, *County and City Data Book* (Washington, D.C.: U.S. Government Printing Office, 1967, 1972, 1983); U.S. Bureau of the Census, *Economic Census: Census of Manufacturers* (Washington, D.C.: U.S. Government Printing Office, 1960-1980).

The decline in manufacturing was echoed by a similar decline in wholesale and retail trade in St. Louis and other frostbelt cities. Only the service sector saw an increase in the number of establishments and employees. However, service employment is two-tiered. At one end, highly skilled professionals work in the legal, accounting, and data-processing fields. At the other end of the spectrum, service-sector jobs pay only minimum wage or just above and involve work in the fast-food industry, hostelry, and retail sales. Nonwhite migrants to northern cities frequently found themselves in the second category.

Demographic and economic changes confronted politicians in many urban locales in the 1960s, 1970s, and 1980s. The federal government, through its various grants, became an even more important source of aid as many mayors grappled with the daunting indicators of distress. St. Louis's mayors struggled along with the rest, hampered by their lack of statutory power and by the many fiefdoms with which they had to work. Because St. Louis is not part of a county, the Missouri legislature created a unique package of development agencies for the city, which further impeded coordination. Often discouraged by the innate conservatism of their region and its fragmentation—both civic and political—the mayors nonetheless helped spearhead some positive redevelopment. Yet all too often the sheer loss in population became the critical criterion for judging success or failure. And that loss continued.

Return to Tradition in the Mayor's Office

A. J. Cervantes, sworn in as mayor in April 1965, was no stranger to ward politics, nor did he pretend to be. Many who knew him said he had a definite flair and that he returned showmanship to the mayor's office. People knew when Cervantes entered a room. His strongest supporters were those for whom Tucker had little interest. Lebanese politicians in the seventh, ninth, and twenty-third wards all supported Cervantes in 1965. His political alliances with that community were complemented by his friendship with the Sansone family. Cervantes also enjoyed the support of the Steamfitters and their business agent Bill Clay. Clay and many other African Americans backed Cervantes each time he ran for mayor from 1965 through 1977. A close associate of Clay identified Cervantes as a good ally and friend. Cervantes' close ties to a number of the old-style ward politicians removed the notion of a separate "mayor's party" from St. Louis's political lexicon. Interestingly, Cervantes also received significant support in his first mayoral contest from two of the "newspaper" wards, the twenty-fifth (where he now resided) and the neighboring twenty-eighth, both in the central section of the city.

From his autobiography, it is clear that Cervantes recognized St. Louis's dire straits. He wrote, "Cities disintegrate socially as well as physically. Urban blight is social as well as physical. We know the symptoms: Prejudice, hatred, rioting, juvenile delinquency, crime in the streets, alcoholism, dope addiction, broken homes, abandoned children, irresponsibility, lack of pride in self, in the neighborhood, in the city."[7] Cervantes acknowledged the phenomenon of two very different St. Louis areas: one a central city growing increasingly black and poor and the other an affluent chain of white suburban communities.[8] Although this dichotomy was real, Cervantes maintained at least a restrained optimism about the city he governed and the efforts he spearheaded to revive it. He named as highlights of his administration certain experimental, model projects, "a modicum of cooperation between the races," and a master plan, "The Challenge of the Seventies."[9] In retrospect, Cervantes' plan and projects may not have packed the payoff he desired, but he never failed to bring energy and buoyancy to his tasks.

Cervantes' relationship with Civic Progress differed from Tucker's. According to one person close to the players then, Cervantes felt that he should enjoy a closer partnership with these business leaders than Tucker because he was a businessman, not a professor. The corporate titans, however, did not share that sentiment. Cervantes' insurance agency and taxicab company made him a small-business man, someone in a very different league from them. In addition, he was part of the city's nitty-gritty politics, and he enjoyed the support of some who were identified with corruption by the newspapers. Cervantes certainly relied on Civic Progress's help with major projects, appreciating the group's ability to generate funds quickly. But the frequency and intimacy of the meetings of the Tucker years did not continue into his administration. Civic Progress's lack of staff or offices also made it more likely that the business group would selectively participate in specific projects and not have a broader role. St. Louis's experience in this regard contrasts sharply with the more corporatist form of governance established in Pittsburgh between that city and the Allegheny Conference. Unlike in St. Louis, Pittsburgh's political power was highly centralized, and that dovetailed with a centralized and institutionalized corporate community.[10] Other cities such as Boston or Baltimore fell somewhere in between.

Tucker's major urban renewal projects already had spent their fury when Cervantes took office. The new mayor instead had to cope with the implementation of the various Great Society initiatives, from the War on Poverty to the Model Cities program. St. Louis's community action agency (CAA) was the Human Development Corporation (HDC). Its initial board and staff were predominantly white. In a relatively short time, African Americans assumed the lead roles at the HDC. A major black newspaper, the *St. Louis American*, had protested the insignificance of black input and "insufficient employment of blacks."[11] The HDC then began to hire activists to channel their energy and regulate conflict. By 1970, "HDC had become an overwhelmingly black organization with few ties to either the social welfare or business community or the political system."[12] Kerstein and Judd concluded that participants in the War on Poverty in St. Louis "had little influence in established community institutions and policy processes."[13] They made the point that few involved in the CAA had run for political office. However, the quid pro quo, machine approach adopted by Bill Clay and other civil-rights veterans actually created a new patronage network of color, of which the HDC and the public schools soon became a part. The traditional fount of patronage dominated by white committeemen and county officeholders no longer included the CAA or the public schools. In 1961, members of the blue-ribbon faction on the school board, led by Daniel Schlafly, put an end to hiring those recommended by committeemen for nonacademic jobs. However, not that much later, friendships with African American officeholders became valuable for those in teaching and administrative positions.

Frequent protests over discriminatory hiring practices by local government were common while Cervantes was mayor. For example, one north St. Louis woman, accompanied by her five children, descended on City Hall and staged a sit-in in the mayor's office.[14] In a machine-politics setting such as St. Louis, the cries for fairness and representation could apply to patronage as well as to more generic job opportunities. In the 1960s, civil-rights demonstrators also targeted private employers such as department stores and the Laclede Gas Company.

The most famous protests during Cervantes' mayoralty concerned the administration of public housing. Irate tenants staged the nation's first rent strike, lasting from February to October 1969. They frequently demonstrated at City Hall. As Lipsitz points out,

> For people living in St. Louis public housing projects in 1969, the accumulated legacy of federal urban renewal and public housing policies made for desperate living conditions. Black families displaced from slums by urban renewal found few relocation opportunities on the private market and consequently flocked into public housing. Inadequate capital reserves for public housing meant high rents and poor maintenance. The housing authority had to raise rents to meet operating costs and to subsidize the increasingly indigent population living in the projects. Officials of the St. Louis Housing and Land Clearance Authority admitted as early as 1966 that they faced "a definite breakdown in the relationship between management and tenants" in public housing.[15]

Settlement of the rent strike resulted in greater inclusion of residents in the administration of the housing projects. The first tenant-management corporation in any housing project in the U.S. also sprang up in the aftermath of the strike. However, the strike was also a harbinger of the severe troubles that came to affect the high-rise housing projects constructed in St. Louis during the Tucker years and similar complexes nationwide. Vacancies, vandalism, and crime became rife in these structures. In 1974, the Pruitt-Igoe complex became the first high-rise project in the U.S. to be torn down.[16]

Cervantes acted quickly after Martin Luther King, Jr.'s assassination in 1968 to keep the peace in the city. St. Louis was one of the few large cities that did not experience significant civil disorder at that time or, for that matter, at all during the turbulent sixties. Following King's death, Cervantes joined black leaders in designing an appropriate commemoration. Tens of thousands marched from the Gateway Arch about seven miles to Forest Park.[17] The march absorbed people's grief and anger. Shortly afterward, Cervantes signed into law a bill making King's birthday a city holiday. He said, "I couldn't get away from the nasty fact that blacks of our city had never got anything but the short end of the stick."[18] Cervantes' empathy with African Americans exceeded that of a number of other white politicians from the south side. Of course, Cervantes had strong alliances with a number of black politicians, including Bill Clay.

Cervantes moved the city in two directions regarding development. Aware of St. Louis's mounting difficulties, he looked at neighborhood stabilization and at tourism as ways to keep revenues on an even keel. In 1971, Cervantes found that the "two pressing priorities" of city government were "the fight against crime and the fight to preserve our neighborhoods."[19] His recognition of the importance of neighborhoods came at a time when neighborhood-based movements appeared in many cities. These groups frequently sought preservation of their areas through public and private reinvestment, and they fought redlining.[20] In St. Louis, Cervantes recognized these burgeoning community groups, but he did not help create them. Some had their roots in the War on Poverty, others were made up of latter-day gentrifiers, while still others sought to stabilize neighborhoods undergoing racial turnover.

Investment in professional sports and the visual and performing arts represents a major mode of urban redevelopment characteristic of the 1990s. Three decades earlier, Cervantes showed some prescience in this regard. He introduced projects to lure additional tourist dollars to the central city. In his 1965 campaign for mayor, he promised to create a group, the St. Louis Ambassadors (originally Flying Ambassadors), to promote the city at home and across the country. The *Post-Dispatch*, clearly in Tucker's camp, ridiculed this idea and, as the accompanying cartoon shows (Figure 8), portrayed "Doc" Lawler, a committeeman and also a Steamfitter; Louis Buckowitz, a longtime ward boss; and black leader and Steamfitter business agent Bill Clay as prototypical Cervantes Ambassadors. Once in office, Cervantes fulfilled his pledge to create the Ambassadors, and in time, they became a permanent part of St. Louis's hospitality and booster network.

Two other projects to increase downtown tourism that the mayor pushed failed to turn out. The projects appealed to him in

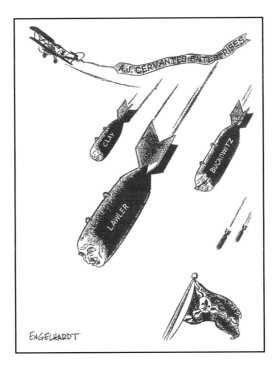

FIGURE 8. *"Flying Ambassadors." The* St. Louis Post-Dispatch *attacks Mayor Cervantes' proposal for the Flying Ambassadors by linking him to machine politicians.* Illustrated by Tom Engelhardt, © 1965, St. Louis Post-Dispatch. Reprinted with the permission of the St. Louis Post-Dispatch, 2002.

part because of his Spanish heritage. With the assistance of some men of means, Cervantes purchased the rather striking Spanish Pavilion featured at the 1964–65 New York World's Fair and brought it to St. Louis. Highly touted for its design when the Fair opened, the pavilion was placed on Market Street near Busch Stadium in the city's downtown. Although many visited the pavilion after its installation, its doors closed for financial reasons prior to its first anniversary in St. Louis. Howard Baer, privy to many meetings of the civic elite, discussed this project at length in his memoirs:

> Harold Koplar, of the Chase Hotel, a close friend of the Mayor, had suggested it would be a spectacular ten-strike to purchase and move the building here.... Cervantes was then newly elected and he was a charger, no idea was too far out for him and he was

never in doubt. He determined to get it and twisted every arm he could grab to get the $2 million he thought he'd need. Oddly enough the business community went along with him in spite of their almost unanimous feeling that the project was ridiculous. Actually they were a little afraid of him and decided to play along.[21]

When the Pavilion appeared to be failing, however, business leaders refused to advance additional capital to create a dinner theater there. The Pavilion eventually was incorporated into a new Marriott Hotel built at the site.

Cervantes' other tourist-oriented acquisition also failed. The mayor paid $375,000 to bring a replica of Christopher Columbus's flagship, the *Santa Maria*, to St. Louis and place it on the riverfront. Soon after its arrival in St. Louis, the *Santa Maria* separated from its mooring during a severe storm. The boat crashed into pylons on the Illinois side of the Mississippi River and was destroyed.[22]

The mayor was on more solid ground when he put forward plans for a major convention center in the heart of downtown. During his term, the voters passed a bond issue to finance that center, later named for him. Cervantes' developmental instincts were basically sound. He realized early on the importance of tourist dollars to central city coffers. In his acquisition of the Spanish Pavilion and the *Santa Maria*, he tried to provide new venues besides the Arch to draw tourists downtown. His projects ultimately failed, but the logic behind them became more important to city leaders in later years.

Cervantes' last major idea for economic development was his most controversial yet, and it lost him significant political support. Again ahead of his day, Cervantes recognized that airport expansion was critical to economic growth. The area's airport, Lambert Field, was owned by the city but located in north St. Louis County. A 1969 study by the Federal Aviation Administration (FAA) determined that the best site for a new airport would be on the Illinois side of the Mississippi River. Cervantes gave his wholehearted support to the project. Other Missouri politicians, including the state's two U.S. senators and union leaders, worked actively against this plan because it would take jobs away from Missouri residents.

The proposed Illinois airport never saw the light of day. The FAA never made an official recommendation. Cervantes took a great deal of heat for favoring the Illinois location. A report by Economic Research Associates at the time said that "The growth of the region continues to be predominantly in a westward direction.... An eastern location would have a positive effect on the present urban core of the cities of St. Louis and East St. Louis."[23] Since that was written, growth westward has continued unabated at the expense of St. Louis City. St. Louis County itself has experienced minimal growth over the past two decades and decline in its older suburbs. With the wisdom of hindsight, Cervantes' advocacy of a second airport in Illinois seems somewhat more understandable than it did at the time.

During Cervantes' mayoral tenure, a major step toward regional cooperation occurred. He initially opposed the idea and then played no role in its adoption. Using the model provided by joint city-county creation of the Metropolitan Sewer District twenty years earlier, state legislators and voters joined together to create a special district for the funding and administration of formerly city-owned cultural institutions. Property taxes of St. Louis City and St. Louis County dwellers would fund a new Zoo-Museum district to oversee the Saint Louis Art Museum and the city's renowned zoo. Later, the Science Center, the Missouri Botanical Garden, and the Missouri Historical Society joined the district as well. Howard Baer played a pivotal role in the creation of this district. According to Baer, Cervantes initially opposed the measure. Baer then asked other politicians to try to influence him.[24] In Baer's words,

> As we went into 1971, and election day began to loom ever closer, his attitude changed. Bob Duffe, his executive assistant, sent word that at least he would not oppose us. The wind was blowing our way, and he wanted to change his mind. However, Al's popularity had been slipping fast, he had made a number of goofs and it was clear—or so we thought—that now his endorsement might hurt us rather than help us. Very politely, then, we suggested to Duffe that, much as we appreciated the turnabout, we would rather City Hall stayed quiet. He understood that very well.[25]

In St. Louis's fragmented political environment, a mayor's power is a tenuous thing, dependent more on personality, alliances, and perceived success than on powers inherent in the office. Ironically, Cervantes' falling star prevented him in the end from being part of one of the few successful regional initiatives in the twentieth century.

Because of his personality and charisma, Cervantes was a larger-than-life figure on St. Louis's political stage. At first, this meant considerable support for his plans, but in his second term, his descent was as sharp as his climb. Cervantes played St. Louis's traditional game of

Aldermanic president Joseph Badaracco, the last Republican to win a citywide office, sits behind Mayor A. J. Cervantes at a 1969 meeting. Photograph by Gene Pospeshil, St. Louis Post-Dispatch, 1969.

supporting friends for office and trying to defeat enemies. However, it appears that he gave it less attention than did one of his predecessors, Bernard Dickmann, nor did he enjoy Dickmann's success. For example, in 1966, Cervantes failed to have his friend Anthony Sansone named chair of the city Democratic committee. In 1967, Donald Gunn, a key Tucker ally, easily was renominated as Democratic candidate for aldermanic president. In that same primary, another Tucker ally, Arthur Sullivan, won the Democratic nomination in the sixteenth ward against a candidate backed by a Sansone. In addition, in the twenty-eighth ward, Brendan Ryan captured the Democratic aldermanic nomination by defeating the incumbent, Peter Simpson, Cervantes' very close friend and former staff member.

Results from the 1969 municipal elections confounded pundits and politicians alike. Mayor Cervantes and Comptroller John Poelker, a former FBI agent, sought reelection. Several Democratic candidates filed to serve out Donald Gunn's unexpired term as president of the board of aldermen. In that contest, old-line ward organizations backed one of their own, seventh-ward committeeman Sorkis Webbe, who also served as public administrator. Webbe had the quiet support of Mayor Cervantes. Anton Sestric, committeeman of the eighth ward, another longtime organization leader, also entered the race, as did African American alderman Joseph W. B. Clark and a liberal candidate, Stephen Darst, the twenty-fifth-ward alderman. The *Post-Dispatch* backed Darst and linked Webbe to their old bête noire, the Steamfitters. Longtime Fitters officials Larry Callanan and Doc Lawler had given their support to Webbe. Webbe won the primary with just 34.3 percent of the vote.

The April 1969 general election provided politicians with a major surprise. A Republican alderman from the sixteenth ward, Joseph Badaracco, defeated Webbe, and Republican candidates for mayor and comptroller, although not victorious, did quite well against Cervantes and Poelker. The *Post-Dispatch* saw the results as "a major turning point in the GOP's repeated efforts to gain a power base at City Hall."[26] In retrospect, it was probably more of a last hurrah for the Republicans than a turning point. Webbe had run a lackluster campaign, while Badaracco was always on the offensive, continually attacking the Cervantes administration.[27] One Democrat told the *Post* that,

> Cervantes still is thought of as a wheeler-dealer. And it didn't help things to have the *Santa Maria* being towed up the Mississippi just a few days before the election. What place does the Mayor have to go to Washington to bid on a ship for a private city group? Besides that, the south side voters are disgusted. They feel that too much attention is being paid by the city to the north side—where the taxes are not paid—than to the south. The property owners in the south want street lights, they want the derelict automobiles removed, they want their streets repaired. They feel they are getting nothing for their tax dollar, and their frustrations with City Hall showed up Tuesday. Poelker was just a victim of circumstance because he was included in the protest although he is mostly a technician, not a policy maker.[28]

Deep south St. Louis contained the last Republican strongholds in the city. The War on Poverty and Model Cities focused attention on black communities in the north. Civil-rights laws and the changes they wrought in public accommodations, employment, education, and voting were very recent occurrences in 1969. As in other northern communities, the racial divide between black and white city dwellers became more marked. In this 1969 election, Webbe, of Lebanese descent, who had strong ties to African American politicians such as Bill Clay and to the Steamfitters, ran poorly on the south side.

Badaracco later defeated Stephen Darst in 1971 to win a full term as president of the board of aldermen. However, he would be the last Republican to achieve citywide office. St. Louis's principal political divisions became even more firmly situated in the Democratic Party. There, ward factions continued to seek allies from other wards and to thwart adversaries. Mollenkopf noted, as V. O. Key, Jr., had years earlier, that one-party politics foster the creation of factions based on personality or racial, ethnic, or status divisions.[29] Key recognized the importance "of political organization and structure" in determining the nature of factionalism in each southern state.[30] Whether Republicans or Democrats dominated elective offices in St. Louis or when the parties competed on relatively even terms, there were factions in each party. Fragmentation of governmental power and a lack of centralization in the dispersal of patronage related strongly to the perpetuation of factions in the Gateway City. This same type of fragmentation was characteristic of New York City politics. There, assembly districts functioned much like wards. The borough presidents handled patronage, and the mayor shared fundamental powers with other officials elected citywide.[31] It is not only one-party dominance that produces factional machine politics. Democrats have been dominant in Chicago and Pittsburgh for decades, and factionalism has not been prevalent in either place. Structure of both government and party is associated with whether factions arise and whether they retain their importance. In St. Louis, as time passed, factional struggles did not always carry the same cachet. The rewards were not as meaningful. However, the city's institutional arrangements and its concomitant culture sustained the familiar political patterns and mitigated against the development of alternatives.

Political Passages

Jack Dwyer, the protégé of Robert Hannegan and Barney Dickmann, first won election as a ward committeeman in 1934. Dickmann appointed Dwyer treasurer in 1938, and he became chair of the city Democratic committee in 1943. Dwyer continued to serve in all these posts until his death in April of 1966. Under Dwyer, the city committee was a potent force. Dwyer always managed to bring the warring factions of his party together. He provided campaign funds to fellow Democrats and was considered a fair broker. He had the respect of the business elite, the newspapers, and the politicians. Although the city committee's role had begun to wane somewhat over the years, Dwyer's leadership sustained it as a key player.

After Dwyer died, the committee's influence declined further. His successor as chairman was John L. "Doc" Lawler, the second-ward committeeman and a business agent of the Steamfitters Union. Lawler defeated Cervantes' ally and friend Tony Sansone, the committeeman of the twenty-fifth ward, for the post. Lawler's background changed the committee's relationship with the business elite. In addition, from Lawler on, no committee chairman would serve as long or dominate the way Dwyer had. However, Lawler was able to exercise influence on gubernatorial appointments to county offices when vacancies occurred during the middle of a term. While at the Democratic National Convention in 1968, he played a key role in the selection of Joe Roddy, committeeman of the seventeenth ward, as clerk of the circuit court. He also facilitated the appointment of the first African American to hold a county office.[32]

The city's Democrats sponsored Truman Day dinners each year. These were major fundraising events. Supporters, job seekers, and those who had, or wished to have, business with the city turned out in droves. Beginning in the seventies, attendance dropped off. The city Democratic committee received fewer contributions and consequently could not fund individual nominees in the fashion it had in the past. As a result, St. Louis's political fragmentation increased; one of the few unifying elements—the committee—had begun to atrophy. The committee was inherently a weak actor because of St. Louis's decentralized patronage arrangements. Individual committee people still referred their constituents for the shrinking pool of patronage positions. Unlike most of the other machine cities, St. Louis's party chairman never had ultimate control over job disbursement.

Democratic Party Festivities

Each year, the city Democratic committee sponsored a Truman Day Dinner at a major hotel. In its heyday, under Dwyer's stewardship, the dinner would be packed with politicians and business people. The ad book was often a half-inch thick, with all funds raised going to the committee. The Truman Day Dinner was the premiere event of the political year.

As the 1960s drew to a close, the value of ward organization endorsements to candidates in the Democratic primary also came into question. Writing in the *Globe-Democrat*, John Angelides noted that some wards in low-income areas still could produce votes for their favorites. However, Angelides found that "the day when most St. Louis Democratic ward bosses could deliver huge majorities for candidates is over at least for a while."[33] Venerable ward leaders such as the ninth-ward committeeman, Martie "Murph" Aboussie, and the tenth's Louis Buckowitz had failed to carry for their candidates in recent elections. In Angelides' view, African American committeemen, such as the twenty-first ward's Benjamin Goins, still enjoyed successes. But when black leaders endorsed a white candidate over a black candidate, they failed to carry their ward.[34] By 1970, political roles evinced signs of change, at the ward level and in the city as a whole. Yet these changes did not affect the city's traditional political rituals.

Change Among the Aldermen

For much of its history, the St. Louis Board of Aldermen had been a repository for ward-organization loyalists. Committeemen played the pivotal role in the disposition of jobs and services. They would slot a loyal follower as alderman, and he would do as told. Through the 1940s, the job required little skill and often received little attention. Federal funding to the cities for urban renewal and public housing, and later the various War on Poverty programs, increased the importance of aldermanic service. Aldermen had to approve program applications and determine budget allocations. Big business became more interested in their actions, as did neighborhood residents directly affected by a number of the initiatives. Yet some old-fashioned organization loyalists continued to serve on the board. They adhered closely to the traditions and procedures created in simpler times. By 1970, a few more independent and educated people had begun to achieve election to the board. They felt stymied, however, by rules that kept relative newcomers in positions of obscurity for lengthy periods.

In 1971, a group of aldermen, forever after referred to as the "Young Turks," began to demand changes in the aldermanic modus operandi. Elected from generally middle-class and majority-white areas, these men began to make a mark on the body they served on: Richard Gephardt (fourteenth), John Roach (twenty-eighth), Milton Svetanics (first), James Komorek (twelfth), Henry Stolar (twenty-fifth). *Globe* reporter Angelides wrote, "Most of them do not have any political debts to pay to ward organizations, because they took advantage of weak ward machinery to win office through personal campaigns. In their wards, the politicians no longer have the same power to boss the faithful and punish dissenters, and they can be their own men."[35]

Independent and better-educated, the Young Turks addressed issues and did not wait their turn to be heard. Their velvet-gloved revolt pointed to the increasing importance of legislation and of the services provided to neighborhoods by ward legislators. The power balance continued to shift to aldermen from committeemen, from patronage to neighborhood-oriented service in the areas of zoning, commercial development, and housing rehabilitation. Another major transition in St. Louis politics was underway. Interestingly, all the Young Turks supported John Poelker for mayor in 1973 over the more traditional political figure, A. J. Cervantes, who sought a third term.

North side committeemen Leroy Tyus, Franklin Payne, Fred Weathers, William Clay, Samuel Goldston, and John Conley. Photograph by Irving Williamson, 1968, MHS Photograph and Print Collection.

Transitions in the Politics of Black and White

During the 1970s, St. Louis's African American politics took on a strong resemblance to the existing ward factionalism characteristic of white wards. Feuds, still cast in racial terms, among black officeholders replaced the unity of Chambers's era.

Unlike more reformed cities with at-large council elections, St. Louis, with its twenty-eight wards and other electoral districts, began to elect African Americans to office at a very early date, 1918. Citywide office, however, eluded African American candidates for almost five decades. Black political ambition was stifled also because white committee people and aldermen clung to power long after their wards became majority black. Liberal use of patronage enabled the white officeholders to hold on. By 1960, the civil-rights movement had changed the nature of the game. No longer content with a part of the spoils, African Americans wanted members of their race to represent them politically. The phenomenon of black wards run by whites ended in the sixties. Many observers felt that the next step might be the election of an African American to the board of education or to a county office in citywide contests.

This transition would not be an easy one; whites made up a clear majority of the voting population. Needless to say, a number of white officials did not accept African Americans as political equals.[36] Writing in the *Globe-Democrat*, John Angelides noted that some white committeemen felt that "a Negro would hurt the ticket and their own power and prestige with voters in their wards. White committeemen have set up standards for Negro candidates that are far more demanding. White candidates on the other hand seemingly have no qualification except that they are white.... White politicians are not indifferent to Negro votes—only to Negro desires."[37]

Factional rivalries among black politicians also made attempts at citywide office more difficult for black candidates. Black factions joined their white counterparts in looking for allies in other wards, and they also put candidates in certain contests to make life difficult for their enemies. In fact, election returns from the 1930s onward show that relatively few people ran unopposed for ward offices in any Democratic primary.

"Doc" Lawler, chairman of the city Democratic committee from 1966 to his death in 1972, convinced his ally Missouri governor Warren Hearnes to name Benjamin Goins, the committeeman of the twenty-first ward, to finish out Joseph Hayden's term as license collector in 1968. Goins had been active in politics since 1956. Several white politicians had been interested in that particular post after Hayden's death, including Edward Roche, first-ward committeeman, and Louis Buckowitz, boss of the tenth ward, at the time serving as the city's parks director. In keeping with the traditional alliance between blacks and Steamfitters, it is not surprising that Lawler, an official in the Steamfitters Union, aided the selection of the first black citywide officeholder.

With Lawler's assistance, Missouri's first congressional district was redrawn in the mid-1960s to make possible the election of an African American. In 1968, William L. Clay successfully sought the seat. He defeated Teamster official and longtime activist Ernest Calloway for the nomination. Clay's personal prominence, as well as his new high office, ensured his status as St. Louis's most formidable black politician. However, he continually had to guard that status.

Observers of St. Louis politics were not surprised that Goins would challenge Bill Clay for political control of the north side. Clay and Goins both had been students of Jordan Chambers. In the August 1972 Democratic primary, six candidates backed by Goins challenged six candidates backed by Clay. This lack of unity allowed Raymond Percich to capture the nomination for sheriff, defeating black state representative James Troupe. In similar

William Clay and Benjamin Goins in more amicable times. Photograph by Irving Williamson, ca. 1970, MHS Photograph and Print Collection.

fashion, Charles Deeba won the public administrator nomination, beating out several black candidates.[38] In the nineteenth ward, state representative J. B. "Jet" Banks, allied with Clay, defeated incumbent Samuel Goldston for committeeman by just twenty-three votes. Goldston, deputy circuit clerk, was an ally of Goins. In an unsolved mystery of St. Louis politics, Goldston was found murdered two months later. He had filed suit in circuit court to overturn the committeeman election.[39] According to newspaper coverage, voting in that primary election in the nineteenth ward had been replete with irregularities, such as people voting multiple times, threats to election judges, and interference with persons waiting in line to vote.[40] Goldston's murderer was never found.

Goins went on to win the office of sheriff in a special election in 1977. Lawrence Woodson, an African American alderman, filled the license-collector slot, giving St. Louis two African American citywide officeholders. When Goins was convicted of financial wrongdoing and sent to prison in 1978, his political career and the rivalry with Clay came to an abrupt end.

Clay characterized his political struggle with Goins in racial terms. For example, in the fall of 1977, Clay "charged that black elected officials in St. Louis had turned into a 'cadre of black hustlers' who think it's more important to socialize with white bigots than to represent black interests."[41] At that point in time, the *Globe-Democrat* reported that Goins considered challenging Clay for his congressional seat. The *Globe* also noted that Clay had been saying that white politicians channeled federal money to downtown and the south side, instead of to north St. Louis.[42]

Clay tended to be more confrontational than Goins. He directly challenged the white political establishment on a number of occasions. Throughout the 1970s, he endured unremitting hostility from the *Globe-Democrat*. The *Globe* charged him with neglecting his district, associating with hoodlums, and being involved with drug activity. Clay sought the help of fellow members of Congress to clear his name.[43] Clay reported that the *Globe* also accused him of "padding his payroll, paying friends and associates who were allegedly ghost employees, and using his staff for political campaigning."[44] The *Globe*'s allegations—never proven—did not abate until the paper ceased publication in 1985.

Clay's civil-rights activism, especially his role in demonstrations at the Jefferson Bank and his subsequent imprisonment, affected his interactions with white politicians and the St. Louis business establishment. Some expressed consternation when he won his seat in

Congress. But Clay was a keen student of St. Louis politics. He understood and adhered to its norms. He allied himself with white politicians as well as blacks to ensure that his supporters had a seat at the table, in terms of projects, jobs, and contracts. After Goins's unwilling departure from politics, Clay was clearly St. Louis's premiere black politician, and his support became more valued by other office seekers. Many later disputes, with state senator Jet Banks and others, centered on the maintenance of his status as well as on the distribution of traditional perquisites.

In St. Louis, issues frequently were not central to either black or white politics. Sometimes, white elected officials portrayed their north-side counterparts in monolithic terms—"the Blacks." However, alliances came and went there just as they always had when whites controlled the organizations. Jordan Chambers had been an undisputed leader with authority acknowledged widely in the African American community. But after his passing, and as the black population grew and spread over more wards, unity suffered. The factors that worked against centralization in the city also worked against strong cohesion in black wards. Generally, force of personality was important to individual political successes. Race sometimes could be a mask covering typical machine interests.

The Rise of the Neighborhoods

At the time that aldermen came into their own and African Americans gained in political prominence, neighborhoods also became better organized. Neighborhood organizations began to place demands on the political structure. St. Louis always has been a city of neighborhoods. Almost all its residential areas have distinct names and relatively identifiable boundaries. At the turn of the century, various ethnic groups were linked with these territorial units. By the latter half of the twentieth century, the strong ethnic identifications had faded, with the exception of the Italian Hill. Race became a better delineator. Neighborhoods in the central corridor became home to blacks and whites, and these remained integrated. Otherwise, the city was a portrait in black *or* white.

The city's ward organizations long had helped constituents with their problems with municipal bureaucracy. But it had been case-by-case assistance. Neither committeemen nor traditional aldermen took seriously the idea of a neighborhood unit working to plan commercial and housing developments. It was not in their lexicon of operating procedures.

The Ward Office

Ward offices (whether in saloons or not) often were gathering places for constituents. One former committeeman spoke of men dropping by in the afternoon to play cards. Ward headquarters were also sites of parties, with entertainment and dancing. The pivotal social role of the ward organization began to fade as television became common in many households and people could entertain themselves at home. In addition, the rush to the suburbs already had begun.

The office of the twenty-fourth ward could be found in the Hill neighborhood, home to many Italian-immigrant families. The office was open at least four nights a week, and the organization provided a number of services to residents unable to visit City Hall. A resident could buy a required city sticker for the family automobile, obtain a needed license, or pay a city tax right in the neighborhood.

Social Service Networking

Accounts from other cities that practiced machine politics detail an informal network of social services that politicians routinely supplied to their constituents. Provision of these services brought loyalty and votes in turn. At the turn of the century, George Washington Plunkitt of Tammany Hall attended every christening and bar mitzvah in his ward and aided every fire victim; fighting fires was a sure vote getter.[1] Despite the introduction of the welfare state in the 1930s, ward leaders in St. Louis continued the tradition of service.

These traditional ward functions were carried out through at least the 1970s in the poorer areas of the city. Aldermen as well as committemen maintained a service network that some would have thought vestigial.

Newspaper accounts have documented that the old way had not died out. For example, the seventh ward was an old river ward populated by various immigrant groups, especially Lebanese and Bohemians or Eastern Europeans (Serbs, Croats, Czechs). Its population was always blue collar and often poor. The *Post-Dispatch* described how Alderman Ray Leisure and Committeeman Paul Simon visited the Municipal Courts Building every day to help constituents.[2] Leisure and Simon tried to get certain cases dropped, or they arranged for new court dates. They frequently visited the office of the prosecuting attorney to intercede for people. Political case dropping apparently occurred frequently. As one official said, "If you can give him the benefit of the doubt, do it."[3] Another committeeman practiced a variation on ticket fixing. Constituents gave him their summonses and money for fines, and the committeeman made the court appearances for them. "These may seem like little things but they are important to the people involved. And they give you a chance to make contact to make a favorable impression."[4]

Alderman Leisure held court every day from 4 P.M. to 6 P.M. "in a little wood-paneled room off his bar." *Post* reporters found that the telephone "rattles each five or ten minutes, [and] a constituent walks through the bar's back entrance every 20 or 30 minutes."[5] Constituents would question the traffic tickets they received, complain of dog bites, and wonder why some city officials had asked their children not to play at a certain baseball diamond.[6]

1. William L. Riordan, *Plunkitt of Tammany Hall* (New York: Dutton, 1963).
2. William Freivogel and Karen Van Meter, "Dispensing Justice Seventh-Ward Style," *St. Louis Post-Dispatch*, July 3, 1974.
3. Ibid.
4. *St. Louis Post-Dispatch*, March 5, 1972; papers of A. J. Cervantes, Washington University Archives.
5. Freivogel and Van Meter, "Dispensing Justice."
6. Ibid.

Yet some form of neighborhood organization had existed in certain parts of St. Louis for many years. The communities made up of wealthy residents on the city's private streets handled their own basic services and made their own maintenance decisions beginning in the 1870s. In the 1940s, the Urban League began to organize block units in some parts of the city, probably to help acclimate newcomers from the rural South to city living. Later, these block units became a key element in the fight against crime. The War on Poverty spurred further organizing in north St. Louis.

However, the burgeoning of neighborhood groups really took place on a large scale in the late 1960s and 1970s. Population shifts accounted for some of this growth, as did increases in crime and declines in city services brought on by decreasing revenues.

Some neighborhoods in the central corridor of the city organized in the face of racial change, white flight, and redlining by real-estate firms, lending institutions, and insurance companies. One such neighborhood was Skinker DeBaliviere, located north of Forest Park and close to Washington University. Black families began moving there in 1963. They were principally working families. The neighborhood began to turn over rapidly. HUD's 235 program enabled some welfare families to acquire single-family homes there, even though they were frequently unable to meet the costs of repairs for homes built almost seven decades before. Multifamily dwellings deteriorated, and crime rose. In 1966, major neighborhood institutions—Washington University, St. Roch Catholic Church, Grace United Methodist Church, and Delmar Baptist Church—joined with concerned residents to form the Skinker DeBaliviere Community Council (SDCC). They also funded the council. Monsignor Robert Peet of St. Roch opened his church to the entire community for meetings and social gatherings. A group of women formed their own agency to advertise for-sale property in the neighborhood to both white and black prospective residents. The SDCC helped organize house tours with accompanying art fairs to showcase the neighborhood. Dinner theaters brought neighbors and friends together. To aid in the fight against crime, block units formed and organized neighborhood watches. Although the neighborhood became about 60 percent black (30 percent being the traditional tipping point), it remained integrated.[45] The SDCC worked closely with the alderman on issues of housing, commercial development, undesirable properties, and the delivery of city services.

Under similar circumstances, an organization took root in the Shaw neighborhood on the city's near-south side in the 1960s. At the start, a small group of neighbors pooled their money and bought drug houses to prepare for resale to families. By the seventies, they had formed block units. St. Margaret of Scotland Catholic Church played an important role in this neighborhood, at first helping to recruit prospective residents and later sponsoring a housing corporation to rehabilitate properties. House tours, particularly a pre-Christmas parlor tour, became a staple. The Shaw became about half white and half black, and it has remained that way.

The Shaw has been part of the eighth ward for many years. Into the 1970s, old-time ward leader Anton Sestric controlled the organization. However, James Conway, a resident of the Shaw, served as state representative and state senator and later became mayor. Generally considered a maverick, he was attuned to neighborhood concerns.

Skinker DeBaliviere has been part of the twenty-eighth ward (although a small portion today is in the twenty-sixth). The twenty-eighth was one of the first wards to become an "independent ward"; ward members began to cast ballots to determine which candidates to endorse. In the 1960s, there was high turnover in ward offices. By the seventies, a series of Skinker DeBaliviere residents began to serve as aldermen: John Roach, Vincent Schoemehl, Daniel McGuire. Committeeman John George Storey also hailed from that neighborhood. In fact, neighborhood and ward interests (as well as participation) were closely intertwined in both Skinker DeBaliviere and the Shaw. In each area, aldermen worked with neighborhood groups. They did not see them as a challenge to their authority but rather as bulwarks for stability.

In other neighborhoods where ward organizations were more traditional, particularly the white delivery wards, committee people and aldermen distrusted the new neighborhood organizations and did not want to work with them. In such situations, these elected officials resembled their Chicago counterparts, who also resented neighborhood groups as potential threats to their influence.[46] The Hill neighborhood long had been home to one of the city's strongest "delivery" organizations. In the 1960s and 1970s, aldermen there did not relish the idea of working with organized neighbors. Yet this did not prevent a viable group—Hill 2000—from emerging and playing a strong role in the preservation of the area and in marketing it to the region. As early as 1965, Father Salvatore Polizzi, associate pastor at St. Ambrose, inaugurated Hill Day. Hundreds flocked to enjoy Italian food and entertainment. This festival eventually was discontinued; because of its success, it attracted larger crowds than it could accommodate. Proceeds from Hill Day went to Hill 2000 and

Father Sal Polizzi in front of St. Ambrose Chruch in 1980. Polizzi fought for preservation of the Hill in St. Louis and Washington, D.C. The St. Louis Mercantile Library at the University of Missouri–St. Louis.

made possible the purchase of properties for redevelopment. Hill 2000 also subsidized the costs of home improvements for current residents.[47] Father Polizzi and the neighborhood residents began to organize when city and federal officials announced a freeway route that would split the neighborhood in two. Although Polizzi and Hill residents failed to reroute the freeway, Polizzi got the federal government to agree to build an overpass to preserve a linkage between the two sections of the Hill.

The historic neighborhoods of Lafayette Square and Soulard became home to urban pioneers beginning in the late 1960s. Each neighborhood had suffered a lengthy decline. In Lafayette Square, many stately homes dating from the 1870s had been turned into rooming houses. In Soulard, the poor from a variety of groups lived in federal-style row houses originally built in the 1850s. In the 1970s, these neighborhoods both were located in the seventh ward, an old-fashioned "delivery" ward. The ward organization was actively hostile to the transplanted suburbanites who had begun to gentrify the areas. For example, residents requested crosswalks and other amenities and could not get them. Agitated, they formed their own political rump groups and began to take on the Webbe organization (then led by Sorkis Webbe, Sr.) and Alderman Ray Leisure. After some initial failures, they helped elect Ed Bushmeyer, one of their own, as state representative in 1978. In 1980, a Webbe candidate, Bob Brandhorst, regained the seat by a slim margin only after the absentee ballots were counted. During the course of that 1980 campaign, a Bushmeyer volunteer, James Shrewsbury (later sixteenth-ward alderman), was badly beaten after he solicited absentee ballot requests at the Sorkis Webbe Senior Center.

After 1980, redistricting moved Lafayette Square to the sixth ward, then represented by a progressive alderman, Bruce Sommer. A few years later, two women active in the restoration groups in their respective neighborhoods—Marit Clark and Phyllis Young—sought and won the sixth- and seventh-ward aldermanic seats. The new middle-class white residents of Lafayette Square and Soulard succeeded in replacing old-style officials. Clark and Young represented a merger of neighborhood and political activity. Years later a Lafayette Square resident writing in the neighborhood newspaper captured the significance of their accomplishment:

> I cannot say enough for Justine Wildeman who uncovered the absentee ballot scam about 1975 [the Seventh Ward syndicate could win an election with a mere four hundred ballots and without any campaigning!].
>
> [Thank you] for Jim Shrewsbury who took a hit man's hit while cleaning up absentee ballots and Ed Bushmeyer for wrestling all of Soulard, Lafayette Square and LaSalle Park out of Mafia clutches and Seventh Ward domination.[48]

In African American areas of the city, ward organizations remained stronger and continued to play the predominant political role. These ward organizations succeeded in turning out the troops on Election Day. Yet neighborhood groups appeared in the northern part of the city too. Groups in Penrose, the Ville, Hamilton Heights, and other neighborhoods became quite active. Two organizations that formed in this era—the West End Community Conference and Northside Preservation—took in multiple neighborhoods in their jurisdictions. Sometimes, those heading community/neighborhood organizations also had ties to leading political figures.

In some wards, such as the central corridor's twenty-eighth, neighborhood groups eclipsed the ward organizations. Eventually politics and neighborhood concerns meshed together in the person of the alderman, who monitored commercial activity, housing development or deterioration, placement of stop signs and traffic signals, and myriad other interfaces with city bureaucracy. The alderman also engaged in political-coalition building and advocacy for citywide candidates. In other wards, such as the twenty-fourth, the neighborhood group became an additional force. Most everywhere in the 1970s, neighborhood concerns began to be heard alongside the traditional ward concerns. St. Louis's decentralized structure permitted the rise of neighborhood groups. The old wards had less clout than they used to and eventually came to accept a new agenda (if they were not supplanted). However, even with this transition occurring in St. Louis, each ward still controlled a certain amount of patronage and still took candidates in all the primary races. Although some functions had shifted, there was considerable continuity. Besides, the figure of the alderman linked neighborhoods and ward organizations in many areas.

Crime and Politics: The Other Side of the Blanket

Many machine-politics cities have had political figures connected to organized crime or those who engaged in illegal activity. Historically, political ties bought protection for various illegal operations. In both Chicago and New York, a number of elected officials have been indicted for their role in protecting vice or from profiting personally from public service. St. Louis too has had its crime figures and its politics sometimes tainted by the criminal element, although indictments have been relatively few.

Irish gangs ruled the roost in St. Louis during Prohibition. Their fights over turf were sometimes brutal. One former gang leader, Edward "Jellyroll" Hogan, entered politics. He was elected a state senator in the forties and served in that position for close to three decades. His checkered past bothered the newspapers but apparently not the voters in his district.

In the 1930s, two organized crime groups with national connections—one Italian, one Lebanese (or Syrian[49])—reached an accommodation regarding a division of activity. A committee would handle disputes between the parties. Jimmy Michaels led the Lebanese contingent. Through marriage, Michaels was related to a number of politicians of Lebanese descent. His sister married Martie "Murph" Aboussie, a longtime ninth-ward committeeman. Their son Martie in turn represented the ninth ward on the board of aldermen for the better part of three decades. Michaels's daughter married Tony Sansone, who served as twenty-fifth-ward committeeman in the

Mayor Cervantes' decision to name attorney Morris Shenker (right) crime commissioner was controversial, given Shenker's connections to the Steamfitters and his representation of criminals during the Kefauver crime committee hearings. Photograph by Peter Ferman, St. Louis Star-Times, 1951.

1960s and who was a close friend and business associate of Mayor Cervantes. In addition, Sorkis Webbe, Sr., and Sorkis Webbe, Jr., elected officials from the seventh ward, were rumored to have Mafia ties. It is difficult to document the reality of such ties, but they are part of St. Louis lore. Politicians did interact with those linked to the mob. In 1968, the *Globe-Democrat* reported that Jimmy Michaels met with Missouri house speaker James E. Godfrey and members of Lebanese descent of the St. Louis delegation to discuss Godfrey's possible candidacy for lieutenant governor.[50]

In its relation to organized crime, as in other ways, St. Louis is more like a small town than a large city. The populace is highly interconnected, particularly those involved in politics. For example, many past and present officeholders have been related to others elected to office. In such an environment, St. Louisans have tended not to be judgmental. They often have based their opinions of others on how they personally have been treated, not on other grounds. Rumors have abounded, but the live-and-let-live philosophy has dominated political relations. The exception of course occurs when someone has directly hurt the politician or one of his or her allies. This toleration proved very costly for A. J. Cervantes and also may have hurt others' dreams of higher office.

A. J. Cervantes' mayoral career and any ambition he might have had for higher office was dealt a crippling blow by a *Life* magazine exposé, "A Two-Faced Crime Fight in St. Louis," which appeared in 1970.[51] Its author, Denny Walsh, who worked for the *Globe-Democrat*, concentrated his piece on Mayor Cervantes and Cervantes' decision to name criminal attorney Morris Shenker as his crime commissioner. Shenker was linked to the Steamfitters and to state senator Hogan in the early 1950s. He had represented a number of the crime figures that appeared before the Kefauver Commission and later served as legal counsel to the Teamsters' president, Jimmy Hoffa. Walsh questioned some of Shenker's complicated business affairs, including investments in Las Vegas hotel-casinos. To Walsh, Shenker was a perplexing choice for crime commissioner. In his memoirs, Cervantes described Shenker as an ideal choice for the job:

> Morris Shenker "was one of my finest appointments. I had known him for years.... I respected his legal talents, his business acumen, and his fund-raising ability for both Jewish and Christian charities. A successful criminal lawyer does not build his practice or gain national reputation by defending Mothers Superior.... The nature of his calling had brought Shenker into contact with newsworthy transgressors, and the juxtaposition of names in the press had over the years given him a veneer of guilt by association."[52]

Shenker was one face of *Life*'s two-pronged attack: Tony Sansone was the other. Walsh concentrated his thunder on Cervantes' friendship with Sansone:

> The man closest to Cervantes, as friend, business associate, campaign manager and unofficial but forceful influence around city hall, is Tony Sansone. A wealthy and socially prominent real estate and insurance man, Sansone is also the mayor's liaison with the two mobs that run the St. Louis underworld....

> Through Sansone, Cervantes has sought and received the counsel of this powerful gang leader [Jimmy Michaels]. In December 1964, just two days after Cervantes declared his candidacy for mayor, he met with Sansone and Michaels to plan campaign strategy.[53]

The *Life* article continued in that vein. Cervantes denied Walsh's charges. In his memoirs, he called them "in part outright falsehood, and the rest a rehash of tired old complaints which my opponents exhumed every time I ran for office."[54]

However, the damage was done. *Life*'s charges echoed in the headlines of many American newspapers. Cervantes sued *Life* for libel, but the suit bore no fruit. In a 1995 interview, Duncan Bauman, publisher of the now defunct *Globe-Democrat*, acknowledged that he had refused to run Walsh's piece on Cervantes and the mob in the *Globe*. Walsh had won a Pulitzer Prize in 1969 for his *Globe* stories on union corruption. But according to Bauman,

> When I read Walsh's series of stories on organized crime, I found he went to great lengths to link Mayor Cervantes to organized crime. I then made some personal phone calls to the sources Walsh said he was using and I found out that Walsh was not reflecting the views of those sources accurately.... We'd print the other installments...but I would not print the one respecting Cervantes.[55]

Whether accurate or not, Walsh's *Life* article did not help Cervantes' popularity with the voters, and he never recovered from it. It was another factor leading to his failure to win a third term as mayor.

St. Louis's underworld again made headlines when a new struggle for power turned bloody. In 1980, Anthony Giordano, who headed the Sicilian branch of organized crime, died of natural causes. Just three weeks after Giordano's death, a car bomb ended the life of Jimmy Michaels as he traveled home on I-55. The car bombings continued. Paul J. Leisure lost his leg when a bomb exploded in his vehicle in August 1981. Charles Michaels was shot in September of that year, and in October, George "Sonny" Faheen also was the victim of a car bomb. In July 1982, Michael Kornhardt was slain as well.[56]

Federal prosecutors successfully sought convictions of Paul Leisure and four members of his gang on racketeering charges, including responsibility for Jimmy Michaels's slaying.[57] Paul Leisure was a cousin of seventh-ward alderman Ray Leisure, and his uncle John Leisure served as state representative. Another uncle was an official in the city's parks department. A struggle for control of Laborers Local 42 appears to have sparked this spree of bloodletting among those tied to organized crime in the early 1980s.[58]

Material found in Paul Leisure's car after it was bombed and a tap on his business telephone led to an investigation of "the possibility of collusion in the city's effort to award a cable television franchise."[59]

qualifications of applicants."[3] Hayden hired a number of people with known police records (more than one-third of his staff), and several of his employees had "been caught cheating the city by reducing payment of the merchants' and manufacturers' tax."[4] Further, one of Hayden's auditors was a convicted felon.[5]

The reports from other county offices were equally disconcerting. Payrolls were padded, some employees performed little work, and political relationships dominated much of the decision making. The *Globe* also noted that "Mayor Raymond Tucker and his Democratic administration long have claimed they are helpless to halt the freeloading which goes on in the city's 'county' and 'state' offices." However, city ordinances had increased the number of county workers beyond those specified in the state statutes, according to the newspaper.[6]

1. Marguerite Shepard, "Political Parasites Infest Patronage Offices in City," *St. Louis Globe-Democrat*, January 21, 1964, p. A1.

2. Marguerite Shepard, "One Party System at Work," *St. Louis Globe-Democrat*, January 21–February 3, 1964.

3. Stephen Darst, "Controversial 'Juggy' Hayden," *St. Louis Globe-Democrat*, 1964, p. 3F.

4. Marguerite Shepard, "Padded Payrolls, Bribery, Cheating Mark Hayden's Office," *St. Louis Globe-Democrat*, January 24, 1964, p. 1A.

5. Marguerite Shepard, "Hayden 'Auditor' Convicted of Felony, Once Voted Illegally," *St. Louis Globe-Democrat*, January 25–26, 1964, p. 1A.

6. "Who Decides Payroll for County Offices?," *St. Louis Globe-Democrat*, January 21, 1964.

The county offices have aided in perpetuating St. Louis's ward politics. In Missouri's other counties, most of these positions have been or have become appointive, and some do not exist at all elsewhere. State officeholders did not make drastic changes to St. Louis's county structure in the twentieth century. Rather, they themselves benefited from their ties to the city's ward politicians. For example, governors have been able to reward supporters by granting them fee offices (sites that offer drivers' licenses and license plates for the set cost plus a small fee) or appointments to the police board or election board, reinforcing particular rewards for support at the polls.

Missouri's court reorganization, which took effect on January 1, 1979, adjusted the city's institutional arrangements to some degree. The position of constable, a comfortable post for a variety of local politicians, was eliminated. Constables had been elected from districts, as had magistrates. On the first day of 1979, the city's magistrates became associate circuit judges. Henceforth, they would be appointed by the governor and confirmed by the voters at periodic intervals. Judicial selection ceased to be a partisan process at this time in both St. Louis City and St. Louis County.[63] City voters no longer filled sixteen positions that once had provided livelihood for ward organization leaders such as Anton Sestric, Jordan Chambers, and Fred Weathers.

The 1979 court reform also combined certain county offices involved in the judicial system. The circuit attorney became the city's sole prosecutor for both misdemeanors and felonies, and the post of prosecuting attorney was eliminated. The positions of clerk of the court of criminal causes and clerk of the court of criminal corrections also ceased to exist. The clerk of the circuit court absorbed the responsibilities of the other two offices.

These changes to the judicial system had been enacted in 1976, although more than two years would pass before they took effect. Political observers familiar with those events attributed the consolidation of county offices to disclosures of irregularities in bail-bonding and dismissal of misdemeanor cases based on political influence. A series of stories appearing in the *Post-Dispatch* in 1974 pointed out shortcomings in the office of the clerk of the court of criminal corrections. The clerk at that time, James Patrick Lavin, had been elected to his post in 1950. He also served as a committeeman. Lavin previously was a Steamfitter. The *Post* charged that Lavin worked less than a full day as clerk almost every day,[64] received $1,000 a year for serving on a commission that had not met in eight years,[65] and that, along with prosecuting attorney Thomas W. Shannon and his staff, had a number of prosecutions at the court of criminal corrections dropped.[66] According to prosecutor Sidney Faber, these prosecutions were dropped at the request of various politicians. Sources told the *Post* "that dropping cases for politicians was 'a fact of life in the Democratic Party machine.'"[67] Officials such as Paul Simon and Ray Leisure, both from the seventh ward, allegedly interceded frequently for their constituents.

TABLE 8-3

County Officeholders, 1969-1981

Office	Officeholder	Other Political Ties
Clerk of the Court of Criminal Causes	James McAteer	Committeeman, eleventh ward
	George Solomon	
License Collector	Joseph Hayden	Committeeman, third ward
	Benjamin Goins	Committeeman, twenty-first ward
	Lawrence Woodson	Alderman
Clerk of the Court of Criminal Corrections	James Lavin	Committeeman, twentieth ward
	Rosemarie Storey	Wife of twenty-eighth ward committeeman
Clerk of the Circuit Court	Phelim O'Toole	Committeeman, fourteenth ward
	Joseph Roddy	Committeeman, seventeenth ward, and former alderman
Recorder of Deeds	Anthony Denny	
	Francis R. Slay	Committeeman, twenty-third ward, and former state representative
	William Schultze	
	Sharon Quigley Carpenter	Committeewoman, twenty-third ward
Prosecuting Attorney	William Geekie	
	Thomas Shannon	
Collector of Revenue	Louis Berra	Committeeman, twenty-fourth ward, and former state representative
	John Travers	Former assistant treasurer
	Ronald Leggett	
Sheriff	Martin Tozer	Committeeman, twenty-sixth ward
	Raymond Percich	Former alderman, twenty-seventh ward
	Benjamin Goins	License collector and committeeman, twenty-first ward

TABLE 8-3

County Officeholders, 1969-1981

Office	Officeholder	Other Political Ties
Circuit Attorney	James Corcoran	Committeeman, twenty-fifth ward
	Brendan Ryan	Former alderman, twenty-eighth ward
	George Peach	
Public Administrator	Sorkis Webbe, Sr.	Committeeman, seventh ward
	Charles Deeba	
	Mark Ostenfeld	Committeeman, thirteenth ward
Treasurer	John Dwyer	Committeeman, fourth ward
	Paul Berra	Committeeman, twenty-fourth ward, and former state representative

John George Storey, committeeman of the twenty-eighth ward, challenged Lavin in the August 1974 primary. Despite the unfavorable publicity he had received, Lavin hung on to his position. Disclosures of irregularities in the county offices were not unusual, of course. Most St. Louisans seem to have taken them in stride, at least in the 1970s. However, combination of the three clerkships along with the nonpartisan court plan did curtail some of the practices mentioned here.

The changes to the county offices meant fewer elective offices, but they did not affect the patronage work force. The number of slots remained unchanged. The ties between county offices and ward organizations also stayed in place. In addition, the eight remaining offices still would be filled in at-large elections. Changes, including the elimination of the elected offices of constable and magistrate, were not extensive enough, however, to fundamentally alter St. Louis's political culture. The particulars shifted a bit; the standard operating procedures did not. Even though endorsements counted for less in 1979 and committeemen had to share their turf more than before with aldermen and committeewomen, those procedures stayed in place. With county offices still in existence, it was easier for traditional political rituals to hang on as well.

The Vanishing Republicans

Joseph Badaracco, who served as president of the board of aldermen from 1969 to 1975, was the last Republican elected to a citywide post. Even while Badaracco held office, the number of Republican aldermen continued an inexorable decline. Table 8-4 demonstrates this trend.

As early as the 1950s, the Republicans retained strength in only a few wards, such as the twelfth and the sixteenth at the southern edge of St. Louis. Until the 1990s, a Republican state senator or state representative sometimes had part of his district in the city and part in the county. But especially after 1975, it is clear that St. Louis had become a solidly Democratic town. In fact, only one seat on the board of aldermen has belonged to someone from the GOP since 1983.

TABLE 8-4

Partisan Representation at the Board of Aldermen

Year	Republicans	Democrats
1945	20	8
1947	20	8
1949	15	13
1951	11	17
1953	7	21
1955	4	24
1957	4	24
1959	4	24
1961	4	24
1963	4	24
1965	2	26
1967	6	22
1969	4	24
1971	4	24
1973	3	25
1975	2	26
1977	1	27
1979	2	26
1981	2	26
1983	1	27

Future mayor John Poelker in April 1973. Photograph by Michael Baldridge, *St. Louis Post-Dispatch,* 1973.

Changes to Electoral Politics

Cervantes' two, one-term successors had neither his gusto nor his showmanship. On the other hand, they also lacked his particular ties to old-style politics. John Poelker, a former FBI agent, city assessor, and four-term comptroller, made his mark as a professional and a technician. He was well respected and frequently served as a talented behind-the-scenes strategist. James Conway, a state senator, had run against members of the Sestric organization in the eighth ward and was regarded as a maverick or a reformer. Both men enjoyed more rapport with newspaper and business leaders than Cervantes. According to several then–politically active people, Poelker had the backing of Civic Progress when he challenged Cervantes. Civic Progress has never—as an entity—contributed to the campaigns of individuals. However, members of the elite body at times have contributed on their own, as they reportedly did in Poelker's case. Poelker promised steadiness and security. He had no embarrassing links to those the elite despised. Poelker also had the endorsement of the Young Turks at the board of aldermen, who were interested in various types of reform.[68]

Future comptroller John Bass and Mayor A. J. Cervantes at the City Workhouse in 1971. Photograph by Robert C. Holt, Jr., St. Louis Post-Dispatch, 1971.

In the March 1973 primary election, James Conway joined John Poelker in opposing the incumbent, A. J. Cervantes. Given Cervantes' waning popularity and Poelker's big-league backers, the results were surprisingly close. Poelker pulled 48,941 votes to Cervantes' 43,340. Conway trailed with 13,367. Poelker's strength lay with white voters, those on the south side and those in the wards in the far north, which still had a sizable white population.[69] Cervantes maintained his strength in the black community.

Despite Cervantes' loss, many blacks rejoiced because John Bass, an African American, defeated three white candidates to garner the Democratic nomination for comptroller. Bass received 41 percent of the vote to 28 percent for twenty-eighth-ward alderman John Roach, 26.5 percent for twenty-seventh-ward alderman Raymond Percich, and 4.5 percent for James Joyce, alderman of the twenty-third ward. In addition to running strongly in the black wards, Bass carried the sixth, seventh, seventeenth, and twenty-fifth wards, all in the city's integrated central corridor. License Collector Benjamin Goins, the first African American to hold citywide office, devoted himself to the Bass campaign. According to the *Globe-Democrat*, Public Administrator Sorkis Webbe, "the behind the-scenes South Side Democratic political power, masterminded the black unity move that put Bass in the race."[70] In the April general election, Poelker and Bass won easily. Poelker defeated the Republican mayoral candidate, aldermanic president Joseph Badaracco.

Following the election, Benny Goins and venerable eighteenth-ward committeeman Frederick Weathers made strong efforts to see that African Americans received key positions in Poelker's administration.[71] Poelker complied with their requests but later alienated Goins and other African American officials when he proposed consolidating the two city hospitals.[72] The city's traditionally black hospital, Homer G. Phillips, had been built when Barney Dickmann was mayor. African Americans had struggled for many years to get the city to build Phillips. In addition, the employment opportunities it offered to African Americans gave Phillips a special significance in the nonwhite community. Poelker also irritated Goins when he failed to select Goins's choice as the first African American director of public safety.[73] By 1976, Comptroller John Bass, whose candidacy had been so championed by Goins, had moved closer to Bill Clay's camp.[74]

Following Bass's unprecedented citywide victory, speculation arose about the likelihood of St. Louis electing a black mayor. Jack Flach wrote in the *Globe-Democrat* that a successful black mayoral candidacy might be some years off. He noted "there has been an exodus to the county of middle and upper-class blacks in the last several years which has siphoned off leadership, money and enthusiasm in some black areas." Flach also noted "the frequent lack of unity among the blacks."[75] This suggestion referred to the Clay-Goins struggle. There was also a lack of black unity in other cities with machine-style politics and factionalism. Cleveland, between the mayoralties of Carl Stokes and Michael White, and New York City, prior to David Dinkins's election in 1989, provided evidence of this disunity. Black politicians in those cities devoted more attention to immediate spoils instead of concentrating on the attainment of the city's highest office.[76] Although a successful black mayoral candidate seemed unlikely in St. Louis in the 1970s, many white politicians were well aware that black voters already could affect the fortunes of white candidates for higher office.

Mayor Poelker's notable care and caution did not free him from criticisms from former allies and from former opponents as well. He faced accusations that he neglected the predominantly black north side during his mayoral tenure. He and his community development director, John Roach, devoted attention to preserving city neighborhoods and funneled considerable resources to the integrated central corridor.[77] These efforts displaced some low-income minority residents. Poelker and his administrators tried to respond to the growing number of neighborhood groups, which made frequent demands on City Hall. Poelker, however, according to observers of that era, seemed to function best behind the scenes. He was an able steward but not a leader.

During Poelker's tenure, the various ward organizations continued their machinations, worrying about whom to slate for county offices and about picking winners. The city's factionalism now extended to black wards as well as white, and the division of the development pie took on greater meaning. For most in the old-time party orbit, this division still symbolized jobs, contracts, and opportunities for friends. For those elected officials who cooperated with neighborhood groups, principally aldermen, questions of land use grew in significance, and the aldermen increasingly became the officials most likely to intercede with the bureaucracy for citizens.

Poelker had indicated he wished to serve only one term as mayor. The 1977 race to succeed him boiled down to a contest between James Conway, who had unsuccessfully sought the mayor's office in 1973, and former mayor A. J. Cervantes. The media and a number of politicians identified Conway as a reformer. In his races for state representative and state senator, he successfully had opposed organization candidates. However, in 1975, he helped his own position by securing the eighth-ward aldermanic seat for ally Tom Connelly in traditional St. Louis style.

In the 1977 mayoral contest, Conway interestingly enjoyed both Republican and liberal Democratic support. He also received endorsements from some black officials, such as Benny Goins and state senator Jet Banks. Conway led in campaign spending, and financial reports indicated that his contributors included bank president Clarence C. Barksdale; the chairman of Anheuser-Busch, August A. Busch, Jr.; and James S. McDonnell of McDonnell-Douglas[78]—all prominent members of Civic Progress. The longstanding practice of candidates giving money to the ward organizations that endorsed them to pay for election expenditures continued in 1977. Both Conway and Cervantes made such payments. For example, Conway gave money to the third and fourth wards on the north side and to the thirteenth on the south. Cervantes contributed to Clay's twenty-sixth ward and to Leroy Tyus's organization in the twentieth.[79] Tyus was a close ally of Clay, and Clay had always been with Cervantes.

In the March 8 Democratic primary, Conway defeated Cervantes handily with 60 percent of the vote. He carried twenty-one of the twenty-eight wards, losing only on the north side. The north side traditionally had been a Cervantes stronghold. Leaders of some of the stronger organization wards throughout the city had gone with

Cervantes. In addition to Clay and Tyus, Cervantes' allies included party chair and city treasurer Paul Berra from the Hill and circuit clerk Joseph Roddy of the seventeenth ward. Only seven wards had endorsed Conway, but both daily newspapers and the *Southside Journal* supported him.[80]

Campaign Transitions

As Conway's victory demonstrated, the value of ward endorsements in a mayoral race clearly had declined by 1977. Part of the change stemmed from erosion in the power of ward committeemen. The committeemen no longer had as many incentives to offer prospective supporters. Perhaps even more important was the fact that candidates could reach the electorate on their own, either through grassroots campaigning or through the mass media.

Liberal insurgents began a new grassroots campaign style in the 1960s. Denied the chance to support antiwar presidential candidates Eugene McCarthy or Robert Kennedy in 1968, they began organizing on their own. The antiwar movement brought new blood into St. Louis politics. Several political veterans credit the events of that time with reshaping St. Louis's electoral process. The new participants resembled at least in part those in the sixth and seventh wards who fought traditional leadership. They became a force in the twenty-fifth and twenty-eighth wards on the city's central western edge.

Campaign styles changed in some of the other wards as well. Paul Berra, city Democratic committee chair, summed it up. "In the old days," he told the *Post*, "an alderman would not have to do any campaigning if he had the ward organization behind him. The ward machine is gradually fading in influence because ward leaders are not in a position to tell voters how to vote, and people are now more educated and do their own analyzing of candidates."[81] The candidates also began to run their own campaigns.

In his 1972 quest for the Democratic nomination for state representative, Steve Vossmeyer appealed directly to ward organization members in the twenty-fifth and twenty-eighth wards for support and directly to the voters by going door to door throughout the district. He prepared his own literature, recruited his own volunteers, and created a follow-up system to keep in touch with every household he visited. Others soon followed his lead. In the years to come, door-to-door efforts and independent mailings would be used in conjunction with media campaigning, particularly for citywide races. The ward organizations were not rendered obsolete, but their effectiveness again declined, initially in better-off sections of the city. Although ward organizations could be bypassed and although they could be beaten, the vast majority of potential candidates continued eagerly to seek their endorsements, and "who's with whom" remained an important conversation topic. Traditional practice endured, although the utility of these rituals had faded.

Black and White Politics Redux

John Bass's election as city comptroller in 1973 had been a major victory for African Americans in St. Louis. In the primary, he had bested two white candidates, and in the general election he easily had overcome a Republican challenger. In fact, he ran only a few thousand votes behind his mayoral running mate, John Poelker. The election results were not as favorable to Bass in 1977. In the Democratic primary in that year, he finished second by 3,600 votes to Raymond Percich, the city's sheriff and former twenty-seventh-ward alderman. Bass had defeated Percich four years before. A third candidate, Kenneth Cohen, a resident of the twenty-eighth ward, received 18,045 votes, votes that could have changed the outcome. Ray Gibson, a fourth candidate, received just more than 3,000 votes. The south side voted overwhelmingly for Percich, and the north side for Bass. In the racially and economically diverse central corridor, the votes split in three directions. Cohen carried the twenty-fifth ward and his home ward, the twenty-eighth, the latter by just 1 vote. Bass carried the sixth and seventeenth wards, while Percich took the seventh and eighth wards. Cohen also amassed a substantial number of votes in these four wards. It is possible that some of Cohen's support might have gone to Bass in this more liberal section of St. Louis.

Bass's defeat did not settle easily with a number of people, including Congressman Clay. Bass had moved from Goins's faction to Clay's while serving as comptroller. On election night, the *Post* quoted Bill Clay as saying, "All the leading white Democrats failed to endorse a black incumbent Democrat. I think there are going to be serious repercussions."[82] In fact, only two white leaders had endorsed Bass, Francis R. Slay of the twenty-third ward and Joe Roddy of the seventeenth.[83] At his victory party, Percich called Bill Clay his major opponent in the primary.[84] Clay had remained a bone of contention to many in the white community; he never bowed to St. Louis's traditional political power brokers.

Clay and Bass refused to let Bass's defeat rest. Instead, they embarked on write-in candidacies, Clay for mayor and Bass for comptroller. Clay expressed reasons for their decision, mixing racial justice with machine politics and its rewards:

> I think we've got the job of educating this community to the fact that the Democratic Party does not want to share equally with black people the fruits of victory. [White south side Democrats had] changed the rules and had failed to honor their promise for a coalition Democratic Party in St. Louis. We're not partners. What we are is cannon fodder. We get votes for them, and they take the victory, the glory and the power. If we won't demand what's rightfully ours, we won't get it.[85]

Conway took the news of Clay's candidacy calmly and mentioned that he had received support for his mayoral campaign from all over the city. He also indicated that he had a good relationship with Congressman Clay.[86]

News of the Clay-Bass write-in effort did not receive unanimous support among black officials, however. Not surprisingly, License Collector Benny Goins was said not to favor such a candidacy.[87] Goins was rumored—accurately as it turned out—to be Percich's replacement as sheriff. Clay reacted angrily to the speculation about Goins.

> You've all seen "Roots" on television where they talked about house niggers and field niggers. Well, we have some house niggers in this town and some of them made a deal to trade the comptroller's office for the office of sheriff. We'd have less blacks working in the sheriff's office than we've got today.[88]

Some pundits, as well as some politicians, felt that Clay's candidacy might cost Conway the mayor's office by siphoning off valuable north-side votes from the Democrats. In fact, Republican Joseph Badaracco had carried some south-side wards in his races for the aldermanic presidency in 1969 and 1971. Badaracco also carried precincts in south St. Louis when he ran for mayor against John Poelker in 1973.

However, all these fears proved groundless. Conway captured 60,567 votes to 16,977 for Clay and 16,910 for Republican James Stemmler. However, in a write-in campaign, Clay succeeded in carrying seven north-side wards, including the twenty-first, where Benny Goins served as committeeman. Conway's wide margin of victory on the south side prevented Clay from hurting him.

Nonetheless, Clay again demonstrated his considerable popularity with black voters and his ability to get them to the polls. He had just one month to convince potential voters to write in his name. In that respect, his campaign was a success.

In the coming months, Clay continued his rivalry with other black politicians, particularly Benny Goins. His attacks continued to contain racial appeals as this excerpt from a speech at a first-ward meeting demonstrates. Clay said, "Black elected officials in St. Louis had turned into a 'cadre of black hustlers' who think it's more important to socialize with white bigots than to represent black interests."[89]

Alderman Eugene "Tink" Bradley of the twenty-first ward was a longtime ally of Benny Goins. In 1980, after aldermanic president Paul Simon resigned to accept a judgeship, Bradley—by virtue of his seniority on the board—became acting president. Bradley then had to contend for his new position in a special election. Thomas Zych, a state senator widely regarded as a maverick, opposed him. Local 73 of the Firefighters Union supported Zych and mounted a door-to-door campaign for him in south St. Louis. Ward organizations there went with Bradley, who was personally popular with many white politicians. However, when the returns were counted, Zych had beaten Bradley. Turnout was exceptionally heavy down south. Although Bradley pulled votes there, Zych pulled many more. But the key to this contest lay on the north side. Turnout was very low there compared to other recent elections. Bradley failed to garner the number of black votes he needed to maintain his office. Friends say the loss broke his heart. He died not long after. In looking at Bradley's contest with Zych and other elections of that period, it becomes clear that Clay could do a great deal to turn out the troops for a candidate. On the other hand, he also could fail to muster support for someone he had endorsed. Thus, a Clay endorsement did not necessarily mean that extraordinary effort would accompany it.

During the decades of white domination of St. Louis politics, African Americans clearly had to play subservient roles. After wresting ward offices from white stalwarts, African Americans not surprisingly absorbed themselves in securing the traditional political fruits of office. In a fragmented system of allocation, rivalries developed among African American politicians just as they had among their white counterparts. For the most part, black areas of the city continued to receive a less-than-equal share of services and patronage.

Reflecting structural and cultural influences, St. Louis saw the rhetoric of civil rights become fused with more traditional concerns. And although Clay and Bass may have fallen short of their goal in 1977, all future candidates had to recognize the clout the congressman could bring to bear. While Clay could not stop Conway in 1977, he played a leading role in doing so in 1981.

Mayor Conway

James Conway's term as mayor stimulated controversy. An intelligent man, he directed much of his effort toward St. Louis's neighborhoods. Monti noted that Conway saw the connection between "the kinds of businesses and institutions that would become the backbone of a new St. Louis and the kind of community that could grow around them."[90] Many of the projects fostered by Mayor Conway were located in the city's central corridor. Conway consciously pursued the maintenance of redeveloped and integrated neighborhoods using federal dollars.[91]

Conway's redevelopment projects often involved displacement of low-income residents, winning him few fans in certain quarters. During his administration, considerable redevelopment and relocation took place in the Tiffany area. The Saint Louis University's medical school complex spearheaded this development. In the throes of these activities, area politicians lobbied to save an old church in the center of the neighborhood, which the redevelopers wanted to demolish. Conway approved the razing of the church, placing a park

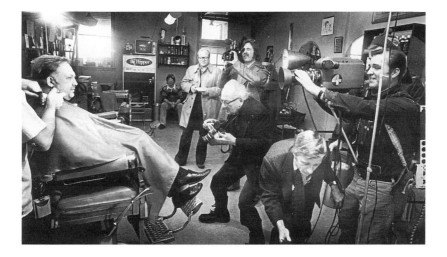

State senator James Conway shaves his beard after entering the mayor's race in 1977. Photograph by Larry Williams, St. Louis Post-Dispatch, 1977.

Many African American residents protested the closure of Homer G. Phillips Hospital by Mayor Conway in 1979. Photograph by Bill Kesler, *St. Louis Post-Dispatch*, 1979.

on the site instead. According to Monti, one political leader who disliked Conway reacted by pushing for Alderman Vincent Schoemehl of the twenty-eighth ward to challenge Conway when he sought reelection in 1981.[92] Along with Geraldine Osborn, alderman of the fifteenth ward, Schoemehl was a persistent questioner of Conway's policies.

Clearly, Conway garnered his share of critics over redevelopment policies. He also had an acrimonious relationship with the comptroller, Raymond Percich. Word about their fractious interchanges circulated widely in the city. Yet these various altercations did not cost Conway his bid for a second term. Instead, he carried out the single action that would galvanize the wrath of the African American community. Conway closed the Homer G. Phillips Hospital on the city's north side. This hospital had been promised to African Americans for years before finally being built when Barney Dickmann was mayor. The building of Phillips had been a strong inducement for blacks to leave the Republican Party for the Democrats in the 1930s.

Homer G. Phillips Hospital had become a strong symbol in St. Louis's nonwhite areas. It was also a rare source of medical training and residencies for blacks until passage of the 1964 Civil Rights Act, which opened many other doors. In addition, the hospital provided a significant number of jobs for the less skilled.

St. Louis also had a white public hospital located on the near-south side in the seventh ward, City No. 1. Both hospitals were nominally integrated by the 1960s, but St. Louis's black community clearly saw Phillips as their hospital. Because of the city's declining population and resources, some business leaders and elected officials favored the closing of one of the two hospitals. Mayor Cervantes wrote,

> The public still views one hospital as black and one as white. An efficient businessman would merge the two: But any effort to do that in St. Louis requires that one or the other be closed. And in a city half black and half white, each racial group refuses to allow 'its' hospital to close.[93]

Alderman Freeman Bosley, Sr. (left), joined the protest against the closing of Homer G. Phillips Hospital by blocking the route for trucks to move equipment to City Hospital No. 1. Photograph by Scott Dine, St. Louis Post-Dispatch, 1979.

The pressure to close a public hospital did not diminish after Cervantes left office. During John Poelker's administration, speculation that he would decrease services at, or close, Phillips met with outrage from black leaders. Yet in 1979, Mayor Conway chose to close this facility permanently. Throughout the next year, protestors appeared at the hospital site on a daily basis. All major African American politicians in St. Louis, from Congressman Clay on down, denounced the closure.

Perhaps Conway did not envision the firestorm that closing the hospital would create. St. Louisans still speculate about why he chose to close Phillips. It was newer than City No. 1, although it could house patients only in wards. (The newer section of City Hospital had some semiprivate rooms.) Some have speculated that the closing resulted from pressure from Saint Louis University medical school professors, who staffed City and did not want to work at Phillips. Others have cited possible pleas from seventh-ward politicians concerned about constituents' jobs if City closed.[94] Whatever the reason, Conway could not walk away from the conflict over the closing of Phillips. The depth of black unhappiness at this move sealed Conway's fate. Alderman Vincent Schoemehl, with the endorsement of Clay and other black politicians, filed against Conway and then defeated him handily. Schoemehl carried white and integrated wards in his victory and carried predominantly black wards overwhelmingly.[95]

An Overview

After Raymond Tucker's reelection defeat in 1965, St. Louis began a series of transitions involving race, neighborhoods, and the strength of ward organizations. It is clear from the example of the Homer G. Phillips Hospital closing and its aftermath that African Americans had become significant political players in St. Louis. Yet their focus—even to some extent in the case of the hospital—was the traditional one of St. Louis's ward organizations: jobs. The importance of committeemen and ward endorsements fell in the 1960s and 1970s, although the traditional election rituals remained. Aldermen, as ombudsmen and as overseers of redevelopment plans, gained in stature. They in turn began to heed the demands of neighborhood groups, which had become strong in various parts of the city. Mayors had to occupy themselves with redevelopment, although with more of an eye to preservation than to displacement and demolition after 1965. Without the national push for renewal and highway building driving programs, St. Louis's mayors appeared weaker and more attentive to other centers of power. Court reorganization reduced the number of county offices from eleven to eight and also eliminated the partisan-elected offices of constable and magistrate. These changes also diminished some of the wards' strength. No other attempts to change city or state law to modernize governance have been successful since.

Despite these significant transitions, the culture of St. Louis politics with its attendant rituals did not change appreciably. Power remained disbursed, and politicians continued in the private-regarding mode. The changes that occurred were not of the magnitude needed to foster major behavioral adjustments. The traditional rewards remained, at least in the eyes of many officials. In 1981, these officials awaited a mayor who tried to combine pragmatic leadership and political mastery. Vincent Schoemehl would be the first mayor since Bernard Dickmann to try to centralize both policymaking and political leadership.

During this period, other machine-politics cities also tried to cope with decaying economies and population loss. In addition, African Americans demonstrated mounting electoral strength in a number of locations. Selection of black mayors moved closer in Chicago, Philadelphia, and Baltimore. In Chicago and Baltimore, white machine politicians made that transition difficult. Former police chief Frank Rizzo governed in Philadelphia, exacerbating racial tensions there. Chicago had to confront the loss of Richard J. Daley, which threw the question of governance up into the air. The vaunted Chicago machine never again achieved the domination of both politics and government that it had had under Daley. In all these cities, however, the mayor had greater powers than St. Louis's mayor. Ready answers to fiscal, racial, and economic problems seemed to elude everyone in America's core cities.

Chapter 9

The Schoemehl Years, 1981–1993
New Wines, Old Bottles

In the late 1970s and early 1980s, some of the media began to refer to St. Louis as an "urban basket case." Its citizenry shared this pessimism. Perhaps the best description of the city's ills at the time Vincent C. Schoemehl, Jr., became mayor in 1981 was offered by historian Kenneth T. Jackson. He called St. Louis:

> a premier example of urban abandonment. Once the fourth largest city in America, the "Gateway to the West" is now twenty-seventh, a ghost of its former self. In 1940 it contained 816,000 inhabitants: in 1980 the census counted only 453,000. Many of its old neighborhoods have become dispiriting collections of burned-out buildings, eviscerated homes, and vacant lots.... The air is polluted, the sidewalks are filthy, the juvenile crime is horrendous, and the remaining industries are languishing. Grimy warehouses and aging loft factories are landscaped by weed-grown lots adjoining half-used rail yards. Like an elderly couple no longer sure of their purpose in life after their children have moved away, these neighborhoods face an undirected future.

> A particularly telling statistic is that, after Chicago, St. Louis is the nation's leading exporter of used bricks.[1]

A number of other midwestern and northeastern cities were also in dire straits. St. Louis's difficulties then seemed more intractable than most, however, to residents and observers alike.

The challenges facing new mayor Vince Schoemehl certainly were formidable when he became mayor in April of 1981. There had been little construction in the city for years, particularly downtown. Schoemehl's predecessors, Poelker and Conway, had laid the groundwork for several key projects that had yet to open. But St. Louis's small-town nature contributed to both its pessimism and a form of stasis. Citizens' most frequent refrain, "But this is St. Louis," did not encourage borrowing from other places.

Elected an alderman in 1975, Schoemehl quickly demonstrated an impatience with the status quo. He came to the board of aldermen after the heyday of the Young Turks but was a kindred spirit. He questioned tradition and standard operating procedures. Along with Geraldine Osborn, alderman from the fifteenth ward, Schoemehl was a frequent critic of Mayor Conway and his programs. When Schoemehl decided to challenge Conway for mayor, he enlisted the support of his sizable family (he was one of eleven children) and a number of his neighbors in the Skinker DeBaliviere area. For at least a year before the mayoral primary, these friends and relatives went door to door in many parts of the city, introducing countless voters to the young candidate from the twenty-eighth ward with the unusual name.

Schoemehl was just thirty-four years old when he became mayor, and many in his staff were around the same age. Some were new to city government but had been part of the campaign. Schoemehl also looked beyond St. Louis to fill key positions, and he continued this pattern throughout his tenure in the mayor's office. He brought tremendous energy to the tasks at hand but sometimes earned the appellation of "Ready, Fire, Aim" because of his lack of patience.

Schoemehl's 1981 primary victory startled many in the city.[2] The breadth of it—he won twenty-seven of the city's twenty-eight wards—amazed many pundits and politicians. Schoemehl benefited from the support of organized labor, particularly Jack Martorelli of the operating engineers and Vergil Belfi of the stationary engineers. They provided his first endorsements, and other unions later followed suit. Some ward organizations endorsed Schoemehl as well, but more went with Conway. Schoemehl's strongest organization supporter was Joe Roddy, called the last of the Irish ward bosses. Roddy, the clerk of the circuit court and seventeenth-ward committeeman, was the first ward leader to back Schoemehl. Congressman Bill Clay had his organization assist Schoemehl as well, in no small part because of the closing of Homer G. Phillips Hospital.

The *Post-Dispatch*, following a familiar pattern, endorsed Conway. The paper liked the fact that he had received support in 1977 from a collection of neighborhoods and the business community. Also, he was "an outsider—at least to the political buddy system that had long dominated City Hall."[3] To the *Post*, Schoemehl was the candidate "with the support of Old-line political regulars who lost influence under Mr. Conway."[4] However, the newspaper failed to note that Conway was supported by a number of political regulars including Louis Buckowitz, Paul Berra, Martie Aboussie, Francis R. Slay, Red Villa, Sorkis Webbe, Jr., and Jet Banks. Jo Mannies, a *Post* reporter, noted that "several past and present department and agency heads appointed by Conway acknowledge that they have close political ties to certain state or local officials—such as J. B. 'Jet' Banks, Alderman Louis Buckowitz, D-10th ward, powerbroker Eugene Slay and even Conway himself."[5] Both candidates had roots in the ward tradition, and each had organizational help.

Because of St. Louis's history and culture, governing the city requires involvement in exchanging favors. Without such exchanges, a mayor would have a difficult time accomplishing anything. St. Louis's fragmentation means that allies are needed to sell projects. Conway had been termed a political outsider because he did not have organization backing in his early races for the state legislature. It is safe to say that by the time of the mayoral primary in 1981 both Conway and Schoemehl had made alliances with Democratic factions. St. Louisans perceive these alliances as necessary tools of governance; to them, they are not cultural artifacts. The support a mayor receives from various aldermen or others in influential positions remains rooted in quid pro quo relationships, principally in exchanges of support for jobs and contracts. Stances on issues sometimes coincide with the alignments and occasionally can eclipse them, as Schoemehl's career will illustrate. But the political standard operating procedures exert a powerful pull no matter the issue. The danger lies in being subsumed by the care and feeding of allies and the desire to thwart enemies.

Schoemehl understood the political game well and, for a time, mastered it better than any Democrat since the Dickmann-Hannegan duo. Schoemehl used the force of his personality to charm department heads and win aldermanic support. One former alderman remarked that "if Vince had a half hour, he could sell you anything." Schoemehl had had a career in sales, and a salesman he remained. He also was effective in addressing large groups. He could build enthusiasm. In this respect, he resembled Cervantes, but his programmatic reach was more extensive than his predecessor's. On trips to other cities, he always was on the lookout for programs to bring to St. Louis or people whose talent he could utilize.

The seeds of future problems for the young mayor lay in two of the promises he made in his first campaign. When he was unable to honor these commitments, some of the public trust in him eroded.

Coupled with ongoing factionalism and racial tension, his popularity began to plummet. While Schoemehl had innovative approaches to address the ills of city living, he was caught in the web of the city's political procedures and his own personality. Ironically, like Dickmann and Hannegan five decades before, Schoemehl appeared to revel in the political machinations, and he also overreached, to his detriment.

The Good New Days: Operations and More Operations

Vince Schoemehl's campaign slogan was "For a Proud St. Louis." Although he did not eradicate the city's pessimism, he did for a time create a belief in possibilities and a feeling of hope. According to a friend, Schoemehl had been somewhat of a liberal activist in his youth. He had worked with the poor and wanted to improve the quality of city life. While in school at the University of Missouri–St. Louis, he helped organize a chapter of Students for a Democratic Society, although he and his fellow members concentrated mainly on university-based grievances such as the quality of cafeteria food.

After taking the oath of office as mayor, Schoemehl acted quickly to improve the image of St. Louis for citizens and visitors alike. He fomented strategies to brighten up the city through Operation BrightSide. BrightSide involved cleaning alleys, removing trash and debris from thoroughfares, and planting trees and flowers all over town. A longtime St. Louis resident enthused, "As winter comes to an end, the grassy slopes along the freeways become a sea of yellow." Daffodil bulbs were planted there in abundance. In fact, St. Louis became the largest purchaser of daffodil bulbs in the world. BrightSide also supplied daffodil and tulip bulbs to residents at cost every year. The resident continued, "The seas of yellow made everyone feel better." Under Schoemehl's direction and under his sister Lucille Green's day-to-day administration, BrightSide helped beautify a declining town. With the aid of donations from Anheuser-Busch and many other firms and individuals, and the expenditure of only limited public funds, BrightSide was a success. In addition, city youth could obtain summer jobs planting and cleaning up around the town. During Schoemehl's three terms in office, the tree-planting never stopped, nor did the planting of tulips, daffodils, roses, petunias, and many other floral varieties. Some St. Louisans, particularly from poorer areas, scoffed at what they felt were frivolous expenditures in the face of more pressing economic and safety needs. However, Schoemehl's successors continued and expanded his horticultural efforts. Suburban communities around St. Louis also began their own planting, and in 1998 Mayor Richard M. Daley started a similar beautification effort in Chicago.

Operation SafeStreet also proved popular with St. Louisans. Using program ideas gleaned in trips to other cities, Schoemehl created, at little cost, a bundle of projects that helped somewhat to reassure a citizenry frightened by crime. Under Operation SafeStreet, every burglary victim could receive at no cost a home-security package that included door locks, window bars, and other protective items. The elderly and the disabled also could have this package installed at their homes for no charge. Other residents could purchase the package for a small fee. SafeStreet also arranged for the installation of automobile alarms for city residents for less than $30. A major element of SafeStreet was crime prevention through neighborhood involvement. Block units received training in how to carry out neighborhood watches in conjunction with neighborhood organizations and the city.

Schoemehl sometimes joked at public meetings that he had created so many operations he could be accused of practicing medicine without a license. Several additional programs that continued after his departure from office were Operation Impact, Operation ConServ, and Operation TeamWork. Operation Impact addressed the rehabilitation of dwelling units in a number of city neighborhoods. This spot rehabilitation tried to stabilize certain areas. Operation ConServ, expanded as Neighborhood Stabilization under Mayor Freeman Bosley, Jr., Schoemehl's successor, fostered the formation of neighborhood housing corporations and provided city staffers to work with neighborhoods in the provision of municipal and police services. TeamWork sponsored recreation teams for children and youth throughout the year.

Schoemehl placed his new programs outside existing city bureaucracy, skirting both civil service and the inertia often characteristic of existing government agencies. This gave the mayor greater flexibility to innovate and to furnish jobs to those sympathetic with his efforts.

These operations exemplified the energy and creativity of the Schoemehl administration. The mayor sold these programs to the city at many venues, including town-hall meetings. His enthusiasm was always palpable. Not unlike Philadelphia's recent mayor, Edward Rendell, Schoemehl was a cheerleader for the city, who helped people feel that life was getting better.[6] Not everyone was convinced, of course. Prophets of gloom continued to complain about population and job loss. Genuine and perhaps intractable problems persisted in St. Louis, as they did in other midwestern and eastern industrial cities.

Development Projects

Schoemehl put in long hours and addressed his development projects with considerable zeal. A feeling of momentum or at least action was always present. During Schoemehl's term, new office buildings began to grace downtown streets. Schoemehl also presided over the opening of Union Station, in its new incarnation as an attractive festival mall, one of a number built by James Rouse, and St. Louis Centre, a downtown shopping mall. These projects were planned prior to his mayoralty but opened during his first term. Schoemehl also sponsored a number of new and rehabilitated market-rate housing projects in the central corridor. Not all citizens were pleased with these efforts. African American critics charged that he neglected the north side, although a number of subsidized residential developments were built in some of the predominantly black wards. Some south siders also felt that their wards were neglected by the administration, although new suburban-style housing was built in the twenty-third and twenty-fourth wards.

A great deal of the administration's development activity involved projects falling under the rubric of tourism. Schoemehl sponsored a major expansion of the city's convention center. He also had to fight to keep professional sports teams in the city and ensure that these teams had desirable venues for their games. In one such effort, Schoemehl had the city purchase the Arena, built in the 1920s, to keep the Blues hockey team in St. Louis and also maintain a home for Saint Louis University's popular basketball team, the Billikens. In the late 1980s, Anheuser-Busch offered to build a new state-of-the-art hockey arena for the Blues close to their baseball stadium downtown. They also wanted to tear down the adjacent Cupples warehouses, built at the turn of the century, to construct additional parking lots for a new arena and for Busch Stadium. Schoemehl balked at the proposed demolition, earning the ire of the brewery and of a large number of Blues fans. He later worked with some of the Civic Progress companies, which called themselves the Kiel Partners (later to become Clark Enterprises). The Kiel Partners decided to build a new arena on the site of the municipal auditorium. The city treasurer's office agreed to build an adjacent parking structure. Although the Blues and the Billikens have enjoyed their new arena with its requisite luxury boxes, some have protested the failure of the Kiel Partners to rehab the adjacent Kiel Opera House, once home to the Saint Louis Symphony and dance and opera performances.

Mayor Vincent C. Schoemehl, Jr., discusses plans for a new downtown arena in 1986. The St. Louis Mercantile Library at the University of Missouri–St. Louis.

The struggle over retention of a National Football League team was also controversial. Schoemehl had had a positive working relationship with St. Louis County executive Gene McNary until McNary tried to build a stadium for the football Cardinals in St. Louis County. The Cardinals, or "Big Red," played their home games at Busch Stadium. The team's owner, Bill Bidwell, wanted a new facility designed exclusively for football with numerous luxury boxes for corporate sponsors. Schoemehl prevented the development of such a facility outside the city limits but could not prevent Bidwell from moving his team to Phoenix. Although St. Louis is more of a baseball town than a football one, the Big Red's departure shocked many in the metropolitan area. St. Louis City, declining in population and less important in its region, wanted to keep its professional teams to ensure its status as a big-league town. Similar reactions occurred in Baltimore and Cleveland when the owners of the Colts and the Browns sought different locales for the teams.

The response to the Cardinals' departure to the desert brought about a unique partnership of the state, county, and city. New county executive H. Milford agreed to pay a quarter of the cost of the bonds needed to finance a new domed stadium to be attached to the convention center downtown. Republican governor John Ashcroft came on board for one half of the cost of the bonds, although as a reluctant partner.[7] Under Schoemehl's successor, this stadium, sometimes referred to as the convention center expansion, became home to the relocated Los Angeles Rams. However, when Schoemehl left office, the almost-completed facility had no team.

In the 1990s, many cities discovered the performing and visual arts as important ways to lure tourist dollars to their towns. Schoemehl was perhaps in the forefront of those recognizing the benefits of the arts. Costing far less to support than athletic teams, arts events also could have greater spillover in terms of fostering restaurants and after-concert venues. In 1985, Schoemehl and county executive Gene McNary cooperated in the formation of the Regional Arts Commission. Funded by a special hotel and restaurant tax, the commission distributes funds to every variety of arts organization in the city and county. Prohibited by law from aiding institutions in the Zoo-Museum district, the commission has been able to assist the Opera Theatre of St. Louis, the Saint Louis Symphony Orchestra, the Black Repertory Theatre, small musical ensembles, and neighborhood arts events. Jill McGuire, a Schoemehl staff member, became the Regional Arts Commission's director.

In 1990, the Schoemehl administration helped create an arts district in the city called Grand Center. Located near the main campus of Saint Louis University, the arts district was immediately home to the recently rehabilitated Fox Theatre. Powell Hall, which became home to the Saint Louis Symphony Orchestra almost a decade before, was just down the street. The arts district has been graced with distinctive signage and lighting. Since its inception, the district has added the Grandel Square Theatre, the Forum art gallery, and a new building housing KETC-Channel 9, the local public television station. A new Pulitzer art repository is taking shape as well. Although the district lacks some of the amenities needed to keep art patrons there after a performance, it is emblematic of the importance of the arts as a development tool.

In addition, against the voices of countless skeptics, Schoemehl worked hard to bring a light-rail system to St. Louis. As the city's contribution, he offered a former railway right of way. The trains began to run four months after he left office and proved a much greater success than anyone would have thought. In addition to carrying commuters, the trains carry thousands bound for sporting events downtown.

Some development projects incur more disfavor than others. Certainly, those with little interest in sports and many of the poor criticized the public funds that supported a new arena and new football stadium. Preservationists were aghast at the plans for the continuation of an open-air downtown mall. The concept of a long and distinctive mall running from the Arch grounds past City Hall actually was first proposed in 1908 by city planner Harland Bartholomew. His ideas took root, and though it took decades to implement them, they were seen as viable throughout. Hearkening back to the City Beautiful movement, Bartholomew envisioned a park area surrounded by ornamental white public buildings and a parkway heading west.

In 1980, development of such a mall again became a major item of discussion. Some of the city's most prominent business leaders, including Robert Hyland, owner of powerful KMOX Radio, supported the concept of the mall and favored tearing down several turn-of-the century buildings—St. Louis's first skyscrapers—to accomplish the goal. The end project would have more commercial activity than had been envisioned earlier amid the mall's greenery. Schoemehl initially objected to the proposed plans and did not want to demolish the architecturally significant buildings.[8] In 1982, the mayor established the Pride of St. Louis Corporation to find compromise among those proposing different scenarios for the area and for the existing buildings. Civic Progress leaders were represented along with members of PRIDE, a joint labor-industry organization that had brought considerable labor peace to the construction industry. Both the *Post-Dispatch* and the *Globe-Democrat* supported a new mall with new construction. In the fall, the board of aldermen and the mayor acquiesced and approved the demolition of several structures. Three buildings, including one designed by Ernst and Young, fell before the wrecking ball. A plaza and amphitheater rose in their place along with a shiny new fifteen-story building that made the mall a half-mall.[9]

When Anheuser-Busch abandoned its plans to build a new hockey arena because Mayor Schoemehl had decided to preserve the Cupples warehouses, Schoemehl referred to the Gateway Mall as his greatest mistake. In his last few months in office, he oversaw the completion of the mall, including placement of distinctive sculptures by Robert Cassilly, a local favorite. Schoemehl came to realize what had been lost by his accession to the earlier demolitions. However, ironically, he almost certainly lost more support by thwarting the arena Anheuser-Busch proposed than he did by allowing turn-of-the-century buildings to come down.

Civic Progress

In his pursuit of downtown development, sports franchises, and an arts district, Schoemehl worked closely with the leaders of Civic Progress. However, he was often the one who initiated requests for their assistance, and the business leaders responded on a project-by-project basis.[10] In a less-than-traditional endeavor, Schoemehl worked with Civic Progress members to support a slate of candidates for the St. Louis School Board in 1991. Court-ordered busing had enraged many white south side residents. They in turn began to support school-board candidates backed by a white citizens group. If this group had been successful in electing its slate in 1991, it would have controlled the board. A Schoemehl staff member as well as business and community leaders screened possible opponents to the white citizens slate. They selected two men and two women, two blacks and two whites, who became the "4 Candidates 4 Kids." Members of Civic Progress contributed handsomely to the 4 Candidates campaign. Neither the business leaders nor the mayor wanted the embarrassment of an intolerant school-board majority. The 4 Candidates 4 Kids were successful at the polls in April 1991.

The school-board campaign provided just the type of project members of Civic Progress preferred, because it was a relatively brief commitment. Although Schoemehl had been perhaps more active in downtown development than any mayor since Tucker, his relationship with Civic Progress was more like that of his immediate predecessors. Contact was related to a specific project and did not entail looking at St. Louis as a whole. After the Tucker era, chief executive officers of Civic Progress companies often were not native St. Louisans. They did not have the same interest in the community as leaders in the 1950s. In addition, business conditions, which entailed a more competitive environment, no longer allowed chief executives the same degree of freedom to be involved in civic projects. Robert Salisbury, professor emeritus of political science at Washington University, wrote in the *Post-Dispatch* that "A generation ago it was useful to both their institutional interests...for the leaders of the major organizations to take on heavy civic responsibilities. If St. Louis prospered, their enterprises would also. They depended on local customers, they hired local people and their corporate image was closely linked with the community's."[11] That was the Tucker era. A changing business world and the loosely structured nature of Civic Progress mitigated against a tightly connected business-government regime.

Nonetheless, in this different era, Schoemehl stood out. Historian Jon C. Teaford included him in his examination of "messiah" mayors, mayors who once again were:

> confidently charting the urban course rather than being pushed helplessly to and fro. They easily won reelection, remained in the mayor's seat year after year, and effectively hobbled opposition. Their electoral successes rested largely on their reputations as urban saviors. They had redeemed their cities from the fiscal doom of the mid-1970s and bolstered municipal credit ratings. They had created a more favorable business climate and thus had nurtured a new downtown building boom.[12]

Teaford's list of messiah mayors also included William Donald Schaefer of Baltimore and Kevin White of Boston. Teaford noted that Schoemehl resembled White. Both these mayors had gained control of their city bureaucracy and amassed considerable political clout.[13] Schoemehl's inclusion in this select group also rested on his ability to trim the city's budget by cutting expenditures, consolidating operations, and privatizing services.[14]

The Morass of Political Custom

On numerous occasions, Schoemehl joked that he had become mayor at the worst possible moment—three months after Ronald Reagan became president. Like other American mayors, he had to deal with the effects of significant cutbacks in federal aid. He also faced a large budget deficit on the day he took office. But these dismal realities proved not to be quagmires for him. Instead, his own campaign promises eventually came back to haunt him. And St. Louis's traditional factionalism took up valuable time and energy. Schoemehl continually tried to augment his support or defeat his enemies.

Schoemehl won the 1981 mayoral primary in no small measure because of his promise to reopen Homer G. Phillips Hospital. Table 9-1 demonstrates the effect of the predominantly black north side vote on the outcome. Schoemehl may have carried twenty-seven of the twenty-eight wards, but his victory margin clearly came from the north side. Conway's closing of Homer G. Phillips Hospital brought Schoemehl the backing of Congressman Clay and other African American elected officials. Schoemehl's initial appointments reflected his gratitude. Irving C. Clay, Jr., the congressman's brother, became director of welfare. State legislator Gwen Giles, a strong Clay ally and

TABLE 9-1

1981 Democratic Primary Mayoral Vote

	Ward	Schoemehl	Conway	Rolen
North side	1	2,924	253	104
	3	2,565	241	70
	4	2,718	360	92
	5	1,366	171	37
	18	2,386	237	73
	19	2,292	414	186
	20	4,122	769	133
	21	4,144	556	167
	22	1,986	193	63
	26	2,538	205	94
	27	3,966	1,131	148
Integrated*	2	1,312	562	27
	6	2,004	1,074	94
	7	1,156	1,099	44
	8	1,385	1,535	34
	17	2,155	724	61
	25	2,133	1,891	84
	28	2,689	841	58
South side	9	1,546	1,319	18
	10	1,980	1,382	20
	11	2,188	1,548	17
	12	3,073	2,701	19
	13	3,119	2,148	26
	14	3,079	2,087	19
	15	2,352	1,651	28
	16	3,250	2,646	31
	23	3,212	2,676	30
	24	2,648	2,251	21

*All integrated wards except the second are in the central corridor. The second is north. After redistricting a year later, the twenty-fifth ward was relocated in south St. Louis.

SOURCE: *St. Louis Post-Dispatch*, March 4, 1981.

Mayor Vince Schoemehl promised to reopen Homer G. Phillips Hospital during his 1981 campaign, but in the end could not because of the cost. St. Louis Post-Dispatch, 1936.

someone who helped bring Clay and Schoemehl together, became the city assessor. Schoemehl also named Larry Williams, a Clay ally, to fill the vacant office of treasurer. Appointing political allies or their friends to significant positions is an old St. Louis custom (and is certainly not unfamiliar in other localities). In similar fashion, Schoemehl also named Joe Roddy's nephew as city counselor.

Schoemehl, however, could not deliver on his promise to reopen Phillips. He believed that his predecessor, James Conway, was correct in consolidating city health care delivery at one acute-care facility. However, Schoemehl repeatedly said that Conway chose the wrong facility to close. Seven weeks before the 1981 primary election, Schoemehl told the *Post-Dispatch* "that he favors reopening Phillips…but only if City Hospital, on the Near South Side, is closed at the same time."[15] He also said that he would support an initiative on the April ballot that would amend the city charter to restore Phillips as an acute-care hospital. On the night of his March primary victory, Schoemehl crystallized his sentiments about the public hospitals. He promised "to reopen the Homer G. Phillips Center as a full-service hospital within nine months if he is elected mayor April 7."[16]

TABLE 9-2

Ward Vote on the Bond Issue to Reopen Homer G. Phillips Hospital
August 2, 1982

	Ward	Yes	No
North side	1	2,367	719
	3	2,054	655
	4	2,851	597
	5	1,796	490
	18	2,819	419
	19	1,857	571
	20	3,292	842
	21	3,216	875
	22	1,829	590
	26	2,385	484
	27	2,223	1,171
Integrated	2 (north)	1,441	1,461
	6	1,967	986
	7	1,279	1,254
	8	1,518	2,018
	17	2,039	1,286
	28	2,742	1,921
South side	9	1,140	1,744
	10	1,637	1,888
	11	1,217	2,130
	12	1,976	4,116
	13	1,563	2,996
	14	1,890	3,223
	15	1,587	2,515
	16	2,079	4,621
	23	2,111	3,730
	24	1,706	2,822
	25*	1,541	2,504

*The twenty-fifth ward moved to the south side after the 1982 redistricting.

SOURCE: *St. Louis Post-Dispatch*, August 2, 1982.

Only a few days later, a letter from the Missouri Health Planning and Development Agency to Mayor Conway was released by Conway's office. According to the *Post*, Mayor Conway had received the letter in February.[17] The state agency said that a newly reopened Phillips would have to meet contemporary accreditation standards. Previously, Phillips had been "grandfathered." As an older hospital, it abided by less-stringent standards. However, having been completely shuttered by Mayor Conway, it could be grandfathered no longer. Compliance with contemporary codes would require at least $30 million of additional expenditures, expenditures on which the Schoemehl team had not counted. Because the letter from the Missouri agency had been received in February, it is somewhat surprising that Conway made no mention of it during the campaign. To this day, Schoemehl and those close to him maintain that they were unaware of the costly accreditation requirements.

Some of Schoemehl's critics saw him as a cynical operator, alleging that he knew of all the difficulties involved in reopening the north-side public hospital. To them, the idea of reopening Phillips was just a Schoemehl reelection gimmick. The Schoemehl side denied that charge and noted that, as mayor, Schoemehl tried for several years to find a way to reopen Phillips. The initiative petition to amend the city charter by designating Phillips as the city's public hospital failed to reach the 60 percent majority the law required, falling 4 percentage points shy, in April 1981.

Mayor Schoemehl later proposed a $60 million bond issue and charter amendment to allow Phillips to be reopened while City Hospital would close. South-side politicians were skeptical of this move: Red Villa, alderman of the eleventh ward, said "it would have a tough time catching on in south St. Louis."[18] When Schoemehl formally unveiled the plan, several black aldermen—including the one representing the Ville area, where Phillips is located—were conspicuously absent. For some, the seeds of doubt already had taken root.

Fifty-three percent of those voting in November 1982 favored the bond issue. Under Missouri law, adoption of the bond issue required a minimum 66 $\frac{2}{3}$ percent favorable vote. Table 9-2 shows that the charter amendment lost in white south St. Louis, but not by a landslide. Opposition was strongest in the southernmost wards, such as the twelfth and sixteenth, which were traditionally not hospitable to any measure that would raise the property tax. Some opposition probably was linked to a disinclination to support a facility to be used primarily by low-income African Americans. There was also opposition in predominantly black north side wards. Certain community leaders there had campaigned for "no" votes because they wanted the city to maintain two public hospitals, both Phillips and City No. 1.

The November 1982 defeats of the bond issue and charter amendment spelled the death knell for efforts to reopen Phillips. Schoemehl admitted, "My mistake was promising to reopen Homer Phillips Hospital last year without looking closely at the issue. When I first made the promise to reopen Phillips, you will recall, it was before the state revealed the hospital's license had been revoked. Throughout the primary, it was believed that opening Phillips was an administrative decision."[19] However, many already doubted him.

Some of those involved in the fight for the hospital, such as third-ward alderman Freeman Bosley, Sr., and Walle Amusa, did not accept the mayor's words. Alderman Bosley remarked that "His campaign promised a 'proud St. Louis,' but quite to the contrary, his Diamond Jim antics and Make-A-Deal Vince maneuvers have shrouded the office with suspicion and distrust."[20] The Post noted that "Amusa said his group [The Campaign for Human Dignity] was not surprised that Schoemehl was abandoning the Phillips issue. 'We stated a long time ago that the mayor was going to do that.'"[21]

So Schoemehl's most important campaign promise could not be met. In a city with considerable racial distrust, this failure grew in significance as time passed. For some, it was all a political trick. However, even certain African Americans who felt Schoemehl was sincere could not understand how he could renege on a promise to the African American community. The memory of Kiel's bond issue, which was supposed to fund a black hospital in the 1920s but did not, contributed to the sentiments about the failure to reopen Phillips. Eventually, the issue of reopening Phillips would cost Schoemehl support from many black voters and even from some south siders.

John Mueller's early study of presidential popularity made two points relevant to Schoemehl's political fortunes in St. Louis. Mueller noted that popularity with the electorate affects a chief executive's ability to govern. He also found that popularity invariably deteriorates over time because the executive takes actions that aggravate a number of different groups. A "coalition of minorities" forms as the number of displeased groups multiplies.[22] Subsequent scholars have demonstrated that certain discrete factors relating to the economy or the keeping of the peace are more significant determinants of presidential popularity.[23] Nonetheless, the idea of a coalition of minorities is pertinent to understanding Schoemehl's popularity. Schoemehl was reelected twice despite such a growing coalition. However, eventually his base crumbled, and issues such as the public hospitals, portrayed within the racial and political framework of St. Louis, took their toll.

In 1981, Schoemehl also had used the issue of a possible decline in the size of the police force against Mayor Conway. He ran television advertisements showing police cars leaving the city. Schoemehl also disagreed with Conway's attempts to increase the city's ability to control the police force, a state entity since 1861.[24] After he became mayor, Schoemehl learned firsthand that revenue constraints clearly affected funding for the police and that he, as mayor, could not control that agency's budget or its salaries, which the state legislature set. Schoemehl used the Hancock Amendment, enacted in 1983 and designed to limit taxes and expenditures in Missouri, to generate some level of fiscal control. Since the salaries of firefighters were linked directly to police pay, a lion's share of the city budget actually was set in Jefferson City. The mayor also had no control over the various line items in the police budget. Frustrated, Schoemehl and supporters visited Jefferson City and subpoenaed all the legislators. This blatant gesture brought neither the mayor nor the city enduring popularity in the state capital or in the hearts and minds of members of the St. Louis Police Officers Association, the largest organized group of police officers. (This group of officers is white; black police officers are members of a separate union.) Later, Schoemehl further increased police ire when, during a dispute over police pensions, he characterized retired officers as "greedy bastards." Again, campaign promises could not stand the test of governance. Another group that once fully supported Schoemehl crossed over to the other side.

Who's with Whom and Why

A city Democratic committee veteran noted that Vince Schoemehl was the first mayor in a long time to be involved with central committee activities. Dickmann certainly had meddled in various committee races, and his close ally and political partner, Bob Hannegan, had chaired the committee for most of Dickmann's mayoralty. During the period after Dickmann, when Republicans held the mayor's office for eight years, Jack Dwyer established strong control over the committee. He served as local party chairman for more than two decades. During his reign, he managed to collect and disperse campaign funds, frequently received from banks, which contributed to his authority. He also had a knack for bringing warring factions together in time for the general election. No successor could ever equal his ability. Doc Lawler of the second ward (and the Fitters) followed Dwyer. Lawler exerted influence over the drawing of First Congressional District boundaries to allow the election of an African American. He also played a significant role in the selection of Joe Roddy and Benny Goins for county offices. But he did not have the reach or general respect given to Dwyer, nor did he have Dwyer's longevity in the office.

Paul Berra was chair of the city Democratic committee in 1981 as well as committeeman of the twenty-fourth ward. Berra had to relinquish both positions when he was elected comptroller that year. Politicking for his successor as party chair began even before the April general election. Schoemehl's involvement in the process was intimated in the press.[25] Two committeemen sought the chairmanship. One was Schoemehl's close ally, Joe Roddy, an elected official since 1953. In 1981, he was clerk of the circuit court and committeeman of the seventeenth ward. Heading the city's largest patronage office, he had been no friend of Conway's because of previous turf battles. He supported Schoemehl's mayoral venture early and enthusiastically. The two men formed a deep bond, mutually beneficial of course, that still exists today.

The other candidate for the party chairmanship was Francis R. Slay. Running independently of the ward organization, he had been elected Democratic committeeman of the twenty-third ward in 1964. In previous decades, relatives of his had been elected to office from the seventh ward. Slay always had been a careful practitioner of coalition politics. He beat the odds when he successfully challenged incumbent Anthony Denny in 1970 to become recorder of deeds. The press questioned Denny's performance in office, but he still enjoyed organizational support from Joe Roddy, among others. Slay previously had served a couple of terms as state representative. Well liked, Slay operated a popular restaurant with his brother in south St. Louis that served as a gathering place for many city politicians. One officeholder noted that Slay had an ability to pick winners, even though he could not always deliver his ward for them. Like many organization people, Slay had supported Conway for reelection.

The battle for the party chairmanship in 1981 had spillover effects in later contests. Aided by the new mayor's influence, Roddy bested Slay by a margin of only two in a public vote. Bill

Clay joined Schoemehl in supporting Roddy. This contest left bitter feelings. Schoemehl had swayed a few votes with his appeals on behalf of Roddy; the new mayor's energy and his upbeat personality aided his cause as well as his position. One old-timer felt that committee people, however, often voted with Schoemehl because they liked him, not because of what they might get in return. Slay felt that several people gave their votes to Roddy although they had previously pledged their support to him. In his concession speech Slay said, "I want to thank all of you who voted for me and all who voted for Joe and stayed with Joe. I'll never forget who stayed with me."[26]

In the following year, a spirited race for circuit clerk developed. In the August Democratic primary, Joe Roddy, the incumbent, faced challenges from Tom Connelly, a close associate of Mayor Conway, and from Freeman Bosley, Jr. The younger Bosley was a recent graduate of Saint Louis University law school. In addition, the presence of a ringer on the ballot, Clara Jo Roddy, complicated the field. Ms. Roddy was an unknown whose presence clearly was designed to draw votes from the incumbent, Joe Roddy. St. Louis, with its machine practices, has had a long tradition of candidates filing for the sole purpose of drawing votes from a front-runner. Sometimes, it was accomplished by running someone with the same name. In other instances, a second or third white or black candidate would be on the ballot to offset the strength of racial voting.

No one has ever been certain who put Clara Jo Roddy in that race for circuit clerk. Many St. Louis politicians believed it was the Bosley campaign. Thirteen years after the fact, a Saint Louis University professor offered another interpretation:

> Bosley's candidacy in the 1982 race for clerk of the circuit court was seen as a stalking horse along with the more obvious spoiler candidate, Clara "Jo" Roddy. The strategy was for Bosley, an African American, to erode Joe Roddy Sr.'s support in predominantly black St. Louis. Of course, Clara "Jo" Roddy was put in the race to confuse voters, serving to drain additional votes away from Joe Roddy and allow Tom Connelly, the other serious white candidate, to win. The strategy backfired, allowing Bosley, who spent relatively little money, to win by less than 1,000 votes because Connelly and Roddy split evenly the vote on the South Side, while Clara "Jo" Roddy; who spent practically nothing, picked up more than 2,000 votes.[27]

Whether the above account is accurate regarding strategy and intent, it nonetheless illustrates the effect of a split white vote and a ringer candidate. The actual vote totals for that circuit clerk's race were:

Bosley	31,121
Joe Roddy	30,175
Connelly	23,227
Clara Jo Roddy	2,345

Congressman Clay had endorsed Roddy, as had most north-side ward organizations. Yet Bosley captured the lion's share of the north-side vote. He had a strong coterie of volunteers, including family, friends, and law-school colleagues, who put in many long hours on his behalf. He also received endorsements from some of the black aldermen, and Bosley's campaign played up the fact that he was an attorney. The candidate himself said, "When you have water problems, you call a plumber. I'm a lawyer, and I want to straighten out the legal problems in the circuit clerk's office."[28] In addition, Bosley's father had been an alderman for five years, and the father's many pronouncements regarding Homer G. Phillips Hospital had created a great deal of name recognition, particularly in the black community.

Francis R. Slay not surprisingly endorsed Connelly in the circuit clerk race, given the fight for chairmanship of the central committee. This enmity has lingered in varying forms to the present day, with the Slay and Roddy factions often on opposing sides.

This race also illustrates the notion that ward organizations in predominantly black areas that endorse a white candidate over a viable black candidate will not carry those wards on Election Day. Using the Goodman (1957) ecological model, Stein and Kohfeld estimated that Bosley received 74 percent of the African American vote in the 1982 race.[29] Primary turnout was high on the north side that year because Congressman Clay had a strong primary challenger in Al Mueller. Clay won easily, but it is likely that his organizational efforts aided Bosley, a candidate he had not endorsed.

The circuit clerk's race heightened tensions among some of the white factions and presented Bill Clay with a potential rival in Bosley. Although Clay supported young Bosley in future races, they never were considered close. Some of the nuances of this contest for circuit clerk may have been lost on the general public; but the outcome influenced future events. St. Louis's fragmented political universe makes it necessary to have alliances and to care about races that seem unimportant in the broader scheme of things. The city's culture continues to stress "who's with whom" and places greater weight on personal relationships than on more substantive matters. That was the case in 1982 and thereafter.

As Roddy's last day as circuit clerk drew near, Mayor Schoemehl named his key supporter clerk and administrator of the municipal courts.[30] The municipal courts handle violations of city ordinances, such as traffic tickets. Roddy had to relinquish his position as seventeenth-ward committeeman to accept the new post, in accordance with city law. He also ended up with a five-thousand-dollar raise. Thanks to the mayor, Roddy remained next door to City Hall and in the heart of St. Louis's political life.

The municipal elections of 1983 provided a reflection of the city's black-white divisions. Nineteenth-ward alderman Michael Roberts, an African American, challenged Thomas Zych, the white incumbent, for the aldermanic presidency. Zych had won the post in 1980 in a special election. He defeated a veteran African American alderman, Eugene "Tink" Bradley, who had stepped into the post by reason of seniority when a vacancy occurred. Zych had ties to a white citizens group in south St. Louis. In this 1983 race, Schoemehl backed Zych, who had endorsed the mayor in 1981. Zych won by just more than one thousand votes. Black alderman JoAnne Wayne also had filed, perhaps as a spoiler. Roberts was a protégé of Jet Banks, who served as nineteenth-ward committeeman. Congressman Clay endorsed Roberts, but some St. Louis politicians wondered about the strength of his commitment. The Roberts campaign emphasized polling and media but did not court north-side organizations, which wanted "walking-around money" to give to workers on Election Day. This contest again illustrates the prevalence of factional divisions throughout St. Louis.

In November of 1982, Alderman Freeman Bosley, Sr., announced that he would challenge Vince Schoemehl for the Democratic nomination for mayor in 1985. The fate of Homer G. Phillips Hospital influenced Bosley's decision. At this time, the *Post-Dispatch* speculated about other potential mayoral candidates for an election more than two years away. The *Post* mentioned such figures as Aldermen Geraldine Osborn and Martie Aboussie as well as Harold Gibbons of the Teamsters Union.[31] When filing finally opened, only Bosley put his name on the ballot.

The mayoral primary took place in March of 1985. Freeman Bosley, Sr., was Schoemehl's main opponent, but also on the ballot was former police chief Eugene Camp, who repeatedly had clashed with Schoemehl. Alderman David Kinealy from the fourteenth ward on the south side also filed. State representative Fred E. Williams then joined the fray. It was widely felt that Williams ran at Schoemehl's behest to draw black votes from Bosley, in the stalking-horse tradition.

Schoemehl scored a landslide win in the Democratic primary. He received 73 percent of the vote, while Bosley had only 22 percent. Bill Clay endorsed Schoemehl and his running mate, the incumbent comptroller Paul Berra. However, Bosley carried eight of the city's eleven predominantly black wards. Schoemehl took everything else, including the eighteenth and twentieth wards on the north side. The eighteenth-ward committeeman, Larry C. Williams, whom Schoemehl had appointed as city treasurer, backed the mayor. In the twentieth ward, Committeeman Leroy Tyus was a close friend of Clay. Luther Boykins, an ally of the mayor's kitchen cabinet adviser, J. Kim Tucci, coordinated the campaign in the twentieth.[32]

Only a few months after this decisive primary victory, the Schoemehl-Clay alliance deteriorated. Ironically, the disposition of the city's remaining public hospital was the precipitating cause. Schoemehl had alluded to the possibility of using private management in public-care facilities before he assumed office. The projected $55 million budget deficit he inherited spurred layoffs, service cutbacks, and thoughts of privatization.[33] Declining revenues and decreases in federal aid, including the termination of general revenue sharing, complicated the fiscal picture. Many cities contemplated cutbacks, layoffs, and contracting out under similar circumstances. Contracting out or privatization can mean a loss of mayoral control and of accountability. In addition, lower wages and fewer benefits frequently generate the cost savings.[34] The municipal goal remains saving money, i.e., efficiency. Even in 1981, Schoemehl said that a private firm "could make the public hospital system more efficient."[35] In fact, City No. 1 was not noted for its excellent physical conditions or quality of care. The main structure was built before 1900, and the entire hospital had no air-conditioning in a city noted for its summer heat and humidity. The hospital came perilously close to losing its accreditation on more than one occasion. In addition, the mayor had difficulty dealing with the Saint Louis University School of Medicine, which supervised treatment at City. The university threatened to withdraw from its agreement with the city and end its services at the hospital.[36]

Two members of Civic Progress, Lee Liberman, head of Laclede Gas Company, and Robert Hyland, head of KMOX Radio, advised Schoemehl on the hospital question beginning in his first term. Originally, Liberman and Hyland scouted locations on the north side, where a new public hospital could be built. Without success, they turned to the possibility of a privatized, joint venture with St. Louis County at an existing facility. St. Louis County also wanted to remove itself from direct patient service and close its own public hospital. A possible site was found in the city on Delmar Boulevard, a major north-south dividing line. The premises belonged to Charter Hospital, formerly St. Luke's. In secrecy, just before the Fourth of July, City Hospital's patients were transported to the new Regional Hospital, and City No. 1 closed its doors for good. A number of city leaders opposed this change. In addition, initial miscues that occurred at the merged facility received considerable play in the press.

Schoemehl had acted without aldermanic authorization. In September, he belatedly brought a plan to the board for endorsement. Alderman Wayman Smith of the twenty-sixth ward (Clay's home ward) sponsored the bill. While the plan was being considered by the Ways and Means Committee at the board of aldermen, Bill Clay announced his objections to the way it was formulated and specified the changes needed for him to give his approval. Some insiders believe that Clay had not been consulted about the move to Regional nor about the proposed private management contemplated there. If true, this would have been a blow to his status as St. Louis's dominant African American politician. Clay's administrative assistant in his St. Louis office, Pearlie Evans, outlined the congressman's objectives:

- That local black physicians and the local affiliates of the American Medical Association have a role in appointing board members for the joint city-county hospital
- That mayoral appointees to the hospital board be confirmed by the board of aldermen
- That the government own the hospital instead of a nonprofit corporation.[37]

Schoemehl chose to travel to Washington, D.C., to meet with Clay. The congressman expressed apprehension concerning the fate of the black-owned Central Medical Center and requested a subsidy for that facility.[38] Clay said that Central Medical Center "could face financial ruin if the Regional plan weren't changed."[39] Clay also was concerned about the employees from City Hospital who had lost their jobs when their facility closed.[40]

Schoemehl and Clay reached a tentative agreement during the mayor's visit to Washington. However, problems remained. Clay told the *Post-Dispatch* that if an agreement was not reached over the ownership of the hospital, he would prepare "a petition drive to force a citywide referendum on the plan if it is approved in its current form by the Board of Aldermen."[41] Schoemehl had acquiesced to Clay's demand for aldermanic approval of nominees to the hospital board and also to a role for black physicians.

The Regional hospital plan received a 19-9 endorsement on its initial aldermanic vote. (A bill is passed on third reading; a final vote is required the following week.) Clay, however, continued with his plans for the petition drive. His assistant, Pearlie Evans, said that Schoemehl's plan to "use a private corporation to run the hospital amounted to 'a corporate takeover' of public health care that black leaders cannot accept."[42] Four black aldermen, including Wayman Smith from Clay's own ward, supported Schoemehl's plan in the initial vote. The opposition included Geraldine Osborn, Schoemehl's comrade in arms in earlier times.

Although the hospital plan was adopted, major fissures had manifested themselves, especially in the relationship between Schoemehl and Clay. The breach was not necessarily irreparable, but it was deep. A privatized public hospital was a threat to Clay's core constituencies. Despite enacting a rather strict civil service system in 1941, St. Louis still had municipal jobs that were politicized to a certain degree. Job applicants had to pass examinations that determined their place on the eligibility list. However, the mayor, an alderman, or other highly placed people provided letters of support for their favorites among the top scorers. In short, a qualified candidate with an influential friend got the job. (Sometimes political supporters of a particular individual could find ingenious ways to adjust the list so that the rule of three would not exclude their candidate.) St. Louis's civil service has operated with a modified version of traditional quid pro quo relationships, but every municipal opening has not always been filled with a touch of favoritism.

Congressman Clay and other African American officials have considered jobs a key focus of their constituent service. It is therefore not surprising that they would look askance at any decline in city jobs, already reduced by layoffs and the closure of Phillips. Further, the cutbacks to the municipal work force in the 1980s disproportionately affected African Americans. As Table 9-3 shows, the number of black employees fell, as did their percentage of the total city work force.

TABLE 9-3

Declines in the St. Louis Municipal Work Force
and in African American Representation, 1979–1990

Category in African American Staff	% Increase/Decrease in African American Staff	% Increase/Decrease in Staff Size
Financial	-25.6%	+13.2%
Streets	-33.1%	-3.2%
Public Welfare	-76.9%	+0.2%
Fire	-24.8%	+13.5%
Natural Resources	-57.7%	-7.9%
Hospitals	-94.7%	-35.3%
Health	-63.9%	+1.2%
Housing	-22.2%	-10.6%
Community Development	-63.5%	-6.5%
Corrections	-4.2%	+11.6%
Utilities	-13.3%	+1.7%
Sanitation	-62.6%	-12.7%
OVERALL WORK FORCE	-57.6%	-11.5%

SOURCE: Lana Stein, "Privatization, Work-Force Cutbacks, and African American Municipal Employment," *American Review of Public Administration* 24 (June, 1994): 181–191.

In 1985, Schoemehl and Clay were the city's most powerful politicians. A breach in their alliance could lead to future political battles involving other factions. In a move reminiscent of Dickmann's overreaching in the 1940 governor's race, in 1986 Schoemehl stood behind multiple challenges to candidates allied to Clay as well as to others not clearly in his own camp. Had he been successful he might have had a genuine machine. But, just like Dickmann, his ambition was thwarted. Schoemehl had put together two decisive mayoral victories, but he could not transfer that support to the candidates he backed for the legislature and county offices. Instead, his actions were seen as a huge power play, and opponents could be found on both sides of the city.

Someone close to those 1986 events related that Schoemehl really wanted to have an ally as state senator, which led him to ask Judy Raker to run against the incumbent, John Bass. Bass was a close friend of Clay's and had served as comptroller from 1973 to 1977.

However, the mayor and his advisers, including restaurateur J. Kim Tucci (Schoemehl's high school coach), did not stop with the state senate race. They chose to challenge a number of other incumbents as well.

Given Schoemehl's close relationship with Joe Roddy, it is not surprising that a candidate was found to run against Freeman Bosley, Jr., the man who defeated Roddy for circuit clerk. In addition, Bosley's father had just run against Schoemehl. Louis Hamilton, a public-relations consultant and former mayoral aide, took on Bosley, and both sides put others in the race as stalking-horses. County officeholder Ronald Leggett, collector of revenue, was a member of the twenty-third-ward organization, whose committeeman was Francis R. Slay. Leggett's allegiances might have been a reason why the Schoemehl camp chose to challenge him as well. Another reason may have been the state law that allows the collector of revenue to pay his expenses from the money his office collects and then to turn the remainder over to the city. Although neither Leggett nor his predecessor ever were accused of any wrongdoing with their office's receipts, having an ally as collector could increase mayoral fiscal control. Schoemehl's aide Jack Keane filed against Leggett.

Perhaps the coup de grâce in these primary challenges was the decision to run city administrator Chester Hines, Jr., against Clay's son and namesake, state representative William Lacy Clay, Jr. Other races were less directly involved in the mayor's quest for greater control. Recorder of Deeds Sharon Carpenter, committeewoman of the twenty-third ward, faced Velmarie King, a modest challenge. To further complicate the scenario, Bosley ally Paula Carter challenged state representative Fred Williams, a friend of Schoemehl. (Clay endorsed Carter.) License Collector Billie Boykins faced Frank Kilcullen, whom she had defeated in 1982. Schoemehl claimed that he supported Boykins, but his opponents questioned his commitment.

Schoemehl's power play drew a quick response. Central committee chair, state representative Tony Ribaudo of the twenty-fourth ward (which included the Hill), allied with Clay to back the biracial slate of incumbents challenged by the mayor. Comptroller Paul Berra, Francis R. Slay, and many other south-side politicians joined to back the incumbents' campaign.

Vince Schoemehl had been remarkably successful in achieving his legislative goals. He used perquisites and personality to sway aldermen, bureaucrats, and business leaders. In a position of little formal power, he managed to accumulate a considerable amount. However, this

TABLE 9-4

Selected Results from the August 1986 Democratic Primary

State Senator	John Bass (I)	57%
	Judy Raker	41%
	Others	2%
Collector of Revenue	Ronald Leggett (I)	57%
	Jack Keane	17%
	Others	26%
State Representative	William Lacy Clay, Jr. (I)	63%
	Chester Hines	37%
Clerk of the Circuit Court	Freeman Bosley, Jr. (I)	61%
	Louis Hamilton	29%
	Others	10%

1986 electoral endeavor aroused a great deal of fear and anger among many outside his circle. Had he been successful, he would have achieved a control none of his predecessors had had. But the audacious plan failed. Every incumbent backed by Clay and Ribaudo and company secured reelection easily. None of these contests was even close, as Table 9-4 shows. The agreement among some white and African American officeholders and ward organizations to support *all* incumbents succeeded handily. For example, Bosley secured 35 percent of the white vote citywide in his reelection as circuit clerk.[43] In addition, Paula Carter defeated Fred Williams.

Congressman Clay portrayed the contest in racial terms. The fight "is between Schoemehl and the black community," Clay said. "If Schoemehl is successful in defeating black incumbents this year, don't think he won't come after others, including the congressman."[44] The 1986 contest represented a struggle for power. By casting it in racial terms, Clay made it resonate for his core constituency and, in turn, made it easier for his organization to draw voters to the polls.

Perhaps Schoemehl might have been more successful had he targeted just one race. However, it appears that that advice was not seriously proffered. Tucci, part owner of the Pasta House restaurant chain, had been involved in the decision making. There is no consensus about the extent of his influence, but his own quotations in the *Post-Dispatch* portray his role as key. "Tucci last week confirmed that it was he, not Schoemehl, who insisted on having the mayor's camp oppose Bosley with a strong candidate. This occurred during a 'summit' meeting with Clay in the mayor's office last fall. 'This was not the mayor's decision; it was my decision,' Tucci said of the Hamilton challenge against Bosley."[45]

The contest for president of the board of aldermen in 1987 presents another portrait of factional division and the racial chasm. Schoemehl endorsed Tom Villa for the position. Villa had been a state representative for a number of years and had served as deputy leader of the Missouri House. He gave up his seat when he ran unsuccessfully for state treasurer in 1984. After Villa's defeat, Schoemehl made him director of public safety. Villa was the son of longtime eleventh-ward alderman Red Villa. The incumbent, aldermanic president Thomas Zych, chose not to run again after facing charges related to the initial award of a cable-television franchise. Former north-side alderman Michael Roberts tried for the post a second time, and white alderman Geraldine Osborn also filed.

With two well-known white candidates, Roberts should have had a good shot at winning citywide office. As it turned out, he lost by no less than sixty votes. (There was a court-supervised recount that came to that conclusion.) Two factors probably contributed to his loss: Roberts did not have Clay's endorsement this time around, and he again failed to court the north-side organizations. Further, his campaign delivered literature in the central corridor questioning Osborn's commitment to equal opportunity. This maneuver backfired against Roberts—only 1 percent of white voters cast a ballot for him. Just 2 percent of black voters chose Villa or Osborn.[46] If there had been greater black turnout, or if Clay had endorsed Roberts, Roberts might have prevailed. Roberts failed to sustain the level of white support he had enjoyed four years earlier.[47] And Osborn failed to seriously dilute Villa's strength on the south side.

The following year, 1988, presented no great electoral challenges for either Schoemehl, Clay, or other faction leaders. Yet Schoemehl's coalition of minorities grew again, in part as a reaction to the 1986 debacle. J. Kim Tucci and his business partners had been strong supporters of Schoemehl for years. Tucci, in fact, became committeeman of the mayor's home ward, the twenty-eighth, in 1983. He and the other "Pasta House boys," as he and his fellow restaurateurs were labeled, raised a great deal of money for

Schoemehl's programs and campaigns, as well as the coffers of those the mayor supported. In the aftermath of the 1986 primary, the friendships seemingly continued, but Schoemehl turned less to those who had supported entering candidates against the incumbents in the 1986 contests. Tucci won reelection as ward committeeman in August 1988. However, in November of that year, a substantial breach between Schoemehl and Tucci became apparent. Tucci and two of his colleagues resigned their positions with St. Louis's booster organization, the St. Louis Ambassadors, as well as the city posts they held (on boards and commissions). In addition, Tucci resigned as twenty-eighth-ward committeeman. In the *Post-Dispatch*, Tucci declared, "I'm just tired and burned out. I will continue to support Vince. I'm just temporarily out of politics."[48]

In hindsight, Tucci's words were misleading. He had ended his close relationship with the mayor. The precipitating incident, according to several sources, was a bill backed by the mayor and introduced at the board of aldermen by his ally, Daniel J. McGuire, alderman of the twenty-eighth ward. This bill would have required fast-food restaurants and similar businesses open late at night to have a permit to serve customers after 10 P.M. The permit could be removed if too many complaints arose. The bill immediately stirred up fervent protests, most notably from Ted Drewes, purveyor of St. Louis's world-renowned frozen custard. Tucci had been out of the country when the bill was introduced, and he apparently felt he should have been consulted about a bill that affected the restaurant industry. The measure itself died a quick death at the board of aldermen, but the coalition of minorities, or enemies, had grown a bit more.

Schoemehl managed to recoup his somewhat battered political fortunes prior to his reelection to a third term. Deal making was key, and his partner again turned out to be Bill Clay. In what quickly came to be known as the "job swap," Paul Berra resigned as comptroller. Schoemehl then appointed an African American, city assessor (and former alderman) Virvus Jones, to that post. He then named Berra to fill Jones's shoes at the assessor's office. Berra had come under fire because of certain pension fund investments and did not wish to run again. According to a source close to the deal making, Clay personally selected Jones to serve as comptroller. In turn, the congressman endorsed Schoemehl for reelection. The possibility that Sharon Carpenter, recorder of deeds, would seek the mayor's office triggered the job swap. She already had elicited north- and south-side support, but the swap ended talk of her candidacy.

As the campaign began, allegations appeared in the press that Jones had not been entirely truthful on some of his campaign literature. He claimed to have a bachelor's degree from Antioch College but had not actually attended the Ohio school. Nor did he have a bachelor's degree, although he had accumulated more than one hundred hours of credit at several colleges. His literature also said he had been wounded and decorated while serving in Vietnam. This was never verified. Further questions were raised about a government loan he had received to redevelop property on Cabanne Street, namely whether any renovation actually had occurred. Despite all these accusations, Jones's campaign did not suffer. The questions about his credibility only resonated in areas of the city where he had the least support. They did not affect the African American vote, and the mayor continued to give him strong support.

In the March Democratic primary, Schoemehl faced Michael Roberts, who had twice run unsuccessfully for the aldermanic presidency. Alderman Steve Conway, son of the former mayor, ran against Jones. A third candidate for comptroller also filed. Peter Percich, son of Comptroller Raymond Percich, who had feuded with Conway's father, appeared to have entered the race as a stalking-horse, drawing white votes from Conway. Schoemehl and Jones clearly ran as a slate. The job swap had precluded other challenges to the mayor, and south-side officials and voters unhappy with Schoemehl had nowhere to turn.

When the primary votes were counted, the mayor had an easy victory, though not on the scale of the 1985 tally. Inclement weather reduced turnout, and Schoemehl's margin decreased in every ward, most notably on the predominantly black north side. (See Table 9-5.) Jones bested his two opponents in the divide-and-conquer manner that had put John Bass in the comptroller's seat sixteen years before. (See Table 9-6.) The 1989 contests are interesting also in terms of cross-racial voting. In the mayor's race, Schoemehl won 31 percent of the black vote citywide, while Jones captured 11 percent of the white vote citywide. Thirty-two percent of the white voters in the integrated central corridor voted for Jones.[49]

Polarization has occurred in a number of St. Louis contests, such as the aldermanic presidency race in 1987. However, cross-racial voting also has taken place, depending on the circumstances of the individual elections. The 1986 races show this, as do these 1989 contests. Schoemehl's support helped Jones with white voters, particularly in the central corridor. Clay's support helped Schoemehl among black voters, as did his selection of Jones as comptroller.

TABLE 9-5

Percentage of Vote for Vincent C. Schoemehl, Jr., in 1985 and 1989 Democratic Mayoral Primaries

	Ward	1985 Percentage	1989 Percentage
North side	1	44.5%	31.3%
	3	32.6%	31.0%
	4	47.6%	31.1%
	5	49.4%	42.4%
	18	55.4%	31.8%
	19	44.4%	34.6%
	20	50.6%	32.9%
	21	46.4%	37.0%
	22	38.3%	32.9%
	26	48.7%	37.9%
	27	47.5%	27.0%
Integrated	2 (north)	67.3%	54.9%
	6 (corridor)	64.9%	57.3%
	7 (corridor)	73.7%	65.6%
	8 (corridor)	82.6%	71.4%
	17 (corridor)	78.1%	72.3%
	28 (corridor)	79.6%	69.2%
South side	9	90.9%	80.5%
	10	91.3%	82.0%
	11	91.3%	85.2%
	12	90.2%	84.5%
	13	89.7%	83.7%
	14	86.0%	85.6%
	15	91.4%	82.6%
	16	91.3%	85.2%
	23	92.8%	84.2%
	24	93.0%	86.8%
	25	91.6%	82.6%
CITYWIDE		69.7%	60.1%

SOURCE: Data supplied by the St. Louis Board of Election Commissioners.

Table 9-6

Election Results for Comptroller
in 1989 Democratic Primary

	Ward	Jones	Conway	Percich
North side	1	1,765	103	70
	2	1,114	468	279
	3	1,509	120	92
	4	1,686	106	63
	5	1,032	132	80
	18	2,072	114	72
	19	1,499	105	64
	20	2,404	180	100
	21	2,551	134	83
	22	1,480	90	91
	26	1,476	118	67
	27	1,941	187	161
Integrated	2 (north)	1,114	468	279
	6 (corridor)	1,146	426	236
	7 (corridor)	867	550	312
	8 (corridor)	646	1,018	286
	17 (corridor)	1,343	626	447
	28 (corridor)	1,458	1,230	237
South side	9	259	735	332
	10	127	615	588
	11	153	774	692
	12	203	1,675	1,251
	13	163	1,138	907
	14	218	1,130	871
	15	325	1,315	592
	16	230	1,897	1,332
	23	251	1,607	1,208
	24	248	1,452	697
	25	154	878	797
TOTALS		29,434	19,391	12,286

Truces may be temporary in city politics. Most black officials, including Freeman Bosley, Jr., endorsed Schoemehl in 1989 because of the job swap. Yet just two months after that Democratic primary, many of these same officials derided the mayor and accused him of playing racial politics. State auditor Margaret Kelly, a Republican, examined the eight county offices. On March 24, 1989, she released a highly critical audit of the office of license collector, headed by Billie Boykins, an African American female. "Kelly estimated that Boykins had failed to collect as much as $9 million in business-license taxes. She called the office the worst she had ever audited."[50] St. Louis circuit attorney George Peach petitioned the Missouri Supreme Court to remove Boykins from office.

At the April 1989 general election, voters narrowly defeated a sales-tax increase. Some observers felt that votes had been lost on the south side because of accounts of the scathing audit. Mayor Schoemehl and president of the board of aldermen Thomas A. Villa decided to transfer duties from Boykins's office to that of the comptroller. The comptroller in turn would assign them to the collector of revenue's office. This measure passed the board of aldermen in June in a vote largely along racial lines. The aldermanic chambers were packed with committeemen and committeewomen from north-side wards. At this juncture, north-side alderman Kenneth Jones accused Schoemehl "of attacking the only African American woman officeholder in the city." He added, "This is consistent with the racist politics that have long existed in the city of St. Louis."[51] To some it was a racial attack; to others it was an attack on patronage. South-side alderman Geraldine Osborn defended the county patronage offices. "She accused Schoemehl of trying to destroy the eight patronage offices to increase his own power."[52]

The Missouri Supreme Court later reversed the city's attempt to strip the license collector's office of its duties, because state law set most of the office's functions. The city could not abrogate the powers of the office. The Court, however, in separate action, did remove Boykins from office. The questions of power and race once again deepened existing fissures in the St. Louis political community. Schoemehl's decisive move following the disclosure of the devastating audit of the license collector's office and the tax-increase defeat cost him further political capital.

By September of that same year, 1989, it became clear that the harmony of the primary campaign had ended. Virvus Jones moved to assert his independence as comptroller and to slow or stymie some of Schoemehl's projects. Most notably, Jones moved to increase minority participation in the building of the new convention-center addition and stadium. He also delayed approval of a variety of expenditures. Schoemehl responded strongly to Jones's independent stances and blamed the comptroller's top aide, Z. Dwight Billingsley, for the friction. He even referred to Billingsley as Rasputin. Jones succeeded in increasing the participation of minority contractors on city projects, but his formerly amiable relationship with Schoemehl (Schoemehl originally had appointed him city assessor after Jones lost races for sheriff and for his aldermanic seat) had fallen apart. One former city official felt that Schoemehl failed to treat Jones as an equal partner on the board of estimate and apportionment, thus arousing his ire. In any case, Jones remained close to the Clay camp. The relative equanimity at estimate and apportionment Schoemehl had enjoyed since 1981 had ended. Nonetheless, Schoemehl and aldermanic president Tom Villa remained frequently in agreement.

St. Louis is a city where power is not centered in the mayor's office. Instead, the mayor continually has to forge and reinforce alliances with representatives of other factions. The bolder one's strokes, the more likely it is that opposition will arise. St. Louis's other officeholders generally have continued to guard their own perquisites. In fact, the city's politicians often conspire among themselves to achieve greater influence or ensure continued electoral success. Mayors in most major cities have to work at maintaining the necessary council majorities to enact legislation they support. In St. Louis, the network of officeholders includes a larger group of people: committeemen and committeewomen, those holding the county offices, and state representatives and senators. The size of the group mandates extra investments of energy and more inducements for possible allies. Potential rivals can emerge from more spots. And race further clouds the scenario; the case easily can be made that blacks have not had the political or governmental opportunities their numbers in the population would indicate. But in St. Louis, the quest for personal rewards—jobs and contracts for friends—can be cloaked in terms of racial justice.

In 1990, Vince Schoemehl decided to run for governor. In this quest, he had a strong coterie of friends, considerable support from organized labor, and a sizable war chest. His primary opponent in 1992 was Missouri's lieutenant governor, Mel Carnahan, who hailed from rural Rolla. Schoemehl waged a strenuous campaign, crisscrossing the state on a regular basis in a tiny plane. He had

County executive H. Milford, state senator Jet Banks, Mayor Schoemehl, and Comptroller Virvus Jones at a 1990 meeting about the expansion of the Cervantes Convention Center. Jones and Schoemehl's relationship soured when, among other things, Jones tried to increase minority participation in the project. Photograph by Karen Elshout Whitely, *St. Louis Post-Dispatch*, 1990.

some out-state support, especially from Bob Griffin, the speaker of the Missouri General Assembly. However, he faced long odds in his quest for the governorship. Rural Missouri still distrusted St. Louis. Few from the Gateway City ever had become governor.

Critical television advertisements paid for by the Carnahan campaign, particularly one featuring retired St. Louis police officers, hurt Schoemehl's chances considerably. He had been close to Carnahan in the polls until that particular advertisement appeared. Carnahan ended up trouncing Schoemehl; St. Louis's mayor received only 37 percent of the statewide vote. The most difficult blow of all was that Schoemehl failed to carry the city of St. Louis and won his own twenty-eighth ward by just nineteen votes. Schoemehl's coalition of minorities, or enemies, nurtured by the city's factional propensity, came out in force against him. J. Kim Tucci hosted fundraisers for Carnahan, and Bill Clay, Virvus Jones, Freeman Bosley, Jr., and most other black officials were for Carnahan as well. The St. Louis Police Officers' Association also assisted their retired brethren in helping to defeat Schoemehl.

Schoemehl was a leader. He pushed many projects from the mayor's office with considerable zeal. He also used jobs and contracts to increase his support but was in many ways the city's first modern politician. He used television, and he raised a gigantic war chest, unheard of before in St. Louis. The *Post-Dispatch* ran a weeklong series in 1986 about his fundraising practices; the newspaper linked a number of his contributions to the awarding of no-bid personal-service contracts.[53] Although Schoemehl knew how the ward organizations operated and he worked them hard, he also reached beyond them to the general public and the business community.

Schoemehl tried to attack St. Louis's decay and abandonment, typical of many midwestern industrial towns. Some of his projects had positive effects that remain in place to this day, and at least in his first two terms there appeared to be momentum. However, strong leaders draw strong opponents, particularly in a fragmented city known for its political infighting. And Schoemehl seemed to enjoy that infighting. As his power grew, his opponents grew in strength, and numbers as well. The sheer number of elected offices in St. Louis makes it difficult for any mayor to assert control for long. The statutory powers of the mayor are not great, and racial tension also makes governance difficult. Power struggles among members of different racial groups are more than just battles over turf; the legacy of superiority and inferiority takes quarrels to a different level.

For a while, Schoemehl exerted greater influence than any mayor since Bernard Dickmann. But the centrifugal tendencies within the political structure rendered his influence nearly moot by the time he left office. In reaching out to conquer the disparate forces, he laid the seeds for his own demise. His audacity also became his undoing. Alderman Red Villa once said, "The kid's got guts and gumption."[54] He also had a knack for gathering talent and ideas wherever he could find them. He was optimistic about the city and introduced programs he thought would benefit it. But he also accumulated enemies and was unable to construct the last winning coalition he needed.

Bryan D. Jones noted that there is "a role for political institutions in shaping the incentive and opportunity structure facing political executives."[55] Many have said that Schoemehl governed by force of his personality. His office provided, as noted above, little formal power. Instead of seeking structural change, he, like Dickmann, sought to control more offices. St. Louis's populist streak worked against that, aided and abetted by officials threatened by his actions. Personality probably is the only tool a St. Louis mayor can use to achieve more centralized authority. After Schoemehl, two black mayors faced the city's divisions with mixed success.

William Donald Schaefer had his own highly effective personality and considerable talent, but also a stronger mayor's office working in his favor in Baltimore. This also was the case for Edward Rendell, the popular mayor of Philadelphia in the 1990s. Rendell had to please a number of officials, but he had greater authority to carry out numerous programs. Neither Rendell nor Schaefer had as cohesive a business group as Pittsburgh's Allegheny Conference to work with, but they did have more institutional tools at their disposal.[56]

Chapter 10

The Advent of African American Mayors
1993 and 1997

Vincent Schoemehl's immediate successors were both African American. Both had backgrounds that did not prepare them well for a St. Louis mayoralty, but for very different reasons. The first problem to surmount was getting elected. Because of its eight county offices, St. Louisans elect an unusually large number of officials in citywide contests. With the three members of the board of estimate and apportionment—mayor, comptroller, and president of the board of aldermen—and the county offices, there are eleven at-large contests. Six African Americans had won posts since the late 1960s but no more than three had held office at any one time. Incumbency, including appointment to the office prior to an election, or a divided white field aided African Americans in these citywide contests.[1]

In major U.S. cities with substantial black populations, election of a black mayor often has not been an easy feat. Sonenshein noted that cities such as Seattle, Denver, or Los Angeles, with African American populations of less than 20 percent, managed to build successful biracial coalitions that aided the election of a black mayor.[2] These cities also had sizable Hispanic and/or Asian populations. Notably, their structure of government was a nonpartisan, mayor-council type. On the other hand, Sonenshein maintained that cities in the Northeast and Midwest "with large African American populations, strong competing ethnic communities, remnants of party organizations, and high levels of white racial animosity" presented models of polarization that made election of an African American mayor quite difficult.[3] Campaigns were often contentious. For example, in Chicago, after African American Harold Washington defeated Jane Byrne and Richard M. Daley for the Democratic nomination in 1983, party loyalties gave way to intense racial division. Many white Democratic officials supported Republican Bernard Epton against Washington in the general election. Some of their partisans wore plain white buttons. Race and fear of reform sparked the support for Epton. A Republican campaign slogan—"Epton Before It's Too Late"—played to white fears of a black mayor.[4] The acrimony did not end with Washington's election. He did not have a majority on the city council, and many of his initiatives could not become law. Thus, the infamous "council wars" dominated governance during Washington's first term.

In some cities with a machine-politics heritage, black politicians themselves focused their attention on the tangible benefits they received from white leaders. Their focus on these individual rewards delayed a serious black mayoral challenge. For example, in New York City regular black Democrats (as opposed to reformers) had a strong interest "in contracts and funding to community-based organizations."[5] With white officials controlling the largesse, some black politicians were reluctant to mobilize independently. Mollenkopf noted that existing political arrangements worked against a minority-liberal coalition there. He described a "factional kaleidoscope" produced by a "weakly organized, one-party system."[6] William Nelson, Jr., found that in Cleveland:

> A loose-knit political organization...took on the character and structure of traditional white-led political machines. The most salient attribute of this new organization was the heavy emphasis on the brokering of political influence in the service of the economic interest of a well-entrenched political elite. Black political leaders associated with this organization ceased championing programs of social reform and community redevelopment, but embraced more pragmatic programs that would enhance their access to high levels of material benefits.[7]

Nelson felt that this behavior delayed the election of a second black mayor in Cleveland after Carl Stokes served from 1967 to 1971.

A similar scenario existed in Baltimore. Orr found that "the tradition of patronage and machines can delay black political empowerment.... Machines can hamper the development of strong independent black political leadership and foster internal division within the African American community."[8] Prior to the election of Kurt Schmoke as Baltimore's first African American mayor, that city's white power structure sometimes "designated 'token blacks'" to impede progressive mobilization.[9]

St. Louis resembles these other machine-politics cities in several ways. Although the first African American was elected to an office in

1918 in St. Louis, black political incorporation proceeded slowly. In the 1930s, Jordan Chambers began to deliver African American votes in exchange for jobs, but he was not the equal of powerful white committeemen. Blacks did not control the committee posts in many majority-black wards until the 1960s. The combination of paternalism and patronage dominated black-ward politics in St. Louis, much as it did in Chicago when William Dawson held sway over black wards. Significant racial division persisted in St. Louis into the 1990s. Even though some whites had voted for black candidates, this cross-racial voting had not yet occurred in contests for the city's highest office.

When the transfer of mayoral power from black to white finally took place in St. Louis in 1993, there was little of the overt rancor that marked Harold Washington's election in Chicago. Many of its residents call St. Louis a small town. Everyone somehow appears to know everyone else, particularly in politics. Most formal interaction is marked by civility. Perhaps that explains the relatively quiet transfer of power from white to black that took place in St. Louis. At least part of white St. Louis's mild reaction to its first black mayor also may have been due to the nature of the mayoral contest itself. Two prominent white contenders ran largely against each other, and their negative commercials may have turned off some of the electorate. On the other hand, the two black candidates seemed above the fray, using more positive messages.

The names of the mayoral contenders in 1993 were familiar ones. Thomas A. Villa, president of the board of aldermen, ran with Vince Schoemehl's endorsement. Tony Ribaudo, a state representative and committeeman of the twenty-fourth ward, was the other white candidate. No friend of Schoemehl's, he had helped engineer the plan to back incumbents in 1986, stymieing the mayor's power play. In this contest, Ribaudo received considerable help from Schoemehl's former crony, J. Kim Tucci. Ward organizations in the twenty-third, sixteenth, and fifteenth wards supported Ribaudo. Officials in his corner included committeeman Francis R. Slay and his alderman son, Francis G., as well as Geraldine Osborn. In addition, African American alderman Bertha Mitchell of the fourth ward signed up with Ribaudo. The Roddys, father and alderman son, and other central corridor aldermen Marit Clark, Phyllis Young, and Daniel McGuire went with Villa.

One of the two African American mayoral candidates was businessman and former alderman Steve Roberts, whose brother Michael had opposed Schoemehl in 1989. Michael Roberts had had little support from the black ward organizations in his race, and Steve had no success there either in 1993. One white alderman from the south side, Paul Beckerle, endorsed Roberts. Roberts had monetary resources but little traditional support.

Freeman Bosley, Jr., the clerk of the circuit court and third-ward committeeman, announced his candidacy in Forest Park in August 1992. Bosley had been elected circuit clerk three times. In his last two outings, he racked up a sizable share of the white vote. Bosley was a graduate of Saint Louis University and the Saint Louis University School of Law, and he had the support of a large body of volunteers. Most of these volunteers were African American, but some white volunteers came from the environmental movement or pro-choice groups.

Demonstrating a curious myopia about the politics of race, a number of observers first concentrated on the chances of Villa and Ribaudo, seemingly dismissing the black contenders. Villa and Ribaudo bought into this myopia as well. Their early campaigns were marked by attacks on each other, including negative television advertisements. All the mayoral candidates crisscrossed the city, appearing in an unusually large number of community meetings. Bosley reiterated one principal theme: the interrelationship between housing, schools, crime, and jobs. He also repeated a refrain he learned from

TABLE 10-1

1993 Democratic Primary: Mayoral Vote

Citywide

Candidate	Vote	Percentage
Freeman Bosley, Jr.	40,118	44.1%
Tony Ribaudo	11,342	12.5%
Steve Roberts	6,839	7.5%
Tom Villa	32,762	36.0%

Percentage of Vote for Bosley by Area of the City

Area	Percentage for Bosley
North	90.1 %
Central corridor	50.5%
South	10.0%

SOURCE: St. Louis Board of Election Commissioners.

his father: "It takes white and black keys to play the 'Star-Spangled Banner.'" Bosley's television ads, appearing late in the campaign, echoed that sentiment. His positive ads contrasted with the negative commercials aired by the two white candidates, Villa and Ribaudo.

Polls released prior to the March balloting predicted an easy victory for Villa. Many politicians and pundits were quite surprised that Bosley ended up carrying the day. Once again in St. Louis, a black candidate won over a divided white field. Roberts ran a poor fourth, not cutting into Bosley's margin in the black community. Table 10-1 shows the vote breakdown. Estimates of cross-racial voting in this contest using the Goodman model show that 42 percent of white voters in the city's central corridor cast ballots for a black candidate, predominantly Bosley.[10] Citywide, 11 percent of white voters selected Bosley. Pundits questioned whether Ribaudo had been coaxed to stay in the race to draw white votes from Villa. Whatever the intent, the effect was the same. The split white vote in south St. Louis, in addition to the cross-racial voting in the center of the city, made Bosley the city's first African American mayor.

Bosley assumed office on a jubilant note. The staff he assembled was principally black, but he retained several white aides who had worked for his predecessor, Vince Schoemehl. Bosley also hired two politically experienced white women, one an environmentalist and the other a leader in the pro-choice cause. Except for the holdovers, the staff was new to city government. Several appointees, including Lloyd Jordan, the chief of staff, and Tim Person, the executive assistant, had been friends of the new mayor for many years.

Richard F. Fenno, Jr., an astute congressional scholar, found that a senator's prepolitical career affected his conduct in office, particularly the ability to form and shape coalitions.[11] In modified fashion, Fenno's theory regarding prior influences helps explain the conduct in office of Freeman Bosley, Jr., and his successor, St. Louis's second African American mayor, Clarence Harmon. Neither had spent any time in city government proper, as legislators or executives. Bosley came from the city's largest patronage office, while Harmon was a career police officer. Neither had perhaps the best preparation to serve as mayor.

Bosley, the County Officeholder

In the tradition of many of the heads of St. Louis's county offices, past and present, Freeman Bosley, Jr., had concentrated his energies on politicking instead of administration. At the time of his

response to the flooding, voters were amenable to the increases in 1993. The additional revenue made possible neighborhood projects and helped the city's fiscal position.

Bosley's honeymoon lasted almost two years. His popularity soared everywhere when the Rams football team decided to come to St. Louis. However, some political insiders had begun to raise questions about the caliber of his staff. The questions had not permeated to the general public but soon would surface.

In an open race for the aldermanic presidency in 1995 (Villa decided not to seek reelection), Bosley endorsed the twenty-third-ward alderman, Francis G. Slay, from south St. Louis, scion of a political family. Slay had attended law school with Bosley. He won easily over several other aldermen, one of whom—Velma Bailey—was black. Slay enjoyed both north-side and south-side support. However, some black politicians criticized Bosley for supporting a white candidate over an African American in this contest. In a city roughly divided between black and white, Bosley helped keep a black and white presence on the board of estimate and apportionment.

Before Bosley's own handling of his office aroused public criticism, the city's second-highest-ranking black officeholder, Comptroller Virvus Jones, faced inquiries that eventually forced him to resign his post. Jones's 1993 reelection campaign provided the principal fuel for the fire. Jones's campaign aides had encouraged Penelope Alcott to run as a stalking-horse, and his campaign bankrolled Alcott's candidacy. The Jones campaign wanted Alcott to pull white votes from Jones's principal opponent, south-side alderman James Shrewsbury. A federal prosecutor indicted Jones for diverting $300,000 of campaign funds to his personal use.[14] Jones pleaded guilty to income-tax evasion because of the diversion of campaign funds, resigned, and spent a few months in a federal penal facility reserved for white-collar criminals. Jones, articulate and personable, had been highly visible and highly popular in the African American community.

Following Jones's resignation, Bosley named the city's budget director, Darlene Green, comptroller. Green also had worked for Bosley when he was circuit clerk. She had never run for political office before. She had a bachelor's degree in business from Washington University with an accounting emphasis. With the appointment of Green, Bosley ensured that he would have two friends on the board of estimate and apportionment.

As an incumbent, Darlene Green faced the voters in a special election in August 1996. Her opponent was Alderman James

Shrewsbury, the alderman whom Jones had defeated three years before. Green won with little difficulty. She appeared to be a well-qualified professional, and television advertisements emphasized her background. To increase black turnout in this primary, Bosley, in accord with St. Louis tradition, sponsored a few candidates for committee posts (committee people face the voters in the state Democratic primary in presidential years). Although his committee candidates failed, their entry in the race created ill will for Bosley among some ward officers. Bosley's organization as well as that of Congressman Clay worked strenuously on Green's behalf. Green's victory was another political triumph for Bosley, but it ended up being his last.

Since the ascendancy of the Democratic Party in St. Louis began in 1933, no county officeholder had become mayor except Freeman Bosley, Jr. Bosley lacked the intimate familiarity with neighborhood concerns and development projects that an alderman or state legislator might have had. However, every St. Louis elected official has some familiarity with the traditional exchange relationships that characterize the city's politics. Some, such as Tucker and Poelker, were more removed from political life than others. However, it is clear that the nitty-gritty politics of St. Louis characterized Bosley's pre-mayoral career more than that of most mayors. As circuit clerk, he could reward friends and perform favors for other politicians. Bosley's personal honesty had not been questioned directly in the media. On the other hand, it is evident that some of his mayoral appointees wanted to reap tangible benefits when Bosley became mayor. Other ethnic groups in earlier times, such as the Irish, certainly had wanted to. However, federal and state laws had changed a good deal since the Irish heyday two generations before. Activity that once was permitted no longer was legal after enactment of federal and state campaign-finance statutes and conflict-of-interest codes. For example, in 1960 Tip O'Neill came to St. Louis as a representative of the Kennedy presidential campaign. He recalled that the campaign accepted both checks and cash. Regarding the cash, no records were kept of who gave what or how it later was spent. This conduct violated no laws then.[15] However, in the aftermath of Watergate, federal and state legislators enacted campaign-finance reforms, and today campaign funding must be reported and is highly scrutinized. Conflicts of interest in the awarding of government contracts were once the norm but now receive careful oversight.

Many of the troubles that touched Bosley's mayoralty were not, in and of themselves, a great danger to him. However, they had a cumulative effect on opinion-makers and voters. His background in the county offices did not prepare him for the attention or criticism he would receive. Coupled with Bosley's street speech, certain events evoked some fear and consternation in sections of the white populace. For-sale signs proliferated as his term progressed, especially in south St. Louis. The political cognoscenti—or at least part of the white contingent—began to look for an alternative mayoral candidate.

An early sign of possible questionable mayoral judgment occurred only a few months after Bosley assumed office. The mayor decided to seek new bids for a second gambling casino for the city, discarding proposals received during Schoemehl's last days in office. Bosley attached the requirement that a hotel be built by the new casino. The *Post-Dispatch* revealed that some of the companies bidding for these development rights had assembled sets of politically well connected local investors, perhaps in a form of insider trading. Such investors included Congressman Bill Clay's daughter, the father of a Bosley aide, and the cousin of a powerful alderman.[16] Although the casino-hotel development never took place, the disclosures about these backers left a bad taste with some citizens.

In August of 1995, a snafu raised questions about competency inside the mayoral office. On August 3, Bosley announced that he would veto a measure passed by the board of aldermen that would increase penalties for home-security-system false alarms. But it was discovered that the mayor actually had signed the bill a week before. His staff claimed that the signature occurred in error and that the bill would not become law because it had not been returned signed to the board of aldermen.[17] That position eventually prevailed.

The alarm-bill problem reminded many of "who's on first." Bosley's next piece of unfavorable press involved a more serious issue. In 1992, while Vince Schoemehl was still mayor, the city began a little-publicized program, Project 87, that provided a new way to shut down suspected drug houses. Building-code violations proved to be useful tools to terminate occupancy when drug dealing was suspected. Mayor Bosley expanded Project 87 in the spring of 1995. On June 23 of that year, a building inspector broke a front-door window in a residence on the near south side at the request of police officers to facilitate an eviction based on code-enforcement violations. The family losing its home complained to City Hall officials. Bosley's director of public safety and a mayoral aide, Walle Amusa (who had been very active in the fight for Homer G. Phillips Hospital), decided that the inspector had acted improperly. They authorized the expenditure of more than $1,000 to repair the door[18] and wanted to allow the tenants to reoccupy the dwelling. Citizens who had benefited from Project 87 protested, as did many on the south side who were worried about the growth in drug-related crime. Whether the inspector's action was excessive or whether members of the Bosley team now had damaged a viable method of ridding neighborhoods of drug houses became the subject of heated debate. Bosley supporters and Bosley detractors differed in their interpretations. Meanwhile, the incident received significant media coverage.

Then, on November 10, 1995, Clarence Harmon, St. Louis's first African American police chief, resigned his office. Harmon had a considerable personal following, particularly in the white community. He had been an advocate of community-based policing. Vince Schoemehl sat on the police board (ex officio) when Harmon was selected as chief. According to one reporter, that tie contributed to the distrust some black politicians had of Harmon.[19] Several members of the police board, appointed by Governor Mel Carnahan, had ties to state senator Jet Banks. Banks was allied with Bosley and had become a latter-day advocate of local control of the police, a cause dear to the mayor. (Bosley had called for local control in his inaugural address.) Harmon had not had a good relationship with Banks.

According to the press, the police board had made life difficult for Harmon by:

- Overruling some of the chief's promotion decisions
- Blocking an officer's transfer
- Implementing a copier system the chief had not favored
- Forcing him to rehire a staff member he had terminated.[20]

Harmon supporters blamed Bosley for Harmon's resignation. At a Rams football game, just after the resignation, some fans booed Bosley when he was introduced to the crowd. A couple months later, the former chief was feted at a well-attended banquet. Ironically, police officials and other proponents of continued state control of the police had touted the traditional institutional arrangement because it separated policing from city politics. Of course, that separation often has been illusory. It certainly did not exist during the Harmon-Bosley contretemps. Harmon's resignation and the criticism of Bosley implied therein hurt the mayor's popularity, especially in the white community.

Other events also hurt the mayor's image, particularly in the central corridor. Cellular telephones had become very popular in St. Louis, as in numerous other locations. Many administrators received cell phones from the city. A court suit by the *Post-Dispatch* and by KSDK-TV forced city administrators to disclose the cell-phone records. The upshot was that some city officials had made many personal as well as possibly unnecessary calls on the taxpayers' dollar. Needless to say, this occurs in every type of business office. However, calls on cellular phones were a good deal more expensive than the normal telephone call. Members of Bosley's immediate staff were among those who misused the cellular phones.

Then, conflict of interest reared its head. Bosley had to dismiss a longtime aide and close personal friend because he served on a committee that awarded a major airport expansion contract to a firm his wife worked for as a subcontractor.[21] Stories also surfaced in the media about parking tickets accumulated by the mayor's mother and about his father's sweetheart deal with a city agency regarding the purchase of a building to house his mattress factory.

In addition, Bosley had created and nurtured a "Midnite Basketball" program in St. Louis. With corporate donations and city funding, the games became quite popular. Participants, who were unemployed and often high-school dropouts, played on basketball teams and received job counseling. In 1996 several employees of this popular program were accused of stealing program funds. The mayor's office tried to place some of the blame on the city's recreation commissioner, and she was terminated. Bosley had recommended the hiring of several employees of the basketball program who were indicted for theft while at their posts. The disclosures of wrongdoing involving this program received prominent media coverage.

Bosley also came under fire in some quarters because he did not appear to be a preservationist. His administration favored the demolishing of several architecturally significant buildings downtown to create additional surface parking lots. Bosley and his development team also were criticized when they proposed building a golf course and market-rate single-family homes in a low-income area north of downtown.

A number of St. Louis elected officials expressed the feeling that Bosley was hurt by some of the staff members he had hired and trusted. Because he was the city's first African American mayor, his hiring pool was limited compared to his white predecessors. He especially wanted people he felt he could rely on. However, he and most of his staff were new to city government and to its demands. They also probably were not cognizant of all the legal restrictions affecting their positions. And observers felt that Bosley failed to watch over his staff. One politician remarked of these employees, "They got too greedy too quickly." Bosley's loyalty to his friends and employees was emblematic of St. Louis's political culture. Loyalty to political friends always has been highly regarded. Yet this loyalty hurt Bosley with the wider public. For example, two of his staff members (and old friends) left the mayor's office under fire. Bosley turned around and gave them nicely paid positions with his reelection campaign. When he was circuit clerk, Bosley, according to a former officeholder, did not pay attention to ability or performance of the friends he hired. With the spotlight always on the mayor's office, any mayor had to watch his staff closely.

Alderman Marit Clark, who represented a central corridor ward on the board of aldermen, announced her candidacy for mayor in the fall of 1995. After Clarence Harmon's resignation as police chief later that autumn, many began to speak of a Harmon run for the city's highest office. Harmon, however, initially supported Clark, wrote a fundraising letter on her behalf, and sponsored a fundraiser for her. As the months passed though, Clark's support among the voters did not appear to increase. Because of Harmon's considerable name recognition and his popularity in white St. Louis, corporate leaders and others urged him to be a mayoral candidate. Finally, in the late summer of 1996, Harmon announced that he would run.

Two African Americans Vie for the Mayor's Chair

In an interesting twist, the candidacies of two African Americans, Freeman Bosley, Jr., and Clarence Harmon, contributed significantly to racial polarization among the electorate. Bosley was the "black" candidate, while Clarence Harmon appealed largely to white St. Louisans. The major unknown before the March 1997 primary was how the central corridor (about two-thirds white) would vote. In 1993, almost half of the white voters residing there cast ballots for Bosley.

The African American community rallied around Bosley's candidacy. He was a hero who spoke their language and made things happen in their neighborhoods. With the exception of aldermanic president Francis G. Slay and former senator Thomas Eagleton, politically prominent whites supported Harmon. A few, such as former mayor Schoemehl, stayed with Marit Clark. She eventually decided to run as an independent in the April general election rather than in the Democratic primary. Harmon's black support was limited. Aldermen Sharon Tyus, Velma Bailey, and Irene Smith, three

African American women who had feuded with the mayor and his staff, endorsed Harmon. A third candidate, Bill Haas, also filed to run in the Democratic primary. He ended up withdrawing just before the primary. His presence enlivened the debates that took place during the campaign. Haas said that, if elected, he would hire Bosley, Clark, and Harmon as his chief aides.

The mayoral campaign was a nasty one. The Harmon camp ran a TV ad called "Night Shade" that specified various shortcomings of the Bosley administration, such as the missing Midnite Basketball money. Bosley's campaign ran two hard-hitting ads about Harmon's sons, both members of the police force. The ads mentioned complaints that had been made about each of them while Harmon was chief. The ads appeared to use information from their confidential personnel files. The charges against them, in fact, had been either withdrawn or never substantiated.

Because of the *Post-Dispatch*'s coverage of some of these events, irate Bosley supporters picketed at the newspaper's offices, and black leaders met with the editor. Implicit in the protests was the belief that Bosley was being singled out because he was black. James Buford, head of the Urban League, said, "the contest was about the power gained by blacks four years ago with Bosley's election and the loss of power that would result from a Harmon victory."[22] Harmon's third wife, a public-relations specialist, was white. This interracial marriage raised ire in certain sections of the black community, particularly after being the central topic on some radio talk shows. Freeman Bosley, Sr., the mayor's father and longtime alderman, referred to Harmon as a "rented Negro."

The Economist had an interesting take on this mayoral election. The magazine reported, "A diminutive, balding, freckled man with a high voice and speech full of street rhythms, Mr. Bosley never connected with most whites. By contrast, Clarence Harmon, older, more articulate and with a professional demeanor, is a Colin Powell figure—or an Uncle Tom depending on your point of view."[23]

On primary day, Harmon won handily, as Table 10-2 demonstrates. The Colin Powell aspect played very well in south St. Louis and also among whites in the corridor. The north side was overwhelmingly loyal to Bosley, but exit polls showed that a higher percentage of blacks citywide chose Harmon than whites had Bosley. The primary election occurred in the presence of hundreds of poll watchers, supplied by the Harmon campaign to prevent electoral fraud, and demonstrated fundamental cleavages based on class and race in St. Louis. Portrayed as a reformer, Harmon claimed to dislike

TABLE 10-2

March 1997 Democratic Primary: Mayoral Vote

Citywide

Candidate	Vote	Percentage
Freeman Bosley, Jr.	43,351	42.9%
Clarence Harmon	56,927	56.3%
Bill Haas	756	0.7%

Harmon's Vote by Geographic Area

Area	Vote for Harmon	Percentage of Harmon's Vote
North side (12 wards)	4,011	7.0%
Central corridor (5 wards)	10,146	17.8%
South side (11 wards)	42,770	75.1%

Bosley's Vote by Geographic Area

Area	Vote for Bosley	Percentage of Bosley's Vote
North side (12 wards)	32,650	75.3%
Central corridor (5 wards)	6,857	15.8%
South side (11 wards)	3,844	8.9%

Note: No part of St. Louis has ever been exclusively white or black. The north side is predominantly black, and the south side is mostly white. However, in the early 1990s a number of African Americans moved to south-side wards—principally the ninth, tenth, eleventh, fifteenth, and twenty-fifth wards.

SOURCE: St. Louis Election Board.

politics. However, during the campaign, he met frequently with committee people and sought ward endorsements. His last public appearance before the primary was at a south-side ward rally replete with officeholders. One of his principal assets appeared to be his integrity, given greater credence by the circumstances surrounding his resignation from the police department. Harmon easily won the general election, defeating Marit Clark and Jay Dearing, a Republican.

The Police Chief

Corporate leaders, middle-class professionals, and many voters had high expectations for the Harmon mayoralty. However, the transition from police chief to mayor was not an easy one for Harmon. He did not exert much effort in the areas of public relations or coalition building, nor was he a cheerleader for the city or even, at times, for programs he favored. His attendance—or lack thereof—at various events puzzled veteran political observers. For example, the mayor did not go to Busch Stadium to greet Mark McGwire when he hit his sixty-second home run or his seventieth, even though so much national attention was focused on St. Louis. (Unlike his predecessors, he did not buy a box at the stadium.) He actually began his term in office by endorsing a Republican candidate, albeit an old friend, for a seat on the St. Louis County Council. Harmon also held a fundraiser for a county officeholder and then failed to appear at the event.

Some of his appointees shared his apolitical background. They were either retired military officers or former members of the police force. Harmon received plaudits for placing the troubled Emergency Medical Service under the direction of the fire department, reducing citizen complaints considerably. He also asked a leading citizen organization—Focus St. Louis—to audit city government to increase effi-

Clarence Harmon in 1991, when he was police chief under Mayor Vincent Schoemehl. Photograph by Ted Dargan, St. Louis Post-Dispatch, *1991.*

ciency and resident satisfaction. Focus continued to work with the administration on implementation of its recommendations. A number of changes were made in some city operations, although government was not reinvented. Political and strategic difficulties delayed attempts to reorganize development activities.

Having a nonpolitician at the helm of a machine-politics town led to some disquieting outcomes. A profile in the *Post-Dispatch* in the winter of 1999 stressed, "Harmon is a man who says he dislikes backslapping politics as usual.... On Harmon's City Hall desk is a placard that proclaims 'There's nothing honorable about politics.'"[24] The mayor told the *Post* that he now realized that he had "to spend more time schmoozing with elected officials whose votes he needs to carry out his initiatives."[25] Asked to grade his performance, Harmon gave himself a C+ but added that "We don't have a scandal a week,"[26] a reference to his predecessor. Harmon also achieved a certain amount of attention because of his penchant for changing his mind. These turnabouts concerned issues such as light-rail expansion and each time irritated other elected officials and members of the city's business elite.

Despite Harmon's gaffes, St. Louis appeared to have stabilized somewhat. The blankets of for-sale signs disappeared from south-side neighborhoods. New groups of immigrants—from Latin America, Asia, Bosnia, and Kosovo—settled in some older neighborhoods, restoring some of their vitality, although decay continued to spread in other locales. Several adjacent historic downtown buildings were saved from the wrecking ball by Charles Drury and renovated together as the flagship Drury Hotel. McCormack Baron, a real-estate development and management firm, began to restore the Cupples warehouses as offices, loft apartments, and a hotel—the same warehouses that Vince Schoemehl saved in defiance of Anheuser-Busch. A convention hotel that would utilize two boarded-up buildings as well as a new edifice finally took shape. The strong economy contributed to the development activity in St. Louis. Despite these positive events, other political figures began to test the waters with thoughts of toppling Harmon if he ran again.

Implications

The difficulties encountered by both Bosley and Harmon in the mayor's office highlight the relationship of the city's political culture and institutions to governance. Bosley's term pointed out that old-style patronage politics could not be a model for mayoral conduct.

Bosley certainly was steeped in those traditions. Harmon's tenure showed that apolitical management neither inspired nor assisted coalition building in a political locale. Bill McClellan, a columnist with the *Post-Dispatch*, frequently writes that there are two political parties in St. Louis, the white Democrats and the black Democrats. While this is a simplification because there are factions on both sides, perceptions do differ between blacks and whites, and actions do not carry the same meaning with all citizens.

A mayor in St. Louis has to be affected by the dearth of formal powers and the importance of personal relationships. He or she must work to create support for major initiatives, and many in the city, not just politicians, expect some kind of reward for their support. However, the varied quid pro quo relationships cannot dominate the mayoral agenda either. A mayor who does not pay heed to local political considerations undercuts his own support. As in any city, there has to be leadership that extols St. Louis and its potential. There also have to be innovative programs and staff interested in issues and general solutions. Bosley knew the quid pro quo. Harmon knew the pitfalls of machine politics but did not understand the importance of politics generally. Each of these African American mayors lacked part of the equation.

A New Direction

In the fall of 1999, aldermanic president Francis G. Slay announced his candidacy for mayor. Part of a political family, Slay knew the ins and outs of city politics. In previous races, he enjoyed support in all areas of the city. He also was an adept money raiser. For a year and a half, he traversed the city, attending events and making his case for change in the mayor's office.

During this period, former mayors Schoemehl and Bosley both intimated that they might run for their previous post. In the end, Schoemehl demurred, but Bosley filed at the last moment. Bill Haas once again threw his hat in the ring. Clarence Harmon, the incumbent, filed as well.

Harmon's diffidence toward his job hurt his chances. He also had not developed a constituency of his own. The City Living Foundation, designed to lure new residents to the city, spoiled his clean record. While he sat on its board, almost $300,000 was expended without the production of one brochure or advertisement. Elected officials allied themselves with Slay or Bosley as the mayoral campaign began in earnest. Slay's war chest permitted him to run

Mayor Francis Slay endorsed the quest for a referendum on home rule for St. Louis on the November 2002 ballot. Photo by Ravetta, courtesy of the Slay for Mayor Campaign.

upbeat advertisements on television for a number of weeks. He also received the support of a leading black clergyman, Earl Nance, Jr., and north-side alderman Kenneth Jones. In addition, Slay received the endorsements of four of the five central-corridor wards, and all but one of the south-side wards.

Bosley began his campaign by apologizing for his previous errors. He pledged that distinguished St. Louisans would help select his staff. His message was positive, and he, as well as Slay, personally canvassed neighborhoods. All the candidates made frequent appearances at meetings and forums.

Harmon's campaign did not share his rivals' upbeat tone. He denounced the "Slay-Bosley" administration and accused Slay, the front-runner, of strong-arm tactics. Many of Harmon's campaign staff departed prior to the primary, voluntarily or otherwise.

On March 6, 2001, the voters had their say. Slay enjoyed a substantial victory, with Bosley finishing second. As Table 10-3 shows, Harmon received only 5 percent of the vote, a surprisingly low figure for an incumbent. Slay, who is white, received the largest share of the white vote, while blacks strongly favored Bosley.

Francis Slay assumed office facing a divided city and deeply entrenched problems. His perceived integrity and ability to develop coalitions are helpful to his cause, but he must function within an institutional environment and a political culture that will circumscribe his ability to lead. The handiwork of his predecessors may serve him in good stead, however. During Bosley's mayoral term, some prominent community leaders worked together to advise him on fiscal matters. Included in this group were several members of Civic Progress, former senator Thomas Eagleton, and African American attorney Steve Cousins. The group turned its attention to St. Louis's governmental structure and prepared a plan for a strong-mayor form of government. Mayor Bosley did not embrace the plan when it was unveiled. However, after his defeat he joined former mayors Conway and Schoemehl to address the governance issue again. The head of brokerage firm Stifel-Nicklaus, George H. "Bert" Walker, spearheaded the effort. The group decided to attempt to give St. Louis true home rule, namely control over the county side of governance and the eight county offices. The Missouri legislature endorsed a statewide referendum on this question for the November 2002 ballot. Slay also endorsed this quest.

Certainly, a less fragmented governmental structure would allow mayors greater authority to act and decrease the points of agreement needed. But who occupies the mayor's office makes a difference as well. St. Louis's traditional institutions may be detriments to executive leadership. In addition, the continuing focus on individual

TABLE 10-3

The Mayoral Primary Vote in 2001

Vote Totals

Candidate	Vote	Percent
Slay	46,272	53.6%
Harmon	4,263	4.9%
Haas	422	.5%
Bosley	35,341	41.0%

Vote by Area

	Slay	Harmon	Bosley
North side	3,639	1,112	26,300
Central corridor	8,342	1,033	5,415
South side	34,291	2,118	3,626

SOURCE: *St. Louis Post-Dispatch*, March 8, 2001, p. A5.

rewards has siphoned energy from more far-reaching problems. The number of people to satisfy in St. Louis is extensive. Surprisingly perhaps, no recent mayor has had appreciable difficulty in getting legislation through the board of aldermen. The reason also is based on the nature of the city's institutions. Because of the city's structure, aldermen have shown greater interest in what happens within their ward boundaries than in many citywide projects. If aldermen are pleased with allocations to their wards, they often will acquiesce on other matters. But opposition can spring from a number of other areas in this fragmented system.

In looking at Bosley and Harmon, it should be noted that African American mayors in a number of other cities have fallen victim to bad decisions or have had indecisive styles. St. Louis is not unique in that regard. Wilson Goode, former mayor of Philadelphia, a seasoned administrator, lost his footing forever after he authorized the dropping of a bomb on a home occupied by members of the MOVE organization. New York's David Dinkins hurt his reelectability when tensions between Hasidic Jews and African Americans reached the fever point following a traffic fatality and the murder of a rabbinical student. The large Hasidic Jewish community felt Dinkins had not acted quickly enough to prevent violence after the traffic accident, in which a car in a Lubavitcher rebbe's motorcade killed a black child. Hamstrung by the city council, Harold Washington, Chicago's first African American mayor, could not carry out his agenda. In addition, he decided to abide by the Shakman decree that put strong limits on patronage hiring in Chicago. Washington did use Community Development Block Grant funds to support nonprofit social service agencies in black areas, a newer kind of patronage.[27]

In St. Louis, the city's first black mayors did not possess ideal backgrounds for dealing with the demands of their position. At the same time, St. Louis's political thicket proved an impediment. There were too many groups to please and too many sites from which opposition could arise. The need to handle individual and group demands produced different reactions from Bosley and Harmon. Neither of their approaches proved successful in the long run. In the meantime, the tremendous need for new residents, housing, and businesses did not receive enough attention. In 2001, St. Louisans chose an experienced white politician to assume the mayoral burden. His success may depend in part on his ability to govern in an institutional quagmire or on whether his predecessors can help eliminate that quagmire.

Chapter 11

Institutions and Governance in St. Louis

A collection of scholars, grouped together as neoinstitutionalists, has reintroduced governmental structure as an important factor in political analysis. Recognizing that rules and structure are not neutral, they have treated institutions as factors that set the parameters in which behavior takes place. Institutions interact with, shape, and are shaped by political culture. Just as individual mores guide individual behavior, political culture helps to define the acceptability of political practices. Institutions and culture, of course, are not the only factors that explain a jurisdiction's decision making. But in terms of U.S. cities, they can play a significant role. The variation in governmental form is striking. Although many cities have followed similar paths in housing and redevelopment, their ability to harness needed tools has varied. Along with economy and demography, institutions can make a difference at the municipal level. Interestingly, Progressive reformers active one hundred years ago recognized the relationship between governmental form and behavior. In many places, they altered the institutional makeup to replace political decisions with business-style efficiency.

St. Louis's political history is a clear exemplar of institutions affecting agenda setting, leadership, and political practices. Because it is both a city and a city acting as a county, St. Louis has been an ideal stage for the practice of machine politics. Although a strong political machine has never developed in the Gateway City, ward-based factionalism has dominated political life there for far more than a century.

St. Louis's ward factionalism has its roots in decisions made in 1876 and 1914. The city's divorce from St. Louis County in 1876 may have been shortsighted. St. Louis City's boundaries were set in stone, and St. Louis has remained a small core of only sixty-one square miles to this day. Perhaps more important, St. Louis assumed county functions specified in state law. State legislators came to determine the salaries of the independently elected county officeholders as well as the specifications of each of the offices.

What cities legally can do in reference to taxing authority, bond capacity, and other salient issues is decided by state government. And their constitutional and legislative guidelines vary tremendously. As an example, Chicago's political machine survived as long as it did because Illinois was slow to change its laws concerning civil service, partisan elections, and the power of political parties.[1] Ester R. Fuchs points out that Illinois law made possible the creation of special districts and public authorities that enabled Chicago to take hold of its finances in a way New York City could not.[2] Missouri law certainly has played a role in aiding and abetting St. Louis's machine politics.

Missouri governors and legislators always have taken an unusually active interest in St. Louis's governance. The state's governor has appointed the board of police commissioners as well as the board of election commissioners, posts considered political plums by donors and other notables. Backing the winning gubernatorial candidate can bring rewards for friends and family of St. Louis politicians. The state constitution also sets up Missouri's political subunits, which in St. Louis are the city's twenty-eight wards. The wards elect the committeemen and committeewomen of both parties. Not infrequently, state legislators hold these committee posts, contributing to a larger interlocking political network. Until the latter half of the twentieth century, committeemen were focal points of the political scene, and every candidate sought their endorsements.

St. Louis's 1914 charter vested fiscal authority in a board of estimate and apportionment made up of the mayor, comptroller, and president of the board of aldermen, three independently elected offices, rather than in the mayor alone. The charter also established twenty-eight wards that today each have an average of thirteen thousand residents. The city's aldermen have long controlled development and occupancy in their respective bailiwicks, producing a narrow and sometimes incoherent focus. The mayor, by vestige of his office, is the first among many actors, all with independent power bases and all active in city affairs.

The competing sources of power in St. Louis have produced a fragmented landscape where allies continually are sought and placated and where there is a premium on maintaining friendships. Fragmentation creates factionalism. With power dispersed, power brokers ally or feud, and "who's with whom" remains a constant topic of conversation. Victory brings the traditional rewards to party people who pick a winner.

The fragmentation and factionalism so prevalent in St. Louis affect planning and implementation. Many demand a piece of the pie, and satisfying claimants takes a significant amount of a mayor's time. St. Louis's unusually large population loss, 60 percent since 1950, and the sizable segment of its citizenry living in poverty affect its revitalization efforts. But so does its institutional array, which prevents much accumulation of power by the mayor.

Two St. Louis mayors in the second half of the twentieth century made discernible impressions on the fabric of the city: Raymond Tucker and Vincent Schoemehl. Tucker's success stemmed from the strong backing of the business elite he enjoyed as well as his espousal of programs taking hold everywhere in urban America. Schoemehl used the force of his personality to affect the city's bureaucracy and its development agenda. Both enjoyed success and stood out from their peers because of the relative rarity of their accomplishments.

Schoemehl and another of his predecessors, Bernard Dickmann, tried to increase the political power of the mayor's office. Both tried to control other offices as a means to their end. Ultimately, both met with failure. They made enemies of competing political figures and paid the price at the ballot box. Tucker and his immediate predecessor, Joseph Darst, tried to gather power by changing the city charter. These reforms failed; charter change had no following among the numerous members of the working class.

Class differences prevented St. Louis from experiencing thorough reform in the Progressive era, as it did in the 1950s. Coupled with the racial divide, these differences gave fodder to officeholders who opposed change and the concomitant diminution of their authority. They convinced their constituents that their democratic rights would be abrogated if reform occurred. The end result is that St. Louis entered the twenty-first century with an archaic form of government, making it difficult for the city to respond to economic and social challenges.

The factional nature of St. Louis politics also mitigated against a strong regime. In other cities, business and government leaders forged alliances to deal with economic development and other critical issues. In St. Louis, Mayor Tucker and Civic Progress worked as one on urban renewal and highway building. After Tucker left office in 1965, however, ties between business and government weakened, and cooperation became episodic.

In the early 1900s, government similar to St. Louis's was the norm in many cities. Weak mayors and fragmented powers were commonplace, as was the practice of machine politics. In that era, numerous cities reformed their practices and left the machine fold. Many of the cities that continued to share a machine-politics orientation after 1915 changed as well. They eventually moved to centralize political authority. The quid pro quo relationships marking machine politics became subsidiary to citywide agendas, even if they did not disappear. Leadership, at least in part, made such centralization possible. Anton Cermak and later Richard J. Daley in Chicago moved allocation of patronage into their own hands. David Lawrence of Pittsburgh centralized patronage and governmental authority. Daley, Lawrence, and Edward Rendell of Philadelphia all used statutory power and political skill to mold an effective vehicle for governing their cities. In addition, Pittsburgh changed its structure early in the twentieth century by adopting at-large elections for the city council. Philadelphia's electorate changed that city's political subunits so they did not match legislative districts. These structural changes provided mayors greater administrative authority. Further, the cities themselves did not fall under the jurisdiction of state governments to the degree that St. Louis did. Missouri became the only state still with jurisdiction over a municipal police force. The state has shared St. Louis's machine-politics tradition, so that state and local officeholders have joined together in dispensing various kinds of favors.

St. Louis today again appears to be seeking reforms that would allow it to mold an institutional structure that gives the mayor more authority and lessens the centrifugal tendencies of present arrangements. Whether the various actors truly can join together in this endeavor remains open to question. Examination of St. Louis's political history demonstrates that its current institutions encourage factionalism and fragmentation. This has been the pattern regardless of the political party at the helm. These institutions also perpetuate the machine-politics tradition and envelop all participants in its rituals. In St. Louis, politicians arising from the civil-rights struggle have placed personal rewards above other issues. This has siphoned energy from the battle for equality. Addressing the crux of economic and social problems is outside the purview of elected officials, who are accustomed to an engrained reward system that generally helps only a small coterie.

Ironically, if St. Louis's institutional framework had been different through the years, some of its policy decisions may have been the same. Cities learn from one another and imitate the others' strategies.

Different institutions may not have prevented the city's loss of jobs and population, and the decay in many neighborhoods may have continued anyhow. But the ability to deal with these deeply engrained problems may have been stronger if the form of government were centralized and streamlined. At the least, attention might have been directed more at policy than at individual rewards.

Institutions and political culture in St. Louis have produced approachable, if chaotic, politics. In this small town cum large city, those in and outside politics can make connections with ease. At the same time, the culture has produced a sense of St. Louis as a rather unique phenomenon. "This is St. Louis" is a frequent refrain from those who grew up in the Gateway City. The way other cities handle matters does not seem appropriate to the old hometown. This conservatism of spirit can be linked to feelings of both pride and inferiority. It is interesting that the 1904 World's Fair appears to be the high-water mark in the city's history for many residents, and the weakness inherent in St. Louis's political apparatus reinforces this part of the civic culture.

St. Louis has dealt with war, severe air pollution, urban renewal, the civil-rights movement, highway building, the war on poverty, and, in the present day, the sports and tourism industries. Its structure of government has not prevented some successful undertakings. But it has undermined some of its most successful political leaders, because battles over position and turf damaged their ability to govern. Leadership is harder to exercise in a fragmented system, and the inherent divisions devour opportunities for greater progress.

Institutional change cannot be a panacea, however. If the city adopts a new charter and gains home-rule power over its county functions, the political culture will not change immediately. The notions of "going along to get along" and "going home from the dance with the one that brung you" are engrained in the behavior patterns of political actors. A new structure of government would lead to a long period of cultural and behavioral adaptation. But as long as institutions remain untouched, cultural change cannot take place at all. Racial and class schisms have worked against significant change to St. Louis's institutional framework. However, in the new century, the severity of the city's problems point to the need for a more effective system. As it stands, St. Louis is an anachronism, a city whose government resembles one from the nineteenth century more than one from the twenty-first. No matter which path it chooses in the future, its political history to date clearly illustrates the significance of institutions and the triumph of tradition, in the spirit of "for auld lang syne."

Appendix
St. Louis Elected Officials

Mayor

Rolla Wells (D) 1901–1909
Frederick Kreismann (R) 1909–1913
Henry Kiel (R) 1913–1925
Victor J. Miller (R) 1925–1933
Bernard Dickmann (D) 1933–1941
William Dee Becker (R) 1941–1943
Aloys Kaufmann (R) 1943–1949
Joseph Darst (D) 1949–1953
Raymond Tucker (D) 1953–1965
A. J. Cervantes (D) 1965–1973
John Poelker (D) 1973–1977
James Conway (D) 1977–1981
Vincent C. Schoemehl, Jr. (D)
 1981–1993
Freeman Bosley, Jr. (D) 1993–1997
Clarence Harmon (D) 1997–2001
Francis G. Slay (D) 2001–

Comptroller

James Y. Player (R) 1914–1917
Louis Nolte (R) 1917–1949
Milton Carpenter (D) 1949–1957
John Poelker (D) 1957–1973
John Bass (D) 1973–1977
Raymond Percich (D) 1977–1980
Rita Houghasian (D) 1980–1981
Paul Berra (D) 1981–1989
Virvus Jones (D) 1989–1996
Darlene Green (D) 1996–

President of the Board of Aldermen

Louis P. Aloe (R) 1917–1924
Walter J. G. Neun (R) 1924–1935
William L. Mason (D) 1935–1941
Michael J. Hart (R) 1941–1943
Aloys P. Kaufmann (R) 1943
Edgar S. Nicolai (R) 1943–1945
Albert L. Schweitzer (R) 1945–1947
Charles Albanese (R) 1947–1955
Donald Gunn (D) 1955–1959
A. J. Cervantes (D) 1959–1963
Donald Gunn (D) 1963–1968
James Noonan (D) 1968–1969
Joseph Badaracco (R) 1969–1975
Paul Simon (D) 1975–1980
Eugene Bradley (D) 1980
Thomas Zych (D) 1980–1987
Thomas P. Villa (D) 1987–1995
Francis G. Slay (D) 1995–2001
James Shrewsbury (D) 2001–

Endnotes

AN INTRODUCTION TO ST. LOUIS'S
POLITICAL CONTEXT

1. Clarence N. Stone, *Regime Politics: Governing Atlanta, 1946–1988* (Lawrence: University Press of Kansas, 1989).

2. Raphael J. Sonenshein, *Politics in Black and White: Race and Power in Los Angeles* (Princeton, N.J.: Princeton University Press, 1993), 5.

3. James H. Svara, *Official Leadership in the City: Patterns of Conflict and Cooperation* (New York: Oxford University Press, 1990), 47.

4. Raymond E. Wolfinger, *The Politics of Progress* (Englewood Cliffs, N.J.: Prentice-Hall, 1974), 100.

5. Edward C. Banfield and James Q. Wilson, *City Politics* (Cambridge, Mass.: Harvard University Press, 1963).

6. Ibid., 121.

7. Ibid., 123.

8. Robert K. Merton, *Social Theory and Social Structure*, rev. and enlarged ed. (Glencoe, Ill.: The Free Press, 1957), 72.

9. Ibid., 74.

10. Ibid.

11. Raymond E. Wolfinger, "Why Political Machines Have Not Withered Away and Other Revisionist Thoughts," *Journal of Politics* 34 (1972): 374–77.

12. James G. March and Johan P. Olsen, *Rediscovering Institutions: The Organizational Basis of Politics* (New York: The Free Press, 1989), 18.

13. Ibid., 40.

14. James Q. Wilson, *Bureaucracy: What Government Agencies Do and Why They Do It* (New York: Basic Books, 1989), 376; R. Kent Weaver and Bert A. Rockman, "Assessing the Effects of Institutions," in *Do Institutions Matter?* (Washington, D.C.: Brookings Institution, 1993).

15. R. Kent Weaver and Bert A. Rockman, "Where and How Do Institutions Matter?," in *Do Institutions Matter?*, 446.

16. Carl E. Van Horn, Donald C. Baumer, and William T. Gormley, Jr., *Politics and Public Policy*, 2d ed. (Washington, D.C.: CQ Press, 1992), 29.

17. Barbara Ferman, *Challenging the Growth Machine: Neighborhood Politics in Chicago and Pittsburgh* (Lawrence: University Press of Kansas, 1996), 9.

18. Daniel J. Elazar, "The American Cultural Matrix," in *The Ecology of American Political Culture: Readings*, ed. Daniel J. Elazar and Joseph Zikmund (New York: Thomas Y. Crowell, 1975), 26.

CHAPTER 1

1. James Neal Primm, *Lion of the Valley: St. Louis, Missouri*, 2d ed. (Boulder, Colo.: Pruett, 1990), 118–19.

2. Dennis R. Judd and Todd Swanstrom, *City Politics: Private Power and Public Policy*, 2d ed. (New York: Longman, 1998), 51.

3. Primm, *Lion of the Valley*, 246–47.

4. Thomas S. Barclay, *The St. Louis Home Rule Charter of 1876* (Columbia: University of Missouri Press, 1962), 2.

5. Ibid., 1.

6. See, for example, *Preisler v. Hayden* 30 s.w. 2d 645 (1958) and *State v. Dwyer* 124 s.w. 2d 1173, 343 MO 973 (1938).

7. Amy Bridges, *A City in the Republic: Antebellum New York and the Origins of Machine Politics* (Ithaca, N.Y.: Cornell University Press, 1987).

8. Alan DiGaetano, "The Origins of Urban Political Machines in the United States: A Comparative Perspective," *Urban Affairs Quarterly* 26 (March 1991).

9. Ira Katznelson, *City Trenches: Urban Politics and the Patterning of Class in the U.S.* (New York: Pantheon, 1981).

10. Martin Shefter, "The Emergence of the Political Machine: An Alternative View," in *Theoretical Perspectives on Urban Politics*, ed. Willis Hawley et al., 2d ed. (Englewood Cliffs, N.J.: Prentice-Hall, 1976), 15.

11. Jon C. Teaford, *The Unheralded Triumph: City Government in America, 1870–1900* (Baltimore: Johns Hopkins University Press, 1984), 176.

12. Ibid.

13. Barclay, *Home Rule Charter*, 25.

14. Lloyd Wendt and Herman Kogan, *Lords of the Levee* (New York: Bobbs-Merrill Company, 1943).

15. Barclay, *Home Rule Charter*, 18.

16. Ibid., 17.

17. Ibid., 16.

18. Ibid., 25.

19. Ibid., 33.

20. Ibid., 39.

21. Ibid., 44.

22. See, for example, Martin J. Schiesl, *The Politics of Efficiency: Municipal Administration and Reform in America 1800–1920* (Berkeley: University of California Press, 1977) and Samuel P. Hays, "The Politics of Reform in the Progressive Era," in *Readings in Urban Politics*, ed. Harlan Hahn and Charles H. Levine, 2d ed. (New York: Longman, 1984).

23. Shefter, "Emergence of the Political Machine," 34–41.

24. Teaford, *Unheralded Triumph*, 312.

25. Lucius E. Guese, "St. Louis and the Great Whiskey Ring," *Missouri Historical Review* 36 (January 1942): 164.

26. Julian S. Rammelkamp, "St. Louis: Boosters and Boodlers," *Bulletin* of the Missouri Historical Society 34 (July 1978): 203–4.

27. Lincoln Steffens, *The Shame of the Cities* (New York: Hill and Wang, 1957), 21.

28. Teaford, *Unheralded Triumph*, 73–74.

29. Edward C. Rafferty, "The Boss Who Never Was: Colonel Ed Butler and the Limits of Practical Politics in St. Louis," *Gateway Heritage* 12 (Winter 1992).

30. Steffens, *Shame of the Cities*, 73–74.

31. Ibid, 76.

32. Jack Muraskin, "St. Louis Municipal Reform in the 1890s: A Study in Failure," *Bulletin* of the Missouri Historical Society 25 (October 1968): 49.

33. Jack Muraskin, "Municipal Reform in Two Missouri Cities," *Bulletin* of the Missouri Historical Society 25 (April 1969): 221.

34. Ibid., 223.

35. Rammelkamp, "Boosters and Boodlers," 201.

36. Ibid.

37. Muraskin, "Municipal Reform in Two Missouri Cities," 223.

38. David T. Beito with Bruce Smith, "The Formation of Urban Infrastructure Through Nongovernmental Planning: The Private Places of St. Louis, 1869–1920," *Journal of Urban History* 16 (May 1990).

39. Alexander Scot McConachie, "Public Problems and Private Places," *Bulletin* of the Missouri Historical Society 34 (January 1978).

40. Eric Todd Sandweiss, "Construction and Community in South St. Louis, 1850–1910" (Ph.D. diss., University of California at Berkeley, 1991), 240–41.

41. Ibid., 206.

42. Alexander Scot McConachie, "The

'Big Cinch': A Business Elite in the Life of a City, Saint Louis, 1895–1915" (Ph.D. diss., Washington University, 1976), 71.

43. Rammelkamp, "Boosters and Boodlers," 207.

44. McConachie, "The 'Big Cinch,'" 71.

45. Curtis Hunter Porter, "Charter Reform in St. Louis, 1910–1914" (master's thesis, Washington University, 1966), 19.

46. Rammelkamp, "Boosters and Boodlers," 208.

47. Porter, "Charter Reform in St. Louis," 38.

48. Kenneth Finegold, *Experts and Politicians: Reform Challenges to Machine Politics in New York, Cleveland, and Chicago* (Princeton, N.J.: Princeton University Press, 1995), 42–43.

CHAPTER 2

1. Merle Fainsod, "The Influence of Racial and National Groups in St. Louis Politics: 1908–1928" (master's diss., Washington University, 1929), 56.

2. Ibid., 57.

3. "Negro Must Go, Is Cry," *St. Louis Republican*, November 17, 1908, p. 7.

4. Ibid.

5. Ibid.

6. Ibid.

7. "Negro Segregation Plan," *St. Louis Republican*, February 28, 1911, p. 10.

8. Joseph L. Arnold, "The Neighborhood and City Hall: The Origin of Neighborhood Associations in Baltimore, 1880–1911," *Journal of Urban History* 6 (November 1979).

9. Lawrence Oland Christensen, "Black St. Louis: A Study in Race Relations, 1865–1916" (Ph.D. diss., University of Missouri–Columbia, 1972), 227.

10. Ibid., 228.

11. Ibid.

12. Ibid., 239, 249.

13. Wayne E. Wheeling, Secretary of the St. Louis Real Estate Exchange, to Mr. William K. Birby, February 5, 1915, Segregation Scrapbook, Missouri Historical Society. Letter is on United Welfare Association stationery and is a form letter.

14. "Segregation to Be Fought in Courts; Won by 24,000," *St. Louis Post-Dispatch*, March 1, 1916, p. 1; Fainsod, "The Influence of Racial and National Groups," 58–59.

15. *St. Louis Republic*, March 1, 1916, in Segregation Scrapbook, Missouri Historical Society.

16. Katharine T. Corbett and Mary E. Seematter, "'No Crystal Stair': Black St. Louis, 1920–1940," *Gateway Heritage* 16 (Fall 1995): 83.

17. Fainsod, "The Influence of Racial and National Groups," 54.

18. Ibid., 65.

19. Ibid., 63–64.

20. Primm, *Lion of the Valley*, 425.

21. Ibid., 435.

22. Louis F. Budenz, "The Assault on the St. Louis Machine," *National Municipal Review* 7 (July 1921): 363.

23. Ibid.

24. Ibid.

25. Ibid., 365.

26. "Dickmann to Take No Sides on Change in Condemnation," *St. Louis Post-Dispatch*, March 4, 1933, p. 1.

27. See Carl Abbott, *Urban America in the Modern Age: 1920 to Present* (Arlington Heights, Ill.: Harlan Davidson, 1987), 15.

28. Primm, *Lion of the Valley*, 447–49.

29. Ibid., 445.

30. Samuel Lubell, *The Future of American Politics*, rev. 3d ed. (New York: Harper & Row, 1965), 49.

31. "Election Results in St. Louis," *St. Louis Post-Dispatch*, November 9,

1932, p. 1.

32. "Democrats Here Take All Offices on Ballot," *St. Louis Post-Dispatch*, November 9, 1932, p. 1.

33. "A Storybook Politician Reminisces," *St. Louis Globe-Democrat*, May 25, 1959.

34. "Dickmann to Take No Side on Change in Commendation," *St. Louis Post-Dispatch*, March 4, 1933.

35. "Dickmann First Bachelor Mayor Here in 50 Years," *St. Louis Post-Dispatch*, April 5, 1933.

36. "Dickmann and Neun Win Easily," *St. Louis Post-Dispatch*, March 11, 1933, p. 1.

37. Ibid.

38. Ibid.

39. David Grant, interview by Richard Resh, *Oral History Program*, University of Missouri–St. Louis (August 24, 1970): 8.

40. Corbett and Seematter, "'No Crystal Stair,'" 84–85.

41. Grant, interview, 9.

42. Corbett and Seematter, "'No Crystal Stair,'" 85.

43. JoAnn Adams Smith, *Selected Neighbors and Neighborhoods of North St. Louis* (St. Louis: Friends of Vaughn Cultural Center, 1988), 70.

44. Ernestine Patterson, "The Impact of the Black Struggle on Representative Government in St. Louis" (Ph.D. diss., Saint Louis University, 1968), 174–75.

45. Grant, interview, 11.

46. Ibid.

47. Eugene "Tink" Bradley, interview by Isaac Darden, *Oral History Program*, University of Missouri–St. Louis (September 22, 1980): 11.

48. "Total of 250,000 Ballots Expected in Tomorrow's Election," *St. Louis Globe-Democrat*, April 4, 1933, p. 1.

49. Ibid.

50. *St. Louis American*, April 1, 1933, p. 1. Cited by William Jefferson Harrison, "The New Deal in Black St. Louis" (Ph.D. diss., Saint Louis

University, 1976), 24.

51. "Dickmann Is Elected Mayor by 15,600," *St. Louis Post-Dispatch*, April 5, 1933, p. 1.

52. *St. Louis Globe-Democrat*, April 5, 1933, p. 1.

53. "Division of Jobs to Be Dickmann's First Large Task," *St. Louis Globe-Democrat*, April 6, 1933, p. 11.

54. Ibid.

55. See Lana Stein, *Holding Bureaucrats Accountable: Politicians and Professionals in St. Louis* (Tuscaloosa: University of Alabama Press, 1991).

Chapter 3

1. "Division of Jobs," p. 11.

2. Ibid.

3. Mickey McTague, "Hope and Barney Spring Eternal! A Brief Resume of Barney Mueller" (unpublished manuscript, 1994), 1.

4. Thomas F. Eagleton and Diane L. Duffin, "Bob Hannegan and Harry Truman's Vice Presidential Nomination," *Missouri Historical Review* 90 (April 1996).

5. "Where in Politics?," in *Your St. Louis and Mine*, ed. Nathan Young (St. Louis, Mo., 1937), 38.

6. William Jefferson Harrison, "The New Deal in Black St. Louis: 1932–1940" (Ph.D. diss., Saint Louis University, 1976), 62.

7. Ibid., 72.

8. Mayor Bernard Dickmann, "Saint Louis Forward: A Report to Its Stockholders" (report, March 5, 1937).

9. Gary Ross Mormino, *Immigrants on the Hill: Italian Americans in St. Louis, 1882–1982* (Urbana: University of Illinois Press, 1986), 180–81.

10. Ibid., 184.

11. Michael Lewis, "No Relief from Politics: Machine Bosses and Civil Works," *Urban Affairs Quarterly* 30 (December 1994): 210–26.

12. Lyle W. Dorsett, *Franklin D.*

Roosevelt and the City Bosses (Port Washington, N.Y.: Kennikat Press, 1977), 70.

13. Ibid., 75.

14. Carlos Hurd, "St. Louis: Boundary Bound," in *Our Fair City*, ed. Robert S. Allen (New York: Vanguard Press, 1947), 236.

15. Steven P. Erie, *Rainbow's End: Irish Americans and the Dilemma of Machine Politics, 1840–1985* (Berkeley: University of California Press, 1988), 131.

16. Ibid., 133–34.

17. Primm, *Lion of the Valley*, 476.

18. Joel A. Tarr and Carl Zimring, "The Struggle for Smoke Control in St. Louis," in *Common Fields: An Environmental History of St. Louis*, ed. Andrew Hurley (St. Louis: Missouri Historical Society Press, 1997), 210.

19. Primm, *Lion of the Valley*, 476.

20. "Area Facts," *St. Louis Post-Dispatch*, November 29, 1997, p. 7.

21. Charles H. Cornwell, *St. Louis Mayors* (St. Louis: St. Louis Public Library, 1965), 34, 38.

22. Chicago residents elected a mayor, city treasurer, and fifty aldermen. Their aldermen may also serve as committeemen. As part of Cook County, they helped select fifteen county commissioners and six county officials. See Banfield and Wilson, *City Politics*, 80.

23. "Republicans Lose All of Important Posts in St. Louis," *St. Louis Post-Dispatch*, November 7, 1934, p. 1A.

24. Ibid.

25. Ibid.

26. Ibid.

27. "Republican Leaders Concede Rout with Majorities Mounting," *St. Louis Globe-Democrat*, November 7, 1934, p. 1A.

28. Ibid.

29. The collector had ninety-seven jobs and a $189,650 payroll; the circuit clerk had eighty-one jobs and a $140,000 payroll. See "Republicans Lose," *Post-Dispatch*, p. 1A.

30. "Republican Leaders Concede," p. 1A.

31. "Dickmann's Aldermanic Slate Victorious," *St. Louis Globe-Democrat*, March 9, 1935, p. 1A.

32. "Mayor's New Organization Disturbs Party," *St. Louis Post-Dispatch*, February 19, 1936.

33. "Mayor Begins Slate Picking in Party Fight," *St. Louis Globe-Democrat*, July 9, 1936.

34. "Cantwell Tells Mayor He Ought to Tend to Job," *St. Louis Post-Dispatch*, July 20, 1936.

35. Ibid.

36. Ibid.

37. Ibid.

38. "English Apparently Defeated in 24th by Gene Gualdoni," *St. Louis Globe-Democrat*, August 5, 1936, p. 1A.

39. "Democrats Win All Offices in St. Louis Sweep," *St. Louis Post-Dispatch*, November 5, 1936, p. 1A.

40. "Mayor Dickmann's Four Years at City Hall," *St. Louis Post-Dispatch*, March 29, 1937, p. 4A.

41. Ibid.

42. "City Primary Election Today," *St. Louis Globe-Democrat*, March 12, 1937, p. 1A.

43. "Mayor's Slate Sweeps All Except 1st Ward," *St. Louis Globe-Democrat*, March 13, 1937, p. 1A.

44. "Priest Leads Dwyer," *St. Louis Globe-Democrat*, August 3, 1938, p. 1A.

45. Ibid.

46. "Democrats Sweep City by 2 to 1 Margin," *St. Louis Globe-Democrat*, November 9, 1938, p. 1A.

47. "'Stop Dickmann' Movement Grows in His Own Party," *St. Louis Globe-Democrat*, July 7, 1940.

48. Ibid.

49. "Ward Politicians Nominate 5 of 9 Candidates for Circuit Judge," *St. Louis Post-Dispatch*, August 7, 1940, p. A1; "M'Donald Is Disgusted with

Political Chicanery," *St. Louis Post-Dispatch*, August 8, 1940.

50. "M'Donald Is Disgusted."

51. "Ward Politicians Nominate," p. A1.

52. Hurd, "St. Louis," 237.

53. "Donnell 3,286 Ahead with 5 Counties Out," *St. Louis Globe-Democrat*, November 10, 1940, p. 1A.

54. "Governor Contest in Assembly Predicted," *St. Louis Globe-Democrat*, November 11, 1940, p. 1A.

55. "Donnell Ahead with 3,489 Votes," *St. Louis Globe-Democrat*, November 12, 1940, p. 1A; "Donnell's Lead Set at 3,504," *St. Louis Globe-Democrat*, November 16, 1940.

56. "Donnell's Lead Set at 3,504."

57. "Governor Contest," *St. Louis Globe-Democrat*, January 9, 1941.

58. "GOP 'Evidence' in Contest Ready," *St. Louis Globe-Democrat*, January 9, 1941.

59. "Says Donnell Should Be Seated First," *St. Louis Globe-Democrat*, January 16, 1941, p. 1A.

60. *St. Louis Globe-Democrat*, January 26, 1941, p. 1A.

61. "State and City Officials Roast," *St. Louis Globe-Democrat*, January 29, 1941, p. 2A.

62. *St. Louis Globe-Democrat*, February 20, 1941.

63. Hurd, "St. Louis," 237.

64. "G.O.P. Outvotes Democrats by 13,500 for Best Showing Since '32," *St. Louis Post-Dispatch*, March 8, 1941, p. 1A.

65. "GOP Candidate to Back Winner," *St. Louis Globe-Democrat*, March 2, 1941.

66. "Republicans Counting on Big Primary Vote," *St. Louis Globe-Democrat*, March 2, 1941, p. 5A.

67. "GOP Hammers at City 'Machine,'" *St. Louis Globe-Democrat*, March 5, 1941, p. 1.

68. "GOP Candidates Blast Dickmann Machine as Campaign Closes," *St. Louis Globe-Democrat*, March 8, 1941, p. 2A.

69. "Civil Service Plan Called Mayor's Scheme to Perpetuate Machine," *St. Louis Globe-Democrat*, November 29, 1940.

70. Ray J. Noonan, "Barney Keeps Right on Going," *St. Louis Globe-Democrat*, July 17, 1965.

71. "Becker Elected Mayor," *St. Louis Globe-Democrat*, April 2, 1941, p. 1A.

72. Paul M. Green, "Anton J. Cermak: The Man and His Machine," in *The Mayors: The Chicago Political Tradition*, ed. Paul M. Green and Melvin G. Holli, rev. ed. (Carbondale: Southern Illinois University Press, 1995), 99.

73. Paul M. Green, "Same Old Players—Same Old Rules," in *The Making of the Mayor, Chicago, 1983*, ed. Melvin G. Holli and Paul M. Green (Grand Rapids, Mich.: William B. Eerdsmans, 1984), 18.

74. Green, "Anton J. Cermak," 101–2.

75. Ibid., 105.

76. Roger Biles, "Edward J. Kelly: New Deal Machine Builder," in *The Mayors: The Chicago Political Tradition*, ed. Paul M. Green and Melvin G. Holli, rev. ed. (Carbondale: Southern Illinois University Press, 1995), 125.

77. Ibid., 116.

78. Michael P. Weber, *Don't Call Me Boss: David L. Lawrence, Pittsburgh's Renaissance Mayor* (Pittsburgh: Pittsburgh University Press, 1988), 70.

79. Ibid., 67.

80. Ibid., 47.

CHAPTER 4

1. "Civil Service Plan Called Mayor's Scheme to Perpetuate Machine," *St. Louis Globe-Democrat*, November 29, 1940.

2. Carlos F. Hurd, "Merit System for the City's Employees Is the Aim of

Charter Amendment No. 3," *St. Louis Post-Dispatch*, August 24, 1941, p. 1C.

3. "City Jobs Given 2,548 in G.O.P. Since April 15," *St. Louis Post-Dispatch*, September 5, 1941.

4. *St. Louis Post-Dispatch*, September 14, 1941, p. 1A.

5. *St. Louis Globe-Democrat*, September 16, 1941, p. 1A.

6. Carlos F. Hurd, "Amendment No. 3 Offers Way to Remove Public Service from Politics," *St. Louis Post-Dispatch*, September 14, 1941, p. 1A.

7. "Simple and Practical Examinations Are Proposed to Determine Applicants' Qualifications" and "Dismissal, Demotion, or Pay Cut Only for Failure to Do Satisfactory Work," *St. Louis Post-Dispatch*, September 14, 1941.

8. Hurd, "Amendment No. 3."

9. *St. Louis Post-Dispatch*, September 14, 1941, p. 3A.

10. Stein, *Holding Bureaucrats Accountable,* chapter 3.

11. William L. Riordon, *Plunkitt of Tammany Hall* (New York: E. P. Dutton, 1963), 11.

12. "Independent Voters to Decide Fate," *St. Louis Globe-Democrat*, September 14, 1941.

13. Carlos F. Hurd, "Election of Aldermen by Wards the Issue of Charter Amendment No. 1," *St. Louis Post-Dispatch*, September 14, 1941, p. 1A.

14. Ibid.

15. "Civil Service Amendment Wins by 2,966 Votes and Election of Aldermen by Wards by 8,687," *St. Louis Globe-Democrat*, September 17, 1941, p. 1A.

16. "Independent Voters to Decide Fate," p. 1A.

17. "Civil Service Amendment Wins," p. 1A.

18. Ibid.

19. Ibid.

20. See, for example, "Civil Service Amendment Wins."

21. "Ward Elections Assure Minority Representation," *St. Louis Globe-Democrat*, September 17, 1941.

22. Thomas H. O'Connor, *The Boston Irish: A Political History* (Boston: Northeastern University Press, 1995), 189.

23. Ibid., 177.

24. Barbara Ferman, *Governing the Ungovernable City: Political Skill, Leadership, and the Modern Mayor* (Philadelphia: Temple University Press, 1985), 19.

25. Ibid.., 205.

26. Weber, *Don't Call Me Boss*, 70.

27. Ibid., 70–71.

28. Ibid., 231–35.

CHAPTER 5

1. Municipal elections occur every two years in St. Louis. The municipal primary occurs in March, now on the first Tuesday but in the 1940s on a Friday. The general election is the first Tuesday in April. The elections occur in odd-numbered years. Half the aldermen, from the even-numbered wards, run at the same time as the president of the board. Elections for the odd-numbered wards are held at the same time as contests for mayor and comptroller.

2. "Kaufmann Ran 47,000 Votes Ahead of Dewey," *St. Louis Globe-Democrat*, November 9, 1944, p. 3A.

3. Richard G. Baumhoff, "Mayor Kaufmann by 31,000 Plurality; Democrats Carry Rest of St. Louis Ticket," *St. Louis Post-Dispatch*, November 8, 1944, p. 1A.

4. "How to Vote for Roosevelt for President, Kaufmann for Mayor," *St. Louis Post-Dispatch*, November 4, 1944.

5. "Kaufmann Wins by 54,512 in City Republican Sweep," *St. Louis Post-Dispatch*, April 4, 1945, p. 7A.

50. Ibid.
51. Herbert A. Trask, "Tucker Overwhelmingly Reelected," *St. Louis Post-Dispatch*, April 3, 1957, p. 1A.
52. Primm, *Lion of the Valley*, 491.
53. William Lambert, "Ex-Con Who Spends Big on Candidates," *Life*, July 28, 1968, 42A.
54. "Larry Callanan Dies; Leader of Pipefitters," *St. Louis Post-Dispatch*, March 3, 1971.
55. Kenneth E. Gray and David Greenstone, "Organized Labor in City Politics," in *Urban Government*, ed. Edward C. Banfield (New York: The Free Press of Glencoe, 1961), 375.
56. Steven Brill, *The Teamsters* (New York: Simon and Schuster, 1978), 357.
57. Gray and Greenstone, "Organized Labor," 375.
58. The state constitution provided for boards of freeholders from the city alone or the city and county to revise existing structural arrangements. Freeholders were to be property owners. In 1990, the property qualification was successfully challenged in the courts, and boards of freeholders became boards of electors made up of voters from the appropriate jurisdiction.
59. "11 Men, 2 Women on Freeholders' Board to Rewrite Charter for City," *St. Louis Post-Dispatch*, April 6, 1949, p. 1A.
60. *St. Louis Post-Dispatch*, April 1, 1949, p. 2C.
61. Charter of the City of St. Louis Proposed by the 1949–50 Board of Freeholders, St. Louis Public Library, II.
62. "Work Well Done," *St. Louis Post-Dispatch*, April 6, 1950, p. 2B.
63. "Darst Declares for New Charter, Stand Cheers Its Advocates," *St. Louis Post-Dispatch*, July 16, 1950.
64. "Democratic Bloc Maps Drive to Defeat Charter," *St. Louis Post-Dispatch*, July 19, 1950, p. 3A.
65. "New Charter Beaten by 51,200," *St. Louis Post-Dispatch*, August 2, 1950, p. 1A.
66. Ibid.
67. Richard R. Dohn, "Political Culture of Missouri," in *Missouri Government and Politics*, ed. Richard J. Hardy and Richard R. Dohn (Columbia: University of Missouri Press, 1985), 179; Peter A. Harkness, "Dollars and Discipline," in *State and Local Sourcebook 1998*, supplement to *Governing*, 11. Harkness states that "Missouri stands out as a state that doesn't spend much in any area.... (It is) in last place in spending as a share of income." Dohn found that "Missouri's government is more conservative than most other states, at least with respect to taxation, expenditures, and innovative programs."
68. Kenneth E. Gray, *A Report on Politics in Saint Louis* (Cambridge, Mass.: Center for Urban Studies, Harvard University, 1961), 9–10.
69. Ibid.
70. Robert H. Salisbury, "The Dynamics of Reform: Charter Politics in St. Louis," *Midwest Journal of Politics*, August 1961, 268.
71. Ibid.
72. Ibid.
73. Gray, *A Report on Politics in Saint Louis*, 15–17.
74. Henry J. Schmandt, Paul G. Steinbicker, and George D. Wendel, *Metropolitan Reform in St. Louis: A Case Study* (New York: Holt, Rinehart and Winston, 1961), 5.
75. Ibid.
76. Ibid.
77. Ibid., 8.
78. Ibid.
79. Robert H. Salisbury, "St. Louis Politics: Relationships Among Interests, Parties, and Governmental Structure," *The Western Political*

Quarterly 18 (June 1960), and "The Dynamics of Reform," 268.

80. Schmandt, Steinbicker, and Wendel, *Metropolitan Reform*, 43.

81. Ibid.

82. Ibid.

83. E. Terrence Jones, *Fragmentation by Design: Why St. Louis Has So Many Governments* (St. Louis: Palmerston & Reed, 2000), 67–68.

84. Ibid., 69.

85. Milton Rakove, "Observations and Reflections on the Current and Future Directions of the Chicago Democratic Machine," in *The Making of the Mayor*, 127.

86. Gary Rivlin, *A Fire on the Prairie: Chicago's Harold Washington and the Politics of Race* (New York: Henry Holt and Company, 1992), 9.

87. Rakove, "Observations and Reflections," 137.

88. Ibid.

89. Kirschten, *Catfish and Crystal*, 438.

90. Ibid.

91. Ibid.

92. Professionals in government often have voiced these sentiments. See, for example, Stein, *Holding Bureaucrats Accountable*. They still reverberate in the early 2000s.

93. Press release, Raymond Tucker Papers, Washington University Archives (March 23, 1957).

94. Salisbury, "St. Louis Politics."

95. C. L. Kelliher, "Tucker Beats Holloran by 1,272—Vote Margin for Third Term Nomination," *St. Louis Post-Dispatch*, March 8, 1961, p. 1A.

96. Ibid.

97. "Tucker Appeals for a Record Vote Tuesday," *St. Louis Post-Dispatch*, March 7, 1965, p. 1A.

98. Robert Huckfeldt and Carol W. Kohfeld, *Race and the Decline of Class in American Politics* (Urbana: University of Illinois Press, 1989).

99. Larry R. Ford, *Cities and Buildings* (Baltimore: Johns Hopkins University Press, 1994), 90.

CHAPTER 7

1. Similar wards on Chicago's west side were called "plantation" wards, but in Chicago they were also part of a hierarchical machine; see William J. Grimshaw, *Bitter Fruit: Black Politics and the Chicago Machine, 1931–1991* (Chicago: University of Chicago Press, 1992), 120.

2. O'Neill, *Man of the House*, 112.

3. William L. Clay, *Just Permanent Interests: Black Americans in Congress, 1870–1991* (New York: Amistad, 1992), 54–55.

4. Ibid., 57.

5. Sonenshein, *Politics in Black and White*, 5.

6. George Lipsitz, *A Life in the Struggle: Ivory Perry and the Culture of Opposition* (Philadelphia: Temple University Press, 1988), 68.

7. "New Charter Beaten by 51,200," *St. Louis Post-Dispatch*, August 2, 1950, p. 1A.

8. Ibid.

9. Salisbury, "The Dynamics of Reform," 268.

10. Ibid., 272.

11. Raymond Tucker Papers, Washington University Archives, Series 1, Box 10.

12. Ibid.

13. Raymond Tucker Papers, Washington University Archives, Series 1, Box 3.

14. Alphonso J. Cervantes with Laurence G. Blochman, *Mr. Mayor* (Los Angeles: Nast Publishing, 1974), 9–10.

15. Ibid., 10.

16. "Aldermen Pass Anti-Bias Public Accommodations Bill by Vote of 20 to 4," *St. Louis Post-Dispatch*, May 19, 1961, p. 1A.

17. "Types of Places Coming under Anti-Bias Law to Be Listed," *St. Louis Post-Dispatch*, May 20, 1961,

p. 1A.

18. Ibid.

19. Ernest Calloway, "It Finally Came to Pass: Board of Aldermen Adopts First Major Civil Rights Ordinance," *The New Citizen,* May 26, 1961, reprinted in Ernest Calloway, *Notes on St. Louis Politics,* privately printed.

20. Ernest Patterson, *Black City Politics* (New York: Dodd, Mead and Company, 1974), 37.

21. Ibid.

22. Elizabeth M. Rene, "The Jefferson Bank Controversy: A Chapter in the History of St. Louis" (paper, May 12, 1977), 3.

23. *St. Louis Post-Dispatch,* August 28, 1963, cited by Patterson, *Black City Politics,* 96.

24. Cited by Patterson, *Black City Politics,* 96.

25. Rene, "Jefferson Bank Controversy," 7.

26. "Mayor Assails Disorder: Says It Harms Drive," *St. Louis Post-Dispatch,* September 1, 1963, p. 1A, cited by Rene, 5.

27. *St. Louis Post-Dispatch,* January 17, 1964.

28. *St. Louis Post-Dispatch,* January 21, 1964.

29. Marion Orr, "Electoral Control and Governing Coalitions: The Struggle for Black Empowerment in Baltimore," in *Racial Politics in American Cities,* ed. Rufus P. Browning, Dale Rogers Marshall, and David H. Tabb, 2d ed. (New York: Longman, 1997), 205–7.

30. Orr, "Electoral Control," 204–5, and Kevin O'Keeffe, *Baltimore Politics, 1971–1986: The Schaefer Years and the Struggle for Succession* (Washington, D.C.: Georgetown University Press, 1986), 22–23.

31. Orr, "The Struggle," 205.

32. James Q. Wilson, *Negro Politics* (Glencoe, Ill.: The Free Press, 1960), 35.

33. Ibid., 53.

34. William J. Grimshaw, "Harold Washington: The Enigma of the Black Political Tradition," in *The Mayors,* 184–85.

35. Wilson, *Negro Politics,* 22.

36. Ibid.

37. Ibid.

Chapter 8

1 U.S. Bureau of the Census, Censuses of Population, (Washington, D.C.: U.S. Government Printing Office, 1950 and 1980).

2. Ibid.

3. Baer, *Saint Louis to Me,* 261.

4. Ibid., 262.

5. U.S. Bureau of the Census, *County and City Data Book, 1983* (Washington, D.C.: U.S. Government Printing Office, 1983).

6. Carol W. Kohfeld and John Sprague, "Urban Unemployment Drives Crime," *Urban Affairs Quarterly* 24 (1988): 215–41.

7. Cervantes, *Mr. Mayor,* 78.

8. Ibid., 35.

9. Ibid., 4–5.

10. See Ferman, *Challenging the Growth Machine.*

11. See Robert J. Kerstein and Dennis R. Judd, "Achieving Less Influence with More Democracy: The Permanent Legacy of the War on Poverty," *Social Science Quarterly* 61 (September 1980): 212.

12. Ibid., 214.

13. Ibid., 215.

14. "St. Louis Deaths: S. Miller-Shabazz," *St. Louis Post-Dispatch,* December 29, 1998, p. B4.

15. Lipsitz, *A Life in the Struggle,* 147.

16. See Cervantes, *Mr. Mayor,* chapter

4, and Eugene J. Meehan, *The Quality of Federal Policymaking: Programmed Failure in Public Housing* (Columbia: University of Missouri Press, 1979).

17. Cervantes, *Mr. Mayor*, 14.

18. Ibid., 17.

19. Teaford, *Rough Road to Renaissance*, 239.

20. Ibid., 242.

21. Baer, *Saint Louis to Me*, 16.

22. Cervantes, *Mr. Mayor*, 132–34.

23. Ibid., 151.

24. Baer, *Saint Louis to Me*, 174–97.

25. Ibid., 192.

26. "Badaracco Wins in an Upset," *St. Louis Post-Dispatch*, April 4, 1969, p. 1A.

27. Ibid.

28. Robert Christman, "City Democrats View Results as Protest," *St. Louis Post-Dispatch*, April 3, 1969, p. 4A.

29. John H. Mollenkopf, *A Phoenix in the Ashes: The Rise and Fall of the Koch Coalition in New York City Politics* (Princeton, N.J.: Princeton University Press, 1992), 77, citing V. O. Key, Jr., *Southern Politics in State and Nation* (New York: Vintage Books, 1949), chapter 14.

30. Key, *Southern Politics*, 298.

31. Mollenkopf, chapter 4 in *A Phoenix in the Ashes*.

32. "Lawler's Death Leaves Gap in Party Leadership," *St. Louis Globe-Democrat*, February 11, 1972.

33. John Angelides, "The Power of the Wards," *St. Louis Globe-Democrat*, August 22, 1969.

34. Ibid.

35. John Angelides, "City Hall Report," *St. Louis Globe-Democrat*, May 15–16, 1971.

36. John Angelides, "City Hall Report," *St. Louis Globe-Democrat*, December 14–25, 1966.

37. Ibid.

38. "Factions Plaguing City Democrats," *St. Louis Globe-Democrat*, August 10, 1972.

39. Terry Ganey and Tim O'Neil, "The Stealth Senator," *St. Louis Post-Dispatch*, September 14, 1997, p. B1.

40. *St. Louis Post-Dispatch*, September 7, 1972.

41. *St. Louis Post-Dispatch*, October 21, 1977.

42. *St. Louis Globe-Democrat*, October 21, 1977.

43. Clay, *Just Permanent Interests*, 324–29.

44. Ibid., 328.

45. See, for example, Douglas S. Massey and Nancy A. Denton, *American Apartheid: Segregation and the Making of the Underclass* (Cambridge, Mass.: Harvard University Press, 1993).

46. See Ferman, *Challenging the Growth Machine*.

47. Teaford, *Rough Road to Renaissance*, 247.

48. Ruth Kamploefner, "The Love Affair Goes On," *The Lafayette Square Marquis* 20 (December 1998): 5.

49. Originally referred to in the popular press as Syrians, and later as the Syrian-Lebanese, most descendants today claim to come from a small village in what is now Lebanon. They are Maronite Catholics and worship at St. Raymond's, which is still located in the heart of the seventh ward, the original Lebanese political stronghold.

50. *St. Louis Globe-Democrat*, February 8, 1968.

51. Denny Walsh, "A Two-Faced Crime Fight in St. Louis," *Life*, May 29, 1970, 26.

52. Cervantes, *Mr. Mayor*, 91.

53. Walsh, "A Two-Faced Crime Fight," 26.

54. Cervantes, *Mr. Mayor*, 90.

55. Jerry Berger, "Dunc's *Globe*," *St. Louis Post-Dispatch*, October 19, 1995.

56. John M. McGuire, "Our Gang," *St. Louis Post-Dispatch*, February 26,

1995, p. E1.

57. Ibid.

58. Some information regarding these events was found in an undated *Post-Dispatch* article located in a private clipping collection loaned to me.

59. Raymond J. Lawrence, "Cable TV Data in Leisure's Car After Blast, Officer Testifies," *St. Louis Post-Dispatch*, from private collection.

60. Ibid.; Bill Bryan, "Evidence in Schepp Trial Links Leisure to Cable TV War," *St. Louis Globe-Democrat*, private collection.

61. Michael R. Montgomery, "Crucial Files Missing, Webbe Lawyer Says," *St. Louis Globe-Democrat*, private collection.

62. Len O'Connor, *Clout: Mayor Daley and His City* (Chicago: Henry Regnery, 1975), 113.

63. Tim Flach, "Magistrate Elections," *St. Louis Globe-Democrat*, July 17, 1978, p. 1A.

64. Karen Van Meter and William Freivogel, "4 and $\frac{1}{2}$ Hour Day on $19,000 Court Job," *St. Louis Post-Dispatch*, May 31, 1974.

65. Tommy Robertson, "Evidence Held Insufficient for Prosecution," *St. Louis Post-Dispatch*, June 14, 1974.

66. William Freivogel and Karen Van Meter, "Cases Dropped for Politicians," *St. Louis Post-Dispatch*, June 30, 1974, p. 1A.

67. Ibid.

68. *St. Louis Globe-Democrat*, September 18, 1972.

69. "Cervantes Is Defeated by Poelker," *St. Louis Post-Dispatch*, March 7, 1973, p. 1A.

70. *St. Louis Globe-Democrat*, April 4, 1973.

71. *St. Louis Globe-Democrat*, October 4, 1973.

72. *St. Louis Globe-Democrat*, October 4, 1976.

73. Ibid.

74. Ibid.

75. Jack Flach, "Black Mayor Here? Not Yet," *St. Louis Globe-Democrat*, April 21, 1975.

76. William E. Nelson, Jr., "Cleveland: The Evolution of Black Political Power," in *The New Black Politics*, ed. Michael B. Preston, Lenneal J. Henderson, Jr., and Paul L. Puryear, 2d ed. (New York: Longman, 1987); Mollenkopf, "New York: The Great Anomaly," in *Racial Politics in American Cities*.

77. Daniel J. Monti, *Race, Redevelopment, and the Company Town* (Albany: State University of New York Press, 1990), 115.

78. Dana L. Spitzer, "Conway Leads in Spending on Mayor's Race," *St. Louis Post-Dispatch*, March 2, 1977, p. 1B.

79. Ibid. It should be noted that campaign-finance reporting began only a couple years before this race, as a result of Watergate. Records are maintained for only five years.

80. Dana L. Spitzer, "Conway Wins by a Landslide; Bass Unseated," *St. Louis Post-Dispatch*, March 9, 1977, p. 1A.

81. *St. Louis Post-Dispatch*, January 22, 1978.

82. Spitzer, "Conway Wins by a Landslide."

83. Gerald M. Boyd, "Write-in for Bass Considered," *St. Louis Post-Dispatch*, March 9, 1977, p. 1A.

84. John M. McGuire, "Perich in Character; Celebration Is Subdued," *St. Louis Post-Dispatch*, March 9, 1977, p. 4A.

85. Gerald M. Boyd and J. Pulitzer, "Clay's Campaign for Mayor May Split City Democrats," *St. Louis Post-Dispatch*, March 10, 1977, p. 1A.

86. Ibid.

87. Ibid.

88. Ibid.

89. *St. Louis Post-Dispatch*, October 21, 1977.

90. Monti, *Race, Redevelopment, and*

the Company Town, 130.

91. Ibid., 158.

92. Ibid., 144–45.

93. A. J. Cervantes, "Memoirs of a Business Mayor," *Business Week*, December 8, 1973.

94. See Stein, *Holding Bureaucrats Accountable*.

95. Huckfeldt and Kohfeld, *Race and the Decline of Class*, 119–121.

CHAPTER 9

1. Jackson, *Crabgrass Frontier*, 217.

2. Jo Mannies, "Schoemehl Upsets Conway," *St. Louis Post-Dispatch*, March 4, 1981, p. 1A.

3. "The Choice for Mayor," *St. Louis Post-Dispatch*, February 1, 1981.

4. Ibid.

5. Jo Mannies, "Conway's First Four Years," *St. Louis Post-Dispatch*, January 11, 1981, p. 1F.

6. For a portrait of Rendell, see Buzz Bissinger, *A Prayer for the City* (New York: Random House, 1997).

7. Primm, *Lion of the Valley*, 574.

8. Ibid., 541.

9. Ibid., 537–545. Primm provides considerable detail and photographs of the demolished structures.

10. Claude Louishomme, "Urban Regimes and Community Decision-making in St. Louis" (unpublished paper, 1992).

11. Robert H. Salisbury, "Our Fading Civic Leadership," *St. Louis Post-Dispatch*, November 26, 1995.

12. Teaford, *Rough Road to Renaissance*, 255.

13. Ibid., 259.

14. Ibid., 266–67.

15. Roy Malone, "Schoemehl Says Voters Would Reopen Phillips," *St. Louis Post-Dispatch*, January 11, 1981, p. 1B.

16. Jo Mannies, "Schoemehl Pledges to Reopen Phillips," *St. Louis Post-Dispatch*, March 4, 1981, p. 1A.

17. Jo Mannies, "State Demands on Phillips May Cause Schoemehl Shift," *St. Louis Post-Dispatch*, March 10, 1981, p. 1A.

18. Gregory B. Freeman, "South Siders Not Buying Proposal for Homer Phillips, Aldermen Say," *St. Louis Post-Dispatch*, April 1, 1982, p. 1A.

19. Gregory B. Freeman, "Mayor to Drop Drive to Reopen Phillips," *St. Louis Post-Dispatch*, November 3, 1982, p. 1A.

20. Gregory B. Freeman, "Alderman Challenges Mayor After Hospital Bonds' Defeat," *St. Louis Post-Dispatch*, November 3, 1982, p. 8A.

21. Freeman, "Mayor to Drop Drive," p. 1A.

22. John Mueller, "Presidential Popularity from Truman to Johnson," *American Political Science Review* 64 (1970): 18–34.

23. Charles W. Ostrom, Jr., and Dennis M. Simon, "Promise and Performance: A Dynamic Model of Presidential Popularity," *American Political Science Review* 79 (1985): 334–58.

24. Jo Mannies, "Schoemehl's Youthful Rise," *St. Louis Post-Dispatch*, November 8, 1981, p. 1B.

25. Jo Mannies, "Democrats Jockeying for Future Openings," *St. Louis Post-Dispatch*, March 22, 1981, p. 1D.

26. Jo Mannies, "Roddy Defeats Slay for Democratic Post," *St. Louis Post-Dispatch*, April 17, 1981, p. 1A.

27. Kenneth F. Warren, "A Long History of Stalking Horses," *St. Louis Post-Dispatch*, December 18, 1995, p. 7B.

28. Gregory B. Freeman, "Bosley Surprises City's Political Pros," *St. Louis Post-Dispatch*, August 5, 1982, p. 15A.

29. Lana Stein and Carol W. Kohfeld, "St. Louis's Black-White Elections: Products of Machine Factionalism and Polarization," *Urban Affairs Quarterly* 27 (December 1991): 240.

30. Gregory B. Freeman, "Roddy Gets

New Job: Clerk of City Courts," *St. Louis Post-Dispatch*, December 30, 1982, p. 3A.

31. Gregory B. Freeman, "Many Names Suggested as Mayoral Candidates," *St. Louis Post-Dispatch*, November 7, 1982, p. 4C.

32. "Schoemehl's Winning Hand: 91% of White Vote," *St. Louis Post-Dispatch*, March 7, 1985.

33. "1,500 City Jobs May Be Cut," *St. Louis Post-Dispatch*, April 23, 1981, p. 1A.

34. See Donald F. Kettl, *Sharing Power: Public Governance and Private Markets* (Washington, D.C.: The Brookings Institution, 1993), 155–78.

35. Jo Mannies, "Schoemehl Talks of Firm to Run Hospitals," *St. Louis Post-Dispatch*, April 4, 1981, p. 4A.

36. See Stein, *Holding Bureaucrats Accountable*.

37. Mark Schlinkmann, "Schoemehl, Clay Plan Meeting on Hospital," *St. Louis Post-Dispatch*, September 14, 1985, p. 1A.

38. Mark Schlinkmann, "Hospital Subsidy Sought," *St. Louis Post-Dispatch*, September 15, 1985, p. 1C.

39. Ibid.

40. Charlotte Grimes, "Clay Claims Accord on Hospital Plan," *St. Louis Post-Dispatch*, September 16, 1985, p. 1A.

41. Mark Schlinkmann, "Clay Glum on Hospital Deal's Outlook," *St. Louis Post-Dispatch*, September 17, 1985, p. 1A.

42. Mark Schlinkmann, "Hospital Pact Wins Initial Vote, " *St. Louis Post-Dispatch*, September 19, 1985, p. 1A.

43. Stein and Kohfeld, "St. Louis's Black-White Elections," 240.

44. Fred W. Lindecke, "Clay Working to Bolster Black Incumbents," *St. Louis Post-Dispatch*, May 17, 1986, p. 4A.

45. Mark Schlinkmann, "Schoemehl, Clay Locked in Political Contest," *St. Louis Post-Dispatch*, July 26, 1986, p. 1B.

46. Stein and Kohfeld, "St. Louis's Black-White Elections," 240.

47. Ibid., 243.

48. Tim O'Neil, "Three Schoemehl Allies Quit Civic Groups," *St. Louis Post-Dispatch*, November 10, 1988.

49. Stein and Kohfeld, "St. Louis's Black-White Elections," 240.

50. Tim O'Neil, "Hot Words over Move on Boykins," *St. Louis Post-Dispatch*, May 28, 1989.

51. Ibid.

52. Ibid.

53. Robert L. Koening, Louis J. Rose, and Michael D. Sorkin, "The Mayor's Money Machine," *St. Louis Post-Dispatch*, May 4–9, 1986.

54. Becky Homan, "Charging Ahead with Vince Schoemehl," *St. Louis Post-Dispatch Sunday PD*, April 25, 1982.

55. Bryan D. Jones, "Causation, Constraint, and Political Leadership," in *Leadership and Politics*, ed. Bryan D. Jones (Lawrence: University Press of Kansas, 1989), 5.

56. See O'Keeffe, *Baltimore Politics*, and Bissinger, *A Prayer for the City*.

CHAPTER 10

1. See Stein and Kohfeld, "St. Louis's Black-White Elections."

2. Sonenshein, *Politics in Black and White*.

3. Ibid., 5.

4. Roger Biles, *Richard J. Daley: Politics, Race, and the Governing of Chicago* (DeKalb: Northern Illinois University Press, 1995), 237.

5. John Mollenkopf, "New York: The Great Anomaly," *PS* 19 (Summer 1986): 595.

6. John Mollenkopf, "New York: The Great Anomaly," in *Racial Politics in American Cities*, 83.

7. William E. Nelson, Jr., "Cleveland: The Evolution of Black Political Power."

8. Orr, "The Struggle for Black Empowerment," 213.

9. Ibid.

10. Lisa C. DeLorenzo, Carol W. Kohfeld, and Lana Stein, "The Impact of Cross-Racial Voting on St. Louis Primary Election Results," *Urban Affairs Review* 33 (September 1997): 120–33.

11. Richard F. Fenno, Jr., *Senators on the Campaign Trail: The Politics of Representation* (Norman: University of Oklahoma Press, 1996).

12. See John Portz, Lana Stein, and Robin R. Jones, *City Schools and City Politics: Institutions and Leadership in Pittsburgh, Boston, and St. Louis* (Lawrence: University Press of Kansas, 1999).

13. Ibid.

14. Tim Bryant and Thom Gross, "Jones Guilty Plea Expected, Comptroller May Get 6 Months in Prison," *St. Louis Post-Dispatch*, September 26, 1995, p. 1A.

15. See O'Neill, *Man of the House.*

16. Joe Holleman, "Full House: Politically Connected Bid for Landing Casinos," *St. Louis Post-Dispatch*, October 27, 1993.

17. Thom Gross, "Official Questions Bosley's Late Veto," *St. Louis Post-Dispatch*, August 22, 1995.

18. Thom Gross, "Project 87: Small City Program Developed into Big Controversy," *St. Louis Post-Dispatch*, October 3, 1995.

19. Jo Mannies, "Back Seat Drivers: Clarence Harmon Says He Quit as St. Louis Police Chief Because of 'Unnecessary and Unwarranted Interference' by the Members of City Police Board," *St. Louis Post-Dispatch*, December 3, 1995.

20. Ibid.

21. Carolyn Tuft, "Bosley Fires Top Aide Tied to Airport Deal," *St. Louis Post-Dispatch*, November 9, 1996.

22. "St. Louis's First Black Mayor Loses Primary," *Washington Post*, March 6, 1997.

23. "No Brothers They," *The Economist* (March 8, 1997): 29.

24. Mark Schlinkmann, "The Mayor at Midterm: Still Learning," *St. Louis Post-Dispatch*, February 28, 1999.

25. Ibid.

26. Ibid.

27. Anne Freedman, "Doing Battle with the Patronage Army: Politics, Courts, and Personnel Administration in Chicago." *Public Administration Review* 48 (1986): 847–58.

CHAPTER 11

1. John M. Allswang, *Bosses, Machines, and Urban Voters* (Baltimore: Johns Hopkins University Press, 1986), 163–64.

2. Ester R. Fuchs, *Mayors and Money: Fiscal Policy in New York and Chicago* (Chicago: The University of Chicago Press), 6.

References
Books, Journal Articles, Dissertations, and Theses

Abbott, Carl. *Urban America in the Modern Age: 1920 to Present.* Arlington Heights, Ill.: Harlan Davidson, 1987.

Allswang, John M. *Bosses, Machines, and Urban Voters.* Baltimore: Johns Hopkins University Press, 1986.

Arnold, Joseph L. "The Neighborhood and City Hall: The Origin of Neighborhood Associations in Baltimore, 1880–1911." *Journal of Urban History* 6 (1979): 3–30.

Baer, Howard F. *Saint Louis to Me.* St. Louis: Hawthorn Publishing Company, 1978.

Banfield, Edward C. *Big City Politics.* New York: Random House, 1965.

Banfield, Edward C., and James Q. Wilson. *City Politics.* Cambridge, Mass.: Harvard University Press, 1963.

Barclay, Thomas S. *The St. Louis Home Rule Charter of 1876.* Columbia: University of Missouri Press, 1962.

Bartley, Mary. *St. Louis Lost.* St. Louis: Virginia Publishing Company, 1994.

Beito, David T., with Bruce Smith. "The Formation of Urban Infrastructure Through Nongovernmental Planning: The Private Places of St. Louis, 1869–1920." *Journal of Urban History* 16 (1990): 263–303.

Biles, Roger. *Richard J. Daley: Politics, Race, and the Governing of Chicago.* DeKalb: Northern Illinois University Press, 1995.

Bissinger, Buzz. *A Prayer for the City.* New York: Random House, 1997.

Bridges, Amy. *A City in the Republic: Antebellum New York and the Origins of Machine Politics.* Ithaca, N.Y.: Cornell University Press, 1987.

Brill, Steven. *The Teamsters.* New York: Simon and Schuster, 1978.

Budenz, Louis F. "The Assault on the St. Louis Machine." *National Municipal Review,* July, 1921, 363–66.

Calloway, Ernest. "It Finally Came to Pass: Board of Aldermen Adopts First Major Civil Rights Ordinance." In *Notes on St. Louis Politics.* N.p., 1961. First published in *The New Citizen*, May 26, 1961.

Cervantes, Alphonso J., with Lawrence G. Blochman. *Mr. Mayor.* Los Angeles: Nash Publishing, 1974.

Christensen, Lawrence Oland. "Black St. Louis: A Study in Race Relations, 1865–1916." Ph.D. diss., University of Missouri–Columbia, 1972.

Clay, William L. *Just Permanent Interests: Black Americans in Congress, 1870–1991.* New York: Amistad, 1992.

Corbett, Katharine T., and Mary E. Seematter. "'No Crystal Stair': Black St. Louis, 1920–1940." *Gateway Heritage* 16 (1995): 82–88.

Cornwell, Charles H. *St. Louis Mayors.* St. Louis: St. Louis Public Library, 1965.

Dahl, Robert A. *Who Governs? Democracy and Power in an American City.* New Haven, Conn.: Yale University Press, 1961.

DeLorenzo, Lisa C., Carol W. Kohfeld, and Lana Stein. "The Impact of Cross-Racial Voting on St. Louis Primary Election Results." *Urban Affairs Review* 33 (1997): 120–33.

DiGaetano, Alan. "The Origins of Urban Political Machines in the United States: A Comparative Perspective." *Urban Affairs Quarterly* 26 (1991): 324–52.

Dohn, Richard R. "Political Culture of Missouri." In *Missouri Government and Politics*, edited by Richard J. Hardy and Richard R. Dohn.

Columbia: University of Missouri
Press, 1985.

Dorsett, Lyle W. *Franklin D. Roosevelt
and the City Bosses.* Port
Washington, N.Y.: Kennikat Press,
1977.

_____. *The Pendergast Machine.* New
York: Oxford University Press,
1968.

Eagleton, Thomas F., and Diane L.
Duffin. "Bob Hannegan and Harry
Truman's Vice Presidential
Nomination." *Missouri Historical
Review* 90 (1996): 265–83.

Eisinger, Peter K. "Local Civil Service
Employment and Black
Socioeconomic Mobility." *Social
Science Quarterly* 67 (1986):
169–75.

Elkin, Stephen L. *City and Regime in
the American Republic.* Chicago:
University of Chicago Press, 1987.

Erie, Steven P. *Rainbow's End: Irish
Americans and the Dilemma of
Machine Politics, 1840–1985.*
Berkeley: University of California
Press, 1988.

Fainsod, Merle. "The Influence of
Racial and National Groups in St.
Louis Politics: 1908–1928."
Master's diss., Washington
University, 1929.

Fainstein, Susan S., et al. *Restructuring
the City: The Political Economy of
Urban Redevelopment.* Rev. ed. New
York: Longman, 1986.

Fenno, Richard F., Jr. *Senators on the
Campaign Trail: The Politics of
Representation.* Norman: University
of Oklahoma Press, 1996.

Ferman, Barbara. *Challenging the
Growth Machine: Neighborhood
Politics in Chicago and Pittsburgh.*
Lawrence: University Press of
Kansas, 1996.

_____. *Governing the Ungovernable
City: Political Skill, Leadership, and
the Modern Mayor.* Philadelphia:
Temple University Press, 1985.

Ford, Larry R. *Cities and Buildings.*
Baltimore: Johns Hopkins

University Press, 1994.

Gray, Kenneth E. *A Report on Politics
in Saint Louis.* Cambridge, Mass.:
Harvard University Center for
Urban Studies, 1961.

Gray, Kenneth E., and David
Greenstone. "Organized Labor in
City Politics." In *Urban
Government,* edited by Edward C.
Banfield. New York: The Free Press
of Glencoe, 1961.

Grimshaw, William J. *Bitter Fruit:
Black Politics and the Chicago
Machine, 1931–1991.* Chicago:
University of Chicago Press, 1992.

Guese, Lucius E. "St. Louis and the
Great Whiskey Ring." *Missouri
Historical Review* 36 (1942):
160–83.

Halberstam, David. *The Powers That Be.*
New York: Alfred A. Knopf, 1979.

Harrison, William Jefferson. "The New
Deal in Black St. Louis:
1932–1940." Ph.D. diss., Saint
Louis University, 1976.

Hays, Samuel P. "The Politics of
Reform in the Progressive Era." In
Readings in Urban Politics, edited
by Harlan Hahn and Charles H.
Levine. 2d ed. New York: Longman,
1984.

Heilig, Peggy, and Robert J. Mundt.
*Your Voice at City Hall: The Politics,
Procedures, and Policies of District
Representation.* Albany: State
University of New York Press, 1984.

Huckfeldt, Robert, and Carol W.
Kohfeld. *Race and the Decline of
Class in American Politics.* Urbana:
University of Illinois Press, 1989.

Hurd, Carlos. "St. Louis: Boundary
Bound." In *Our Fair City,* edited by
Robert S. Allen. New York:
Vanguard Press, 1947.

Jackson, Kenneth T. *Crabgrass
Frontier: The Suburbanization of the
United States.* New York: Oxford
University Press, 1985.

Jones, Bryan D., and Lynn W.
Bachelor. *The Sustaining Hand:
Community Leadership and*

Corporate Power. 2d ed. Lawrence: University Press of Kansas, 1993.

Judd, Dennis R. "Reform or Revolution: Whatever Works." *St. Louis Journalism Review* 30 (1999): 14.

Judd, Dennis R., and Todd Swanstrom. *City Politics: Private Power and Public Policy.* 2d ed. New York: Longman, 1998.

Katznelson, Ira. *City Trenches: Urban Politics and the Patterning of Class in the United States.* New York: Pantheon, 1981.

Kelleher, Daniel T. "St. Louis' 1916 Residential Segregation Ordinance." *Bulletin* of the Missouri Historical Society, April, 1970, 239–48.

Kerstein, Robert J., and Dennis R. Judd. "Achieving Less Influence with More Democracy: The Permanent Legacy of the War on Poverty." *Social Science Quarterly* 61 (1980): 208–20.

Key, V. O., Jr. *Southern Politics in State and Nation.* New York: Vintage, 1949.

Kirschten, Ernest. *Catfish and Crystal.* Garden City, N.Y.: Doubleday, 1960.

Kohfeld, Carol W., and John Sprague. "Urban Unemployment Drives Crime." *Urban Affairs Quarterly* 24 (1988): 215–41.

Lewis, Michael. "No Relief from Politics: Machine Bosses and Civil Works." *Urban Affairs Quarterly* 30 (1994): 210–26.

Lipsitz, George. *A Life in the Struggle: Ivory Perry and the Culture of Opposition.* Philadelphia: Temple University Press, 1988.

Logan, John R., and Harvey L. Molotch. *Urban Fortunes: The Political Economy of Place.* Berkeley: University of California Press, 1987.

Lubell, Samuel. *The Future of American Politics.* 3d ed, rev. New York: Harper & Row, 1965.

Lubove, Roy. *Twentieth Century Pittsburgh: Government, Business, and Change.* New York: John Wiley & Sons, 1969.

March, James G., and Johan P. Olsen. *Rediscovering Institutions: The Organizational Basis of Politics.* New York: The Free Press, 1989.

Massey, Douglas S., and Nancy A. Denton. *American Apartheid: Segregation and the Making of the Underclass.* Cambridge, Mass.: Harvard University Press, 1993.

Masters, Nicholas A., Robert H. Salisbury, and Thomas H. Eliot. *State Politics and the Public Schools.* New York: Alfred A. Knopf, 1964.

Mayhew, David R. *Placing Parties in American Politics.* Princeton, N.J.: Princeton University Press, 1986.

McConachie, Alexander Scot. "The 'Big Cinch': A Business Elite in the Life of a City, Saint Louis, 1895–1915." Ph.D. diss., Washington University, 1976.

_____. "Public Problems and Private Places." *Bulletin* of the Missouri Historical Society 34 (1978): 90–103.

Merton, Robert K. *Social Theory and Social Structure.* Rev. and enlarged ed. Glencoe, Ill.: The Free Press, 1957.

Mollenkopf, John H. *The Contested City.* Princeton, N.J.: Princeton University Press, 1983.

_____. "New York: The Great Anomaly." In *Racial Politics in American Cities,* edited by Rufus P. Browning, Dale Rogers Marshall, and David H. Tabb. New York: Longman, 1990.

_____. *A Phoenix in the Ashes: The Rise and Fall of the Koch Coalition in New York City Politics.* Princeton, N.J.: Princeton University Press, 1992.

Monti, Daniel J. *Race, Redevelopment, and the Company Town.* Albany: State University of New York Press, 1990.

Mormino, Gary Ross. *Immigrants on the Hill: Italian Americans in St.*

Louis, 1882–1982. Urbana: University of Illinois Press, 1986.

Muraskin, Jack. "Municipal Reform in Two Missouri Cities." *Bulletin* of the Missouri Historical Society 25 (1969): 213–23.

———. "St. Louis Municipal Reform in the 1890s: A Study in Failure." *Bulletin* of the Missouri Historical Society 25 (1968): 38–49.

Nelson, William E., Jr. "Cleveland: The Evolution of Black Political Power." In *The New Black Politics*, edited by Michael B. Preston, Lenneal J. Henderson, Jr., and Paul L. Puryear. 2d ed. New York: Longman, 1987.

O'Connor, Edwin. *The Last Hurrah.* Boston: Little-Brown, 1956.

O'Connor, Thomas H. *The Boston Irish: A Political History.* Boston: Northeastern University Press, 1995.

O'Keeffe, Kevin. *Baltimore Politics, 1971–1986: The Schaefer Years and the Struggle for Succession.* Washington, D.C.: Georgetown University Press, 1986.

O'Neill, Tip, with William Novak. *Man of the House: The Life and Political Memoirs of Speaker Tip O'Neill.* New York: St. Martin's Press, 1988.

Orr, Marion. "Electoral Control and Governing Coalitions: The Struggle for Black Empowerment in Baltimore." In *Racial Politics in American Cities*, edited by Rufus P. Browning, Dale Rogers Marshall, and David H. Tabb. 2d ed. New York: Longman, 1997.

Orren, Karen, and Stephen Skrowneck. "Beyond the Iconography of Order: Notes for a New Institutionalism." In *The Dynamics of American Politics*, edited by Lawrence C. Dodd and Calvin Jillson. Boulder, Colo.: Westview Press, 1994.

Patterson, Ernest. *Black City Politics.* New York: Dodd, Mead and Company, 1974.

Patterson, Ernestine. "The Impact of the Black Struggle on Representative Government in St. Louis." Ph.D. diss., Saint Louis University, 1969.

Porter, Curtis Hunter. "Charter Reform in St. Louis, 1910–1914." Master's thesis, Washington University, 1966.

Portz, John, Lana Stein, and Robin R. Jones. *City Schools and City Politics: Institutions and Leadership in Pittsburgh, Boston, and St. Louis.* Lawrence: University Press of Kansas, 1999.

Primm, James Neal. *Lion of the Valley: St. Louis, Missouri.* 2d ed. Boulder, Colo.: Pruett, 1990.

Rafferty, Edward C. "The Boss Who Never Was: Colonel Ed Butler and the Limits of Practical Politics in St. Louis, 1875–1904." *Gateway Heritage* 12 (1992): 54–73.

Rammelkamp, Julian S. "St. Louis: Boosters and Boodlers." *Bulletin* of the Missouri Historical Society 34 (1978): 200–210.

Rene, Elizabeth M. "The Jefferson Bank Controversy: A Chapter in the History of St. Louis." Research paper, 1977.

Riordon, William L. *Plunkitt of Tammany Hall.* New York: E. P. Dutton, 1963.

Salisbury, Robert H. "The Dynamics of Reform: Charter Politics in St. Louis." *Midwest Journal of Politics,* 1961, 262–75.

———. "St. Louis Politics: Relationships Among Interests, Parties, and Governmental Structure." *The Western Political Quarterly* 18 (1960): 498–507.

Sandweiss, Eric Todd. "Construction and Community in South St. Louis, 1850–1910." Ph.D. diss., University of California at Berkeley, 1991.

Schiesl, Martin J. *The Politics of Efficiency: Municipal Administration and Reform in America, 1800–1920.* Berkeley: University of California Press, 1977.

Schmandt, Henry J., Paul G.

Steinbicker, and George D. Wendel. *Metropolitan Reform in St. Louis: A Case Study.* New York: Holt, Rinehart, and Winston, 1961.

Schwartz, Joel. *The New York Approach: Robert Moses, Urban Liberals, and Redevelopment of the Inner City.* Columbus: Ohio State University Press, 1993.

Shefter, Martin. "The Emergence of the Political Machine: An Alternative View." In *Theoretical Perspectives on Urban Politics*, edited by Willis D. Hawley et al. 2d ed. Englewood Cliffs, N.J.: Prenctice-Hall, 1976.

Smith, JoAnn Adams. *Selected Neighbors and Neighborhoods of North St. Louis.* St. Louis: Friends of Vaughn Cultural Center, 1988.

Sonenshein, Raphael J. *Politics in Black and White: Race and Power in Los Angeles.* Princeton, N.J.: Princeton University Press, 1993.

Sorauf, Frank J. "The Silent Revolution in Patronage." In *Urban Government*, edited by Edward C. Banfield. New York: The Free Press, 1969.

Steffens, Lincoln. *The Shame of the Cities.* New York: Hill and Wang, 1957.

Stein, Lana. *Holding Bureaucrats Accountable: Politicians and Professionals in St. Louis.* Tuscaloosa: University of Alabama Press, 1991.

_____. "Privatization, Work-Force Cutbacks, and African American Municipal Employment." *American Review of Public Administration,* June 1994, 181–92.

Stein, Lana, and Carol W. Kohfeld. "St. Louis's Black-White Elections: Products of Machine Factionalism and Polarization." *Urban Affairs Quarterly,* December 1991, 227–48.

Stone, Clarence N. *Regime Politics: Governing Atlanta, 1946–1988.* Lawrence: University Press of Kansas, 1989.

Svara, James H. *Official Leadership in the City: Patterns of Conflict and Cooperation.* New York: Oxford University Press, 1990.

Swift, Elaine K., and David W. Brady. "Common Ground: History and Theories of American Government." In *The Dynamics of American Politics*, edited by Lawrence C. Dodd and Calvin Jillson. Washington, D.C.: CQ Press, 1994.

Teaford, Jon C. *The Rough Road to Renaissance: Urban Revitalization in America, 1940–1985.* Baltimore: Johns Hopkins University Press, 1990.

_____. *The Unheralded Triumph: City Government in America, 1870–1900.* Baltimore: Johns Hopkins University Press, 1984.

Weber, Michael P. *Don't Call Me Boss: David L. Lawrence, Pittsburgh's Renaissance Mayor.* Pittsburgh: University of Pittsburgh Press, 1988.

Weir, Margaret. "Ideas and the Politics of Bounded Innovation." In *Structuring Politics: Historical Institutionalism in Comparative Analysis*, edited by Sven Steinmo, Kathleen Thelen, and Frank Longstreth. New York: Cambridge University Press, 1992.

Welch, Susan, and Timothy Bledsoe. *Urban Reform and Its Consequences: A Study in Representation.* Chicago: University of Chicago Press, 1988.

Wilson, James Q. *Bureaucracy: What Government Agencies Do and Why They Do It.* New York: Basic Books, 1989.

Wolfinger, Raymond E. *The Politics of Progress.* Englewood Cliffs, N.J.: Prentice-Hall, 1974.

_____. "Why Political Machines Have Not Withered Away and Other Revisionist Thoughts." *Journal of Politics* 34 (1972): 365–98.

Index

Aboussie, Louis, 129

Aboussie, Martie, Jr., 164, 209

Aboussie, Martie "Murph": as committeeman, 164; as ward leader, 152

AF of L, 78; Central Trades and Labor Union, 104

African Americans: advances of, 124–125; as aldermanic candidates, 69; alliance with Steamfitters Union, 155; appointees, 128; on board of aldermen, 64; and city charter (proposed 1957), 106; civil-rights struggle of, 121–133; as committeemen, 152; and Democratic Party, 22–26, 125; electoral strength, 187; factions and white counterparts, 154; and Human Development Corporation (HDC), 142; and jobs, 212, 213; lack of unity, 177; and machine politics, 26, 133; mayors, 187, 227–48; migration to the north, 125; movement to the county, 177; officeholders, 121, 124–25, 154; political incorporation, xxi, 229; and political power, 125; and population, 13, 124–25; and public hospital, 19, 26; realignment of voters, 71; representation of, 124, 125, 154; and Republican Party, 17–18; rivalries among, 182; role of, 13; and structural change, 109; and submachine in Chicago, 45–46; and Teamsters Union, 103; as voters, 177; and white domination of St. Louis politics, 18

Albanese, Charles, 70, 71, 82, 99

Alcott, Penelope, 234

aldermanic boundaries, new, 72

aldermanic courtesy, 98, 107, 113

aldermen: change in functions, 186; and Civic Progress, 99; functions of, 152; functions of in 1970s, 164; importance of, 99; and neighborhood groups, 99; personal campaigns of, 153; and power, 119; ward election of, 49, 137. *See also*

board of aldermen

aldermen, Republican: decline in number, 174

aldermen at large: election of, 20

Allegheny Conference, 93–94

American Bar Association, 104

American Medical Association, 211

Amusa, Walle, 204

Anheuser-Busch, 192

antiwar movement: and St. Louis politics, 179

arena, sports: and Billikens, 194; and Blues, 194, 195

arts district, 196, 198

Ashcroft, John: and domed stadium, 195

Badaracco, Joseph, *148*, 176; defeats Sorkis Webbe, 149; as president of board of aldermen, 150

Bailey, Velma, 234, 239

Bakewell, Claude, 81

Baltimore: African American leaders in, 134; form of governance in, 142

Banfield, Edward C.: *City Politics*, xviii, xix

Banks, J. B. "Jet," 209, *223*; defeats Samuel Goldston, 156; and William Clay, 156–57

banks vs. unions, 68, 75–84

Bartholomew, Harland, 197; city planner of St. Louis, 95

Bass, John: as comptroller, 176; election (1973) and defeat (1977) of, 180–81, 182; and William Clay, 177, 180, 213

Baumann, Duncan: as publisher of *St. Louis Globe-Democrat*, 167

Becker, William Dee: elected as Republican mayor, 43; perishes in glider crash, 69; supports municipal merit system, 54–55

Beckerle, Paul, 230

Belfi, Vergil, 190

Berra, Louis, 31

Berra, Paul, 179, 206, 210, 214, 217

Bidwell, Bill, 195

Big Cinch, 10, 11, 12, 18, 46–47, 84, 105, 107, 109, 119

Billingsley, Z. Dwight, 222

biracial coalitions: as aids to black mayoral elections, 227

black, blacks. *See* African Americans

Blues: and Arena, 194

board of aldermen, 212, 250; African American representation, 64; Democratic majority on, 37, 71–72; *See also* aldermen

board of estimate and apportionment, xvii, 227, 250; Democratic control of, 37, 70; partisan representation on, 174; Republicans on, 27, 70; ways and means committee, 211

board of freeholders: and Metropolitan St. Louis survey, 108; and multi-functional special district, 108; and municipal charter, 3; support of, 103–4

board of freeholders, 1950: and newly proposed charter, 104

board of freeholders, 1956: and newly proposed charter, 105–6

boodle, 5, 8–9

Borough Plan to Revitalize St. Louis, 109–10

Bosley, Freeman, Jr., 193, 207, 208, 214, 215, 216, 236–38; and airport expansion contract incident, 238; background as handicap, 236; candidate for mayor, 244; and cellular-telephone incident, 237–38; as mayor, 231–39; as mayoral candidate, 230–31; and "Midnite Basketball" program, 238; and neighborhood concerns and devel-opment, 235; staff questions, 234–35, 238–39

Bosley, Freeman, Sr., 204, 209, 210, 214

Boston: form of governance in, 142; reforms in, 7, 65

boundary closure, 3

Boykins, Billie, 214, 221

Boykins, Luther, 210

Bradley, Eugene "Tink": and board of aldermen, 23; death of, 182; on Jordan Chambers, 24; and ward organizations, 182, 209

Brandhorst, Bob, 163

Brennan, William J., 38

Brown v. Board of Education, 16

Buckowitz, Louis, 50; and Easter egg hunt, 100; ward leader, 152

Budenz, Luis F., 19

Buford, James, 240

Building and Construction Trades, 104

Burke, James, 38

Burke, Patrick J., 69

Burns, Clarence "DuBro," 134

Busch, August, 77–78

Busch, August, Jr., 97

Busch Stadium, 145

Bushmeyer, Ed, 163

business: and government alliance, xv–xvi, 67; and labor, 84; and rede-velopment, 97

busing, 198; in St. Louis, 232

Butler, Ed, 8–9

Byrne, Jane, 227

cable-television investigation, 168

Callanan, Lawrence (Larry), *80*; and Steamfitters, 79, 80

Callanan, Thomas, 104; as officeholder, 79, 80; linked to Morris A. Shenker, 81; political role, 81; and Steamfitters Union, 99

Calloway, Ernest, 103

Camp, Eugene, 210

campaign-finance reforms, 235

Campaign for Human Dignity, 204

campaign transitions (1977), 179–80

candidacies, write-in, 181

Cantwell, Harry J., 38

car bombings, 167

Cardinals, St. Louis, 195

Carnahan, Mel: campaign of, 223; primary opponent to Vincent Schoemehl, 222

Carpenter, Milton, 71

Carpenter, Sharon, 214, 217

Carter, Paula, 214, 215

Cassilly, Robert, 197

Caston, Jasper C., 69

central cities, 141, 157, 180; conditions in, 85; population decline in, 137–38

central committee activities and relationships, 205–25

Central Medical Center, 211

centralization of power: failure of in St. Louis, xi, 27, 34, 64–65, 66, 84, 137, 150, 253; in other cities, xv, xviii, 65, 66, 110–11

Cermak, Anton: assassinated in 1933, 45; and centralized machine in Chicago, 66; as mayor of Chicago, 45–46; multiethnic political machine of, 45–46; and patronage under, 45, 252

Cervantes, A. J., 97; and African Americans, 141, 144; and Anthony Sansone, 148; campaign platform (1965), 115; "The Challenge of the Seventies," 141; and Civic Progress, 116, 141–42; and convention-center plans, 146; and crime, 165–67; failure of third term, 167; and Illinois airport, 146–47; loss of 1974 election, 176; as mayor of St. Louis, 141–50; and Morris A. Shenker, 166–67; and multifunctional special district plan, 108–9; opponent of Raymond Tucker, 114, 115; and patronage, 147–48; peace-keeping of, 143; and the press, 116; projects of, 141; and public accommodations, 129; on public hospitals, 185; and Spanish Pavilion, 145–46; and urban redevelopment, 144–45; and William Clay, 144

Cervantes Convention Center, 223

"Challenge of the Seventies, The," 141

Chambers, Jordan "Pop," 104, 109, 155, 157, 133; leader among

African Americans, 22–24, 30, 135, 229; as machine politician, 23; and patronage, 23–24

charter (proposed 1950), 104–5, 127

charter (proposed 1957), 106–7, 127

Charter Hospital, 211

charter of 1876, 4–6

charter of 1911, 10–11

charter of 1914, 250; alternative to, 105–7; amendments to, 49–66; decentralization of power, 13; fragmentation under, 13; political structure under, 13; provisions of, 11, 59; ward-based factionalism under, 13

charter reform commission (1949), 127

Chicago: African American leaders in, 134–35; and centralization of governmental power, 110–11; Democratic Party in, 46; as machine-politics city, xv, xvii, 45–47; and plantation wards, 121–23; racial division in, 227; reforms in, 7, 66; WPA jobs in, 32

churches: and race issues, 14

Citizens Liberty League, 22

City Beautiful movement, 12, 197

city-county relationships: Divorce of 1876, xi, 3–4, 249–50

city Democratic committee: Bernard Dickmann candidates for, 38; factions, 37; and nominees funding, 151; opposition in, 37; patronage, 37

city earnings tax: reinstituted, 109

city governments: changes in, 6–12; Progressive reform movement, 7

City Hospital No. 1, 185, 211

City Plan of St. Louis (1947), 95

Civic Federation, 9

Civic League, 10

Civic Progress, 97, 194, 211; and A. J. Cervantes, 141–42; and aldermen, 99; created by Joseph Darst, 93; and James Conway, 178; organization of, 93–95; and strong-mayor form of government, 246; and urban renewal, 87–88, 93, 251; weak institutionalization of, 95 civil rights: black community's campaign for, 123; laws, 149; and Raymond Tucker, 127; struggle, 68, 121–35; white politicians' resistance to, 121

civil service: adoption of, 137; outcomes affected, 64; and Progressive reform movement, 49; safeguards to reform, 56; ward support of, 57–58, 59

Civil War, 2

Clark, Crittenden, 16–17

Clark, John T., 56

Clark, Joseph W. B., 149

Clark, Marit, 163, 239

Clark Enterprises, 194

class and ethnic divisions, 9–12, 88, 114, 251

Clay, Irving C., Jr., 199

Clay, William Lacy, Jr., 214

Clay, William Lacy, Sr., 124, 135, 208–11, 215; and A. J. Cervantes, 132, 141, 144; allegations against black elected officials, 156, 182; arrested, 131; and Benjamin Goins, 155, 156, 177, 182; candidacy for mayor, 181; and civil-rights activism, 130, 156; as committeeman, 132; in Congress, 156–57; and CORE, 130; and demonstrations at Jefferson Bank, 156; elected to board of aldermen, 130; elected to Congress in 1968, 132, 133; endorsements of, 182, 216; importance to ward-based factional politics, 132; influence of at the polls, 182, 183; and James Conway, 181; and John Bass, 177; loss of mayoral election, 181; and NAACP, 130; and patronage, 132, 133, 142; political concerns of, 133; popularity with black voters, 182; and Raymond Percich election, 180; respected among African Americans, 132; and Steamfitters Union, 132; and Vincent Schoemehl, 190, 210, 212, 213

Cleveland: as machine-politics city, xv, xvii; Progressive reforms in, 7

Committee on Human Relations, 131

committeemen: decline in importance of, 186; Democratic, 38; North side, 153; and patronage, 12. See also ward committeemen

Community Action Agency (CAA): and Human Development Corporation (HDC), 142

Community Action Stewards Assembly, 102

Compromise of 1820, 2

comptroller election of 1989, 219–20

Congress of Industrial Organizations (CIO), 69, 75; and American Federation of Labor (AF of L), 78

Congress of Racial Equality (CORE): leaders jailed or released on bond, 131; as supporter of Arthur Kennedy, 122; and public-accommodations bill, 130–31

Connelly, James, 208

Connelly, Tom, 178, 207

Constitution, Missouri. See Missouri Constitution of 1875

convention center: expansion of, 194

Conway, James, 176, 189; and black officials, 178; and Civic Progress member contributors, 178; elected as mayor, 181; and Homer G. Phillips Hospital, 199; as a maverick and reformer, 175; as mayor, 183–86; mayoral race of, 178–79; redevelopment projects of, 183–84; and Shaw neighborhood organization, 161; and William Clay, 181

Conway, Steve, 218

CORE. See Congress of Racial Equality

corruption in urban politics, 81–82

council: district elections for, xvii, xix

Council on Civic Needs, 103

county officeholders (1940–50), 74

county officeholders (1969–81), 172–73; and banks faction, 75; racially and ethnically diverse, 169

county offices, 227; Bernard Dickmann's lack of control of, 39; contesting for, 72–74; as impediment to hierarchical machine, 39; irregularities in, 173; selection criteria for, 169; and ward politics,

170

court reform, Missouri, 171, 187

Cousins, Steve, 246

crime, organized: in St. Louis, 165, 168

crime prevention, 193

cross-racial voting, 218, 229, 231

Cullen, James, 168

Cupples warehouses, 197; restoration of, 243

Curley, James Michael, 65

Daley, Richard J., xvii; and Chicago's black community, 134; and patronage, 252; political machine under, 111; and reforms in Chicago, 66; suspected of mob associations, 168; and William Dawson, 134

Daley, Richard M., 227

Darst, Joseph M., 88, 93, 97; and "anti-Callanan ticket," 83; and charter revision attempt, 103, 104; elected mayor (1949), 71, 103

Darst, Stephen, 149

Dawson, William, 135; and black public hospital, 24, 31; compared with Jordan Chambers, 134; as leader among blacks, 24–25, 46

Dearing, Jay, 241

decentralization, 164

Deeba, Charles, 156

delivery wards, 114, 116–17

Democratic Party: charges against by Republicans, 24; in county offices after 1950, 169; factional cleavages among, 75–84; move of black voters to, 22–26; power in office of committeeman, 72–74; state offices, 69; and Tom Pendergast, 24

Democratic primary (1986), 215

Democratic primary mayoral vote (1981), 199–200

Democratic primary mayoral vote (1993), 230–31

demographic decline, xi, xxi, 138, 140

Denny, Anthony, 206

De Sapio, Carmine, 168

desegregation plan of 1981, 232

development: criticisms of, 196; downtown, 198; under Vincent Schoemehl, 194–97

Dewey, Thomas E., 69

Dickmann, Bernard F., 20–21, 148, 205; accomplishments of, 251; and black public hospital, 24, 31; and the black vote, 21–22, 24–30, 31; centralization attempts of, 34; centralized political machine under, 27; civil-service legislation proposed, 54; and corrupt machine politics, 43–45; downtown redevelopment under, 27; elected as mayor, 21, 25; gubernatorial race involvement of, 41–42, 47; as lobby for WPA funds, 32; major program initiatives of, 33; and New Deal programs, xxi; opposition to, 37, 38; and political and civic worlds, 118; reforms under, 27; and Robert Hannegan, 28–29; and St. Louis Real Estate Exchange, 24; third mayoral contest, 42–45; and Tom Pendergast, 32, 43; and United Welfare Association, 54; and weak-mayor form, 26

Dinkins, David, 247

district elections for council, xvii, xix, 13, 17

Divorce of 1876, xi, 3–4, 138, 249–50

Donnell, Forrest C., 41–42

Donnelly, Phil M., 83

Dougherty, John F., 70

Dowd, Edward, 83

downtown. See development

Drewes, Ted, 217

Drury Hotel, 243

Dwyer, Jack. See Dwyer, John J.

Dwyer, John J.: and African American ward, 121, 122; as ally of bankers and business leaders, 78; Bernard Dickmann supporter, 38; campaign contributions to, 76; and Christmas baskets, 10; death of, 168; defeats Arthur Kennedy, 122–23; as leading figure in party affairs, 73, 77; and patronage, 121, 122, 123; political career and leadership, 150, 205,

206; as Raymond Tucker supporter,
111; supporter of downtown development, 76; supporters of, 38; as
treasurer, 40

Dyer, L. C., 14

Eagleton, Mark: charged as Callanan-Shenker ally, 90; opponent of
Raymond Tucker, 89; qualifications
of, 89

Eagleton, Thomas, 246

Eberhart, Walter, 128

economic changes in St. Louis: political
effects of, 119, 124, 137, 140

economics and demographics, xi, xxi

education; segregation in, 16

1876 Divorce. *See* Divorce of 1876

elections: of aldermen by voters in own
wards, 28; municipal election of
1955, 97; in newspaper and delivery
wards, 116–17; of 1932, 20–26; of
1950, 114; of 1957, 114; 1957
general election, 99; 1957 primary,
99; of 1961, 114; of 1965, 114

Emergency Medical Service, 242

employment practices: discrimination
in, 126, 127, 130, 131

English, John P., 37, 38

environmental initiative, 33

environmentalists: and Forest Park, 233

Epton, Bernard, 227–28

ethnic divisions, 4, 9

ethnic groups, 125; and party support,
28–29; linked with territorial units,
157

Evans, Pearlie, 212

Evers, Fred W.: as city Republican
committee chairman, 43; opposes
civil-service system, 57, 62; opposes
ward elections, 62

exchange relationships, xvii, xviii

factionalism, Saint Louis's, 68, 119,
133, 154, 170, 191–92, 199, 222

Faheen, George "Sonny," 167

Farris, Charles, 96, 97

Federal Aviation Administration (FAA),
146

Federal Housing Act of 1949, Title I,
87

Federal Housing Administration
(FHA), 85, 86

federal programs: effects upon central
cities, 85–86

Fitters. *See* Steamfitters Union

Fleishman, Alfred, 78

flood of 1993, 233–34

Focus St. Louis, 242

Folk, Joseph W., 8

Ford, Louis, *130*

Forest Park: land-use controversy, 233;
master plan for, 232–33

4 Candidates 4 Kids, 198

fragmentation, xv, xvii, xviii, 105; continuation of, 119; effect of, 121;
and factionalism, 191, 250, 251; of
St. Louis politics, 110, 247; under
Schoemehl, 191

freeways: bond issues for, 96; effects of,
86–87; in St. Louis, 67

Gateway Arch, 32, 96

Gateway Mall, 197

"Gateway to the West," 1

General Assembly. *See* Missouri General
Assembly

general election (1938), 40

general election (1969), 149

Gentleman, John A., 39

Gephardt, Richard, 152

German immigrants, 2

German population: and Republican
vote, 17, 28–29

Gibbons, Harold, 84; and "banks vs.
unions," 84; leader in St. Louis
politics, 84; and Teamsters Union,
84, 102, 209

Giles, Gwen, 199

Giordano, Anthony, 167

Godfrey, James E., 165

Goins, Benjamin: finishes term of
Joseph Hayden, 154; and John
Poelker, 177; sent to prison, 168;

and William Clay, 155, 177

Goldstein, Nat, 18

Goldston, Samuel, 156

Goode, Wilson, 247

government, unreformed, xv, xvi, xvii

government contracts, 235

government regimes, xv–xvi

governmental form: and behavior, 249; and minority political incorporation, xvi; and political style, xvi; strong-mayor form, xv, xvii; variation in, 249

governmental reforms, 251, 252

Grand Center, 196

Grant, David, 22, 23, 104

Great Depression, 20; and job provision, 32

Great Society initiatives, 142

Great Whiskey Ring: in St. Louis, 7–8

Green, Darlene, 234, 235

Green, Lucille, 192

Griffin, Bob, 223

Gualdoni, L. Jean, 31, 38

gubernatorial election of 1940–41: conflicts over, 41–42

Gunn, Donald, 148; defeats Charles Albanese, 99; supporter of Raymond Tucker, 114; winner in election of 1955, 97–98

Haas, Bill, 239

Hamilton, Louis, 214, 216

Hancock Amendment, 205

Hannegan, Robert, 41, 42, 205; as chairman of city Democratic committee, 38; gubernatorial race involvement of, 41–42, 47; and Harry Truman, 29; at 1941 election rally, 44; political skills of, 29

Harmon, Clarence: apolitical back-ground of, 242, 244; campaign of, 245; incumbent, 244; as mayor, 240–41; as mayoral candidate, 239–40; performance of, 243; as police chief, 237; police chief to mayor, 242–44; supporters of, 239–40; and Vincent Schoemehl,

242

Harrison, William Jefferson, 24

Hayden, Joseph T. "Juggy," 168, 169–70

Hempelmann, Clara, 69

Hennerich, Paul J., 37

Hickok, James, 97

Highway Act of 1944, 86

highway building, 119

Hill Day, 161

Hill neighborhood, 96, 161. *See also* Italian Hill

Hill 2000, 162

Hines, Chester, Jr., 214

Hoffa, Jimmy, 80, 166

Hogan, Edward "Jellyroll," 79, 164

Holloran, Mark R., 114

Home Owners Loan Corporation (HOLC), 86

home rule, 246

Homer G. Phillips Hospital, 30–31, 199; and African American protests of closure, 184–85, 186; bond issue supporting, 202–5; closure, 184–86, 209; virtues of, 184–85

housing projects in St. Louis, 143

Human Development Corporation (HDC), 142

Hyland, Robert, 197, 211

I-44. *See* Ozark Expressway

Igoe, William L., 38

immigrants, xviii, 5, 12, 31

immigration patterns, 1, 2

improvement associations: in Baltimore, 14, 15; and blacks, 14

institutional change: in behavior, xix; failure of, 84; and government reform, 88; in leadership, xix; in policymaking, xix; under Raymond Tucker, 92; and urban renewal, 88

institutions: in American and urban politics, xvi; and governance, 249–53; and political culture, xi, xix–xxi, xxii, 84

Irish Catholics, 2

Irish Democrats, 28–29, 168; political strength of, 73
Irish gangs, 16, 164
Italian Hill, 157, 158. *See also* Hill neighborhood
Italian population, 31

Jackson, Jesse, 135
Jefferson Bank, 131
Jefferson National Expansion Memorial, 32
Jim Crow laws, 17
job swap, 217, 221, 229
jobs: allocation of, 99; control of, 88, 92, 111; and John Dwyer, 121; loss of, 101, 193, 212, 253; and representation, 124; for youth, 192
Jones, Kenneth, 221, 245
Jones, Virvus, 217, 222; allegations about, 218; at Cervantes Convention Center meeting, *223*; as comptroller victor, 219–20; and minority contractors, 222, 223; sent to prison, 168, 234; and white votes, 218; and William Clay camp, 222

Kansas City machine, 24
Kaufmann, Aloys P.: as aldermanic president, 68–69; as acting mayor, 69, 70; as mayor, 75
Keane, Jack, 214
Kefauver, Estes, 79, 83
Kefauver Commission, 166, 168
Kefauver Crime Investigating Committee, 81
Kelly, Edward: machine politics of, 45; as mayor of Chicago, 45, 134; patronage under, 45; and reforms in Chicago, 66
Kelly, Margaret, 221
Kennedy, Arthur, 121–22
Kennedy, Robert, 179
Kiel, Henry, 13, 20
Kiel Opera House, 194
Kiel Partners. *See* Clark Enterprises
Kilcullen, Frank, 214
Kinealy, David, 210

King, Martin Luther, Jr., 143, 144
King, Velmarie, 214
Koeln, Edward, 36, 97
Komorek, James, 152
Koplar, Harold, 146
Kornhardt, Michael, 167

Laborers Local 42, 167
Lafayette Square neighborhood, 162, 163
Lambert Field, 146
Land Clearance for Redevelopment Authority (LCRA), 96
Lavin, James Patrick, 168, 171
Lawler, John L. "Doc," 151, 155, 206
Lawrence, David: as Allegheny County Democratic chairman, 46; as father of Pittsburgh Renaissance, 65; and governance, 252; patronage under, 46; reorganization of Democratic Party under, 46
Lawson, DeWitte T., 71
LCRA. *See* Land Clearance for Redevelopment Authority
leadership, 246, 253
League of Women Voters, 103; as civil-service advocate, 54, 56
Lebanese immigrants, 29, 141
Lee, Charlotte Corcoran, 38
Leggett, Ronald, 214
legislature. *See* Missouri legislature
Leisure, John, 167
Leisure, Paul J., 167
Leisure, Raymond, 101, 163; helps constituents, 159; and Paul Leisure, 167; and public accommodations, 128
Liberman, Lee, 211
Life: A. J. Cervantes exposé, 166–67
light-rail system, 196, 243
"Little Dixie," 2
Lonesome, Buddy, 122–23
Los Angeles Rams, 196
low-income groups, 87
Lowe, Walter, 70
lugs, 54

machine politics, 252; as deterrent to black political leadership, 123, 228–29; in St. Louis, 8–9, 123, 249

machine-politics cities, xvi–xix, 45–47, 65, 228; St. Louis as case study, xxi–xxii; transitions in, 187

Martorelli, Jack, 190

Mason, William L., 37

mayor-council form, xix

mayoral elections: factors influencing, 118–19

mayors, African American, 227–48; backgrounds of, 247; problems of, 247

McAteer, James, 102

McCarthy, Eugene, 179

McDaniel, Lawrence, 41

McDonnell, William A., 93

McGuire, Daniel, 161, 217

McGuire, Jill, 196

McLemore, Joseph L., 22, 56

McNary, Gene, 195

Mellon, Richard King, 65, 116

"messiah" mayors, 199

Metropolitan St. Louis survey, 108

Michaels, Charles, 167

Michaels, Jimmy, 164, 166, 167

Milford, H., 195, *223*

Mill Creek valley, 96

Miller, Jimmy, 38

Miller, Louis E., 57

Miller, Victor, 26, 27

minority political incorporation, xvi, xxi, 137

minority residents, 124, 138, 139

Missouri: machine-politics tradition, 252; as right-to-work state, 75; taxes and expenditures, 205

Missouri Constitution of 1875, 3, 4

Missouri General Assembly, 223

Missouri law: role of in St. Louis governance, 250

Missouri legislature: Confederate leanings, 2; and home rule, 246; rural-dominated, 2

Missouri Restaurant Owners Association: and public-accommodations bill, 129–30

Missouri Supreme Court, 221

Mitchell, Joseph: and Citizens Liberty League, 22

Mitchell, Parren, 134

Model Cities program, 142, 149

Mueller, A. Barney, 128

municipal elections: Democratic success in, 27; nonpartisan, 49; of 1937, 39; of 1969, 148–49

municipal politics, 3, 5

NAACP, 127, 128, 130

Nance, Earl, Jr., 245

Nash, Patrick, 45, 46, 66

Nation of Islam, 135

National Association for the Advancement of Colored People. *See* NAACP

National Defense Highway Act of 1956, 86

neighborhood divisions, 4

neighborhood organizations, 137, 193; distrusted by ward organizations, 161; eclipsed ward organizations, 163; and political structure, 157, 160

neighborhood-oriented service, 153

neighborhood stabilization: under A. J. Cervantes, 144; under Freeman Bosley, Jr., 193

neoinstitutionalists, 249

Neun, Walter J. G., 21

New Deal programs, 32

newspaper wards, 114, 116–17; small number of, 118

newspapers: effect of on civil rights, 121; influence of on elections, 70

New York City: as machine-politics city, xv, xvii, 54; politics, 150; reforms in, 54

1904 World's Fair, 253

Nolte, Louis, 25, 26, 39; as comptroller, 70

Northside Preservation, 163

O'Keefe, Kevin, 134
O'Neill, Tip, 77–78, 123
Operation BrightSide, 192
Operation ConServ, 193
Operation Impact, 193
Operation Push, 135
Operation SafeStreet, 193
Operation TeamWork, 193
Osborn, Geraldine, 209, 212, 216, 221; as critic of Conway's policies, 184, 190
O'Toole, Phelim, 73–74
Ozark expressway (I–44), 113

partisan elections, xvi, xvii, xix, 11, 12
party politics, 1941–53: jobs and personal service centered, 67; voting practices, 28–29; ward-based, 67
patronage, 5, 221; among black politicians, 133, 228–29; in black-ward politics, 121, 229; centralization of in other cities, 11; liberal use of among white officeholders, 154; and perpetuation of factions, 150; under Raymond Tucker, 122
patronage jobs, 50, 102, 111; controlled by committeemen, 72–74; at county and state offices, 72, 73; and elections, 24, 28; at St. Louis Board of Education, 72
Peach, George, 221
Peet, Robert, Msgr., 160
Pendergast, Tom; downfall in Kansas City, 41; and federal patronage in Missouri, 32; federal prosecution of, 32; as Kansas City Democratic boss, 32; and Kansas City's machine, 24; supporter of Franklin D. Roosevelt, 32
Percich, Peter, 218
Percich, Raymond, 155, 176, 180
Perry, Ivory, 126
Philadelphia: and centralization of governmental power, 110–11; as machine-politics city, xv, xvii; Progressive reforms in, 7; under Republican rule, 20
Phillips, Homer G.: black public

hospital named for, 26, 31; and Citizens Liberty League, 22. *See also* Homer G. Phillips Hospital
Pipefitters Union, 75
Pittsburgh, xv, 45–47; Democratic unification of, 46; form of governance in, 142; Progressive reforms in, 7; WPA jobs in, 32
plantation wards, 122–23; in Chicago, 121
Plunkitt, George Washington, 57, 159
Poelker, John, 149, 189; and Benjamin Goins, 177; and black voters, 177; and city neighborhoods, 177; as comptroller, 99; criticisms of, 177; endorsed by Young Turks, 153, 175; as mayor, 175–78; supported by Civic Progress, 175
political culture, xi, xix, xxii; in American and urban politics, xvi
political equality: hampering factors to, 121
political fragmentation: increase of, 151
political institutions: fragmented, 137
political life in St. Louis: role of culture in, 137, 187; role of structure in, 137
political machines: and the WPA, 32
political parties, 12
political paternalism: in St. Louis, 121
political reform attempts, 103–11
political structure change: in other cities, 252; prevention of, 111; under Raymond Tucker, 84, 110
political system of St. Louis: alliances within, 119; case study of, xxi–xxii; class divisions, xxi, xxii; compared with other cities, xv; development (1876–1914), xxii, 1–12; evolution of, xi; factional, xi, xv, xvi, 28; fragmented power, xv, xxi, 4, 84; patronage of, 119; racial divisions, xxi, xxii
Polizzi, Salvatore, 161, 162. *See also* Hill neighborhood
Pope, Harry, 127, 128
population loss, 140, 193, 195, 253; effects of, 251

poverty: effects of, 251; in St. Louis, 139

Powell, Colin, 240

power balance: from committeemen to aldermen, 153

Pride of St. Louis Corporation, 197

Priest, H. Sam, 39; at 1941 election rally, *44*

private-regarding ethos, xviii

production facilities; inside central cities, 86

Progressive Era, 12, 251

Progressive reform movement, xvi, xviii, 7, 49, 82, 249

Prohibition, 36, 164

Project 87, 236–37

Pruitt-Igoe public-housing project, 97, 101, 143

public-accommodations bill, 127, 128–30; enforcement of in St. Louis, 129–30; opposition to, 129, 130

Public Employees' Welfare Association, 37

public-regarding ethos, xviii

public transportation, 128; in central cities, 86

Pythian Hall, 124

quid pro quo relationships, xvii, 17, 19, 33, 133; and mayor, 92, 244

race, 13–26, 139, 186, 215, 221; and divisions, 229, 239–40, 251; and electoral choices, 118–19; and electoral policies, 16; and ethnicity in St. Louis, 13; and politics, 221, 227–28; problems with, 149, 160, 182

Raker, Judy, 213

Reagan, Ronald, 199

redevelopment, 140, 183–84, 186

redlining, 86, 126, 160

Redmond, Sidney, 56

regimes, 92–95

Regional Arts Commission, 196

Regional Hospital, 211, 212

Rendell, Edward: and governance, 252; as successful mayor in Baltimore, 225

Republicans: and black voters, 22–26; and Great Depression, 20; lead in 1946, 73; and machine politics, 44; in 1914–32, 13–26; patronage opportunities under, 28; and political change, 44

rewards, personal, 246–47, 252

Ribaudo, Tony, 214, 215, 228; supporters of, 229

River Des Peres, 19

Roach, John; as alderman, 152, 176; and city neighborhoods, 177; and Skinker DeBaliviere neighborhood, 161

road building, 86–87

Roberts, Michael, 209, 216, 218

Roberts, Steve, 229–30

Roddy, Clara Jo, 207

Roddy, Joseph P., 101, 129, 206–209, 214; as Raymond Tucker supporter, 111; as Vincent Schoemehl supporter, 190

Roosevelt, Franklin D., 34; elected president, 20, 21; favored by city voters, 69; 1936 landslide of, 39

Rouse, James, 194

Ryan, Brendan, 148

Saarinen, Eero, 32, 96

St. Ambrose Catholic Church: and Italian Hill neighborhood, 161, 162

St. Louis: archaic form of government, 251; census of (1940), 189; census of (1980), 189; ills of, 1981, 189; national rank of, 189; small-town nature of, 110, 189–90

St. Louis Ambassadors, 145, 217; criticism of HDC, 142

St. Louis Cardinals. *See* Cardinals, St. Louis

St. Louis Centre, 194

St. Louis Globe-Democrat: attitude toward demonstrations, 131; on City Hall employees, 26; on Clay-Goins political struggle, 156; on

Jimmy Michaels, 165; on 1934 election, 36; supports civil service, 55; on Thomas Dewey defeat, 69; ward elections analysis, 62

St. Louis governance, 250

St. Louis Housing and Land Clearance Authority, 143

St. Louis police officers, 223

St. Louis Police Officers Association, 205, 223

St. Louis politics: factional nature of, 251

St. Louis Post-Dispatch, 240; attitude toward demonstrations, 131; on Bernard Dickmann, 22; on CIO PAC, 70; on Democrat successes in 1932 and 1933, 36; on Donald Gunn's civic interests, 98, 99; endorses Raymond Tucker, 90; on Harry Schendel's record, 81; on John Dwyer, 76; on politics of Albert "Red" Villa, 102; on Republican rout, 70; and segregation ordinance, 14; on Shenker-Callanan defeat, 81; on "Shenkerism," 82; and the split ticket, 70, 75; supports civil service, 55; supports James Conway, 190–91; supports Raymond Tucker's redevelopment agenda, 99; on urban-renewal bond issue, 90–91; ward elections analysis, 62

St. Louis Real Estate Exchange: and race issues, 14, 15, 16; and segregation ordinance, 24

St. Louis Republic: on fears of white residents, 14; and segregation ordinance, 14

St. Louis School Board: candidates for, 198; hiring practices of, 142–43

Saint Louis University: integration in, 126; and Metropolitan St. Louis survey, 108; and redevelopment, 183–84, 210

St. Margaret of Scotland Catholic Church, 161

St. Roch Catholic Church, 160

sales-tax measures: under Freeman Bosley, Jr., 233–34

saloons, 63

Sansone, Anthony, 164–165; and A. J. Cervantes, 148, 166

Sansones, 141

Santa Maria, 149; to St. Louis, 146

Sartorious, John, 129

Scearce, F. Elliott, 57

Schaefer, William Donald, 225

Schlafly, Daniel, 142

Schmoke, Kurt, 134, 228

Schmoll, John, 36

Schoemehl, Vincent C., Jr.: accomplishments of, 251; as alderman, 190; and black community, 215, 216, 221; black voter support of, 204, 218; campaign for governorship, 222; campaign methods of, 190, 192, 199; and centralization of policymaking and political leadership, 187; at Cervantes Convention Center meeting, 223; coalition of minorities, 216; constructive programs of, xxi; decline of support for, 203–5, 221, 223; defeated by Mel Carnahan, 223; formidable challenges to, 189–90; influence of, 224; innovative approaches of, 192–93; leadership of, 224; as mayor, 189–225; personality of, 251; and police force, 205; and the political game, 191–92, 205, 209, 210, 211, 214, 217; political personality of, 224; racial distrust of, 204, 221; and reopening Homer G. Phillips Hospital, 199, 201, 202, 212; supporters of, 190; views on the public hospitals, 201; and Virvus Jones, 222; votes for mayor, 1985, 1989, 218–19; vs. James Conway, 184, 186; and William Clay, 213

school board, St. Louis. *See* St. Louis School Board

schools, 88; integration in, 126; segregated, 126

Schweitzer, Albert L., 70

segregation, 110; in St. Louis, 121, 126; and freedom riders, 128

segregation ordinance, 13–16, 24

Sestric, Anton, 104, 148; and Shaw neighborhood organization, 161; as ward boss among Slavic and Lebanese, 31–32

Shannon, Thomas W., 171

Shaw neighborhood organization, 160–61

Shelley v. Kraemer, 126

Shenker, Morris A., 104, 166–67; as committeeman, 79; and Edward "Jellyroll" Hogan, 166; and Kefauver crime committee hearings, 81; and Steamfitters, 166; as trial lawyer, 79, 82

Shenker-Callanan-Hogan machine, 72, 79, 83

Shenker-Callanan machine, 72, 79, 82, 83

Shenker-Steamfitters alliance, 83

"Shenkerism," 82

Shrewsbury, James, 163, 234–35

Simon, Paul, 159, 171

Simpson, Peter, 148

Skinker DeBaliviere Community Council (SDCC), 160

Skinker DeBaliviere neighborhood, 160, 161

Slay, Eugene, 168

Slay, Francis G., 234; as candidate for mayor, 244; as mayor, 245–46; supporters of, 245

Slay, Francis R., 206, 207, 208, 214

Slay, Joseph R., 70

slum removal, 87, 96, 119

Smith, Al, 20

Smith, Irene, 239

Smith, Wayman, 211, 212

social-service networking, 158

Socialist Party, 9

Sommer, Bruce, 163

Soulard neighborhood, 96, 162

Spanish Pavilion, 145–46

sports franchises, 194, 198

Sportsmen's Park, 97

spot zoning, 98, 107

state control: of city functions, 2, 4, 12; of St. Louis police force, 2, 5

state laws; and city governance, 250, 252

Steamfitters Union, 75, 99, 101, 104; and black civil-rights activists, 80; decline in influence, 101, 102; as electoral threat, 80, 83; federal indictments of, 80; infighting among, 90; and jobs/contracts, 79; and Lebanese faction, 80; supporters of A. J. Cervantes, 141

Steamfitters' Voluntary Political, Educational, Legislative, Charity, and Defense Fund, 80

Stokes, Carl, 228

Stolar, Henry, 152

Storey, John George, 161

streetcars: effect upon migration outward, 3

strong-mayor form of government, 246

structural change: and African Americans, 109

structural decentralization, 67

suburban communities, 85–87; movement to, 137; white and affluent, 141

Sullivan, John B., 73

Sullivan, Leonor K., 96

Svetanics, Milton, 152

Teamsters Union, 209; and African Americans, 103; for community improvement, 102, 103; decline of, 103

Thompson, Bill, 45

Tiffany area: redevelopment and relocation in, 183–84

Tobermann, Walter, 70

Truman, Harry S: leads Democrats to victory in 1948, 73; as vice-presidential selection, 29

Truman Day dinners, 151

Tucci, J. Kim, 214, 215, 216, 217, 223

Tucker, Raymond: on A. J. Cervantes, 115; abatement program of, 33; academic career of, 89; accomplishments of, 251; and African American community, 132; allies of, 111–13; and board of aldermen, 111–13; business and newspaper

support of, 88, 89; campaign and election of, 89–92; and charter revision attempt, 103–7; and Civic Progress, 111; and civil rights, 127, 130; defeats Thomas Callanan in 1957, 99; dependence on reform constituency, 111; and development programs, 84; and downtown development, 198; and employment bias, 130, 131; and freeloading, 170; with group of aldermen, *98*; influence of, 97; and Mark Eagleton contest, 89–90; as mayor, 1953–65, 85–119; out of office, 137; and patronage, 122; and picketers, 130, 131; political career of, 89; political philosophy of, 111; and political structure reform, 103–11; and politicians, 111–13; on politics and politicians, 118; popularity of, 97; and the press, 111; and public-accommodations bill, 127, 128; reaction to arrest at bank, 131–132; and reform, 119; role in 1955 election, 97; as smoke commissioner, 33; and St. Louis factions, 118; and urban renewal, xxi, 87–88, 119, 142; and Vincent McMahon, *114*; and ward factionalism, 113; as winner of 1953 general election, 92; as winner of 1953 primary, 90–91
Turpin, Charles, 16, 22
Twenty-sixth Ward Improvement Association, 14
Tyus, Eugene, 168
Tyus, Leroy, 210
Tyus, Sharon, 239

unemployment: linked with crime, 139
Union Station, 194
unions: activity, 168; corruption, 167; influence on city officials, 103; and postwar urban renewal, 84
United Railway Company, 18
United Welfare Association, 14, 15
Urban League, 56, 128, 240; block units of, 160
urban renewal, 87, 138; bond issues for, 96; capital grants for, 96; and Civic Progress, 251; newspapers'

interest in, 75; sites, 96–97; and union power, 84

Vaughn, George, 22, 24
Veterans Administration (VA), 85–86
Villa, Albert "Red," 59, 101, 129; and his neighborhood, 102; on Vincent Schoemehl, 224
Villa, Thomas A., 216, 221, 222, 229
Vossmeyer, Steve; campaign style of, 179
voting irregularities, 156

Waechter, James, 90
Walker, George H. "Bert," 24
Walsh, Denny: on A. J. Cervantes, 166–67; on union corruption, 167
Walsh, Thomas V., 39
Walsh, William, 38
War on Poverty, 142, 149, 152, 160
ward-based factionalism, xi, xvi, xxi, 1, 4, 5, 12, 27, 45, 46, 84, 147; in African American politics, 154–57; in Democratic Party, 150; and political life in St. Louis, 133, 249; and Raymond Tucker, 113
ward-based politics: effect of, 121, 123, 133; parochial concerns of, 99
ward committeemen: decrease in power among, 64; patronage of, 54, 57; power erosion of, 179; role in ward affairs, 99. *See also* committeemen
ward organizations, xvii, 28–29, 163, 178, 186; and African Americans, 163; aldermanic elections in, 59–65; and aldermen, 106–7; and campaigning, xv; and charter, 104; in Chicago, 5; civil-service effect on, 57; and committeemen, 92; election-day activities, 60; election-materials funding, 51–52; and endorsements and alliances, xv, xvii, 50–63, 64, 119, 186, 190; and favors, 92; legislators, 153; and machines, 179; and patronage, xv, xvii, xix, xxi, 4, 11, 24, 28, 50, 57, 59, 63, 64, 104–5; political fragmentation in, 53, 64; and recreational and charitable functions,

100; sample ballots of, 51; types, 114; voting practices, 61; and William L. Clay, Sr., 130

Warehouse and Distribution Workers Union, Local 688, 104; opposition to Donnelly, 83–84

Washington, Harold, 227, 229, 247; first black mayor in Chiago, 135; governance under, 228

Washington University, 160; integration in, 126; and Metropolitan St. Louis survey, 108

weak-mayor form, xvii, xxi, 11, 26, 67, 187, 252

Weathers, Fred, 111, 177, 132

Webbe, Anthony, 29–30

Webbe, Sorkis, Jr., 165, 168

Webbe, Sorkis, Sr., 148–49, 163, 165, 168

welfare families: housing of, 160

Wells, Rolla, 13, 17; and machine politics, 18–19; as mayor, 10; and Republican rule, 17–19; and segregation ordinance, 14

West End Community Conference, 163

West Enders: as the "Big Cinch," 10

White, Kevin, 65

White Castle: picketing at, 130

Williams, Fred E., 210, 214, 215

Williams, Larry C., 201, 210

Woodson, Lawrence, 156

Works Progress Administration (WPA), 32

World War II, 67

World's Fair. *See* 1904 World's Fair

Young, Phyllis, 163

Young Turks: group of aldermen, 152, 190; as supporters of Arthur Kennedy, 122

Zoo-Museum district, 147

Zych, Thomas, 168, 209, 216; defeated Bradley as aldermanic president, 182; and Local 73 of Firefighters Union, 182

photo: Jan Frantzen

Lana Stein is Professor of Political Science and Department Chair at the University of Missouri–St. Louis. She has lived in St. Louis since 1987, coming to UM–St. Louis from the University of Georgia. Her Ph.D. is from Michigan State University. Stein specializes in urban politics and public administration and has published a number of articles, book chapters, and books, including *Holding Bureaucrats Accountable: Politicians and Professionals in St. Louis* and *City Schools and City Politics: Institutions and Leadership in Pittsburgh, Boston, and St. Louis* (with John Portz and Robin R. Jones).